Praise for Michael L. Brown
and *Saving a Sick America*

"Dr. Michael L. Brown delivers a healthy antidote to the sickness that is plaguing America. This book is much more than religious moralism; it's a call to authenticity and a biblical application of the gospel for our time. *Saving a Sick America* is the prescription we need so that God will heal our land."

—Jack Graham, pastor of Prestonwood Baptist Church

"This book lives up to its title. It correctly diagnoses the cause of America's ills and also prescribes the cure. Dr. Michael L. Brown describes our descent into paganism—with all of its debilitating consequences—but also sees that our only hope of saving America is to return to the Word of God. This is a message not just to the nation, but especially for our evangelical churches that have become content with a mediocre form of Christianity that is too weak to cure our nation's ills. If we accept the prescription Dr. Brown lays out, our churches and our nation will slowly begin the recovery process. Only God's Word can save us."

—Dr. Erwin W. Lutzer, pastor emeritus,
Moody Church, Chicago, Illinois

"Dr. Michael L. Brown inspires people to seek out the truth about God and faith."

—Ted Cruz, US Senator from Texas

"At a moment when many American Christians are looking for a safe retreat from the culture and its wars, Dr. Michael L. Brown offers a robust and compelling case that Christians must work for good in culture and politics, even at the darkest moment. At the same time, he insists that our culture cannot be fully healed without the transforming power of the Holy Spirit in both the church and our individual lives. Should we work for positive change or pray for spiritual renewal? The answer is not either-or. It's both-and."

—Jay Richards, PhD, *New York Times* bestselling author
and senior fellow at the Discovery Institute

"By accurately diagnosing just how sick America is, Dr. Michael L. Brown can now offer a hope-filled prescription for moral and cultural change based on the timeless principles of the Word of God. While some are throwing in the towel and calling on the church to retreat, Dr. Brown sees the current darkness as the church's great opportunity to arise and shine. America has fallen, but it can rise again."

—DR. ROBERT JEFFRESS, PASTOR OF FIRST BAPTIST CHURCH, DALLAS

"*Saving a Sick America* is a modern-day wakeup call for the church. Dr. Michael L. Brown rightly recognizes that we live in dire times, and yet he offers a hopeful prescription for how the church can seize this moment for good. This book is insightful, convicting, and yet inspiring. My hat is off to Dr. Brown for having the courage to write this book."

—SEAN MCDOWELL, PhD, PROFESSOR AT BIOLA UNIVERSITY,
POPULAR SPEAKER, AND BESTSELLING AUTHOR OF MORE THAN
18 BOOKS INCLUDING *A NEW KIND OF APOLOGIST*

"Dr. Michael L. Brown has produced an extremely readable book that reminds Christians that before we can change our cultural and political world we have to get things in order at our own houses. He does not deny the importance of political engagement, but reminds us that unless we have a revitalized church such engagement will not have lasting effects. We would do well to take Dr. Brown's advice to look within before looking outside our churches to become the type of church that can heal our ailing society."

—GEORGE YANCEY, PhD, PROFESSOR OF SOCIOLOGY
AT THE UNIVERSITY OF NORTH TEXAS

"America is getting weaker and weaker spiritually, politically, economically, militarily, and socially—Or is it? Dr. Michael L. Brown carefully documents this reality and depicts how God historically has moved in and through his people to get a national house in order after a foundation of prayer was laid. Society has been sick before, to the point that leadership in its day would say the nation was at the precipice of destruction. Then 'God moved,' and the issues in society were addressed. Yes, we are sick, but the cure is eminent. Dr. Brown has done an outstanding job of challenging the followers of Jesus to believe and follow God. This is a revolutionary book that can change America. I heartily recommend it."

—TOM PHILLIPS, VICE PRESIDENT/BILLY GRAHAM LIBRARY, AUTHOR,
REVIVAL SIGNS: JOIN THE COMING GREAT AWAKENING

"Dr. Michael L. Brown's *Saving a Sick America* is unlike any other book I have read. Many books have diagnosed the decline in the moral and spiritual state of our country and culture. Dr. Brown does that as well, but responds with an optimism that is unique. He urges the reader to take a long-term view, reminding us that many movements once thought to be on the right side of history ended up on the ash heap of history instead. Dr. Brown calls for a transformation and renewal of America—not through politics, or even (primarily) through the pulpit, but from the bottom up. If we will "get our own houses in order," he declares—by relying on scripture and prayer, and recapturing attitudes of gratitude and personal responsibility—we can see revival again. God can indeed bring healing to a sick America—maybe sooner, if Christians will read this book and take it to heart."

—PETER SPRIGG, SENIOR FELLOW FOR POLICY STUDIES,
FAMILY RESEARCH COUNCIL, WASHINGTON, DC

"Dr. Michael L. Brown is one of the leading prophetic voices in our nation crying out for a moral and cultural transformation. This book is a wake-up call to the church and I strongly urge you to read it. Don't be left on the sidelines. Get in the action and be part of what I believe will be the greatest move of God in history!"

—JONATHAN BERNIS, PRESIDENT AND CEO OF JEWISH
VOICE MINISTRIES INTERNATIONAL

"Dr. Michael L. Brown has written a powerful diagnosis of today's fragmenting, failing culture—the state of our families, the collapse of a common moral code, the turn inward to selfishness and moment-to-moment hedonism. None of that is working. We are less happy, less generous than our parents and grandparents—though they often faced poverty, injustice, and even war. We have fewer children and spend less time with them. We marry less often and divorce much more quickly. We dispose of unwanted children through abortion and even infanticide. The promises of secular reformers, that we would thrive and prosper if we only climbed out from under outmoded moral codes and traditions, have failed. Now we wonder if any of us still has the strength to fight. Dr. Brown does, and he shows us the source of his strength: a firm belief in the Word of God, richly understood in the light of centuries of Christian history and reflection, anchored in a rational understanding of the natural law that God wrote on the human heart. Christians of every tradition would benefit from this book."

—JOHN ZMIRAK, PHD, AUTHOR OF *THE POLITICALLY
INCORRECT GUIDE TO CATHOLICISM*

"Dr. Michael L. Brown is one of the most prolific writers and clear thinkers in the world today! His scholarship, combined with a prophetic grasp on current events, converge to release a powerful and wide array of writings that profoundly affect the soul. This book clearly articulates many of the pressing concerns we have in our nation and offers biblical solutions. Love him or hate him, when you read his material you will be greatly challenged to shift your thinking!"

—Dr. Joseph Mattera, National convener of the United States Coalition of Apostolic Leaders and lead pastor of Resurrection Church of New York

SAVING
A SICK
AMERICA

OTHER BOOKS BY MICHAEL L. BROWN

Breaking the Stronghold of Food: How We Conquered Food Addictions and Discovered a New Way of Living (with Nancy Brown)

The Grace Controversy: Answers to 12 Common Questions

Outlasting the Gay Revolution: Where Homosexual Activism Is Really Going and How to Turn the Tide

The Fire That Never Sleeps: Keys to Sustaining Personal Revival (with John Kilpatrick and Larry Sparks)

Can You Be Gay and Christian? Responding with Love and Truth to Questions About Homosexuality

Hyper-Grace: Exposing the Dangers of the Modern Grace Message

Authentic Fire: A Response to John MacArthur's Strange Fire

In the Line of Fire: 70 Articles from the Front Lines of the Culture Wars

The Real Kosher Jesus: Revealing the Mysteries of the Hidden Messiah

A Queer Thing Happened to America: And What a Long, Strange Trip It's Been

Answering Jewish Objections to Jesus, Volumes 1–5

"Jeremiah," in *The Expositor's Bible Commentary Revised Edition*

60 Questions Christians Ask About Jewish Beliefs and Practices

Revolution in the Church: Challenging the Religious System with a Call for Radical Change

The Revival Answer Book: Rightly Discerning the Contemporary Revival Movements

Revolution! Jesus' Call to Change the World

Go and Sin No More: A Call to Holiness

From Holy Laughter to Holy Fire: America on the Edge of Revival

Israel's Divine Healer

It's Time to Rock the Boat: A Call to God's People to Rise Up and Preach a Confrontational Gospel

Our Hands Are Stained with Blood: The Tragic Story of the "Church" and the Jewish People

Whatever Happened to the Power of God: Is the Charismatic Church Slain in the Spirit or Down for the Count?

How Saved Are We?

The End of the American Gospel Enterprise

Compassionate Father or Consuming Fire: Who Is the God of the Old Testament?

SAVING A SICK AMERICA

A PRESCRIPTION FOR MORAL AND CULTURAL TRANSFORMATION

MICHAEL L. BROWN, PhD

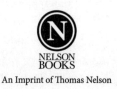

NELSON
BOOKS

An Imprint of Thomas Nelson

In memory of my wonderful, precious mom,
Rose G. Brown, September 25, 1922–November 18, 2016.
She was the epitome of a proud Jewish mother.

CONTENTS

FOREWORD

——

DR. MICHAEL L. BROWN BOLDLY CALLS THE CHURCH AND ALL WHO love freedom to return to the unshakable foundation upon which freedom stands. He makes it perfectly clear that we as believers are on a divine assignment to make a salt-and-light impact on the lives of others. That which is precious must be preserved, and that which is evil and destructive must be exposed as we illuminate the way to peace and security.

In the truest sense of the word, Dr. Brown is a *prophetic voice* crying out in the wilderness of deception, division, relativism, idolatry, and, in many ways, unparalleled rage. He candidly addresses what should be serious concerns to every person who understands the importance and value of freedom. While clearly declaring unadulterated, transforming truth, he demonstrates a prevailing spirit of redemption. He speaks with both courage and compassion. I believe he is being carried not only by the Spirit of transforming truth, but also unconditional love.

Dr. Brown is one of the most prolific writers I know, and it amazes me how effectively he addresses our national ills, personal challenges, and lack of clear vision and understanding of the times on the part of the church. Just as the men of Issachar were anointed to "understand the times" (1 Chron. 12:32), Dr. Brown is gifted to help believers understand the world we live in today. He does not curse the darkness; he exposes its damaging effects and shares the illuminating light that truth offers. With a supernatural anointing, he gives wise, biblical solutions to the challenges we face.

In recent years Dr. Brown has become a dear friend. It has been one of my greatest blessings and privileges to pray with him while seeking the wisdom only God can give as we both grow in the knowledge of Christ and His perfect will. As you read *Saving a Sick America,* I believe you will be inspired, challenged, and moved to become a part of the answer to Jesus' prayer in John 17—that we as believers will come together in supernatural unity as the stage is set for the greatest spiritual awakening in history.

JAMES ROBISON
Founder and president, LIFE
Outreach International
Founder and publisher, The
Stream (stream.org)
Fort Worth, Texas

PREFACE

IF YOU ARE LOOKING FOR A BOOK FILLED WITH PESSIMISM, GLOOM, and despair, this book is not for you. If you are looking for a book filled with divine optimism and hope, this book is absolutely for you, since in the pages that follow I lay out a vision for the moral and cultural transformation of America: a vision based on the Scriptures and based on the belief that another great awakening, perhaps the greatest awakening in our nation's history, could still be ahead. Given the greatness of our God, why does this seem so far-fetched and impossible?

I'm quite aware that there are many believers today who feel that America, along with the rest of the world, is on an inevitable downward course, that the prophetic scriptures indicate that things will only get worse, and that there is no hope for nation-shaking revivals. I am not one of those believers, and as I read the Word and commune with the Lord, my heart is filled with expectation and hope, and I firmly believe that the best is yet to come.

To be sure, I am a realist, and I pull no punches in this book. In fact, one of the goals of *Saving a Sick America* is to help us realize just how sick we are—spiritually and morally and culturally. But our nation is not sick beyond the point of recovery, and if God's people will start living by God's Word and relying on God's Spirit, there is no telling what could happen to our country.

The unexpected events of 2016, culminating with the election of the most unlikely presidential candidate in our history, remind us that anything can happen and that history is not written in stone. Why, then, shouldn't we believe in the possibility of powerful spiritual change as well? If America can be shaken to the core almost overnight in what many pundits refer to as a political revolution, why can't America be shaken with a gospel-based, moral and cultural revolution?

While in prayer one morning early in 2016, I sensed the Lord whispering to me, "Write a book on the fall and rise of America," and I was immediately gripped with the concept. I needed to lay out in the clearest, most graphic terms just how far we have fallen, especially from our earliest days as colonies and a fledgling nation. But then, through the Scriptures, I needed to lay out a prescription for radical change. In all candor, at many points in writing *Saving a Sick America*, I cried out to the Lord, confessing my inability to solve the problems at hand and my need for divine wisdom. To the extent this book proves helpful, transformative, and life-giving, all the credit belongs to him.

I deeply appreciate the excellent work of my agent Brian Mitchell of the WTA Group, who did a masterful job of finding the right publisher for the manuscript, and I am profoundly grateful to the team at Thomas Nelson for their enthusiasm, professionalism, and expertise in bringing this book to light. My thanks to Webster Younce, Heather Skelton, Chris Thillen, and Brigitta Nortker in the editorial department and to Jeff James, Aryn Van Dyke, and Tiffany Sawyer in marketing. May the Lord reward all your efforts by impacting the lives of many.

I am also indebted to the entire ministry team at AskDrBrown, enabling me to focus on the things the Lord has called me to do; to my home community, FIRE, for continuing to pursue our world-changing vision; and to Nancy, my best friend since 1974 and my wonderful bride since 1976. And to each of you reading this book, thank you for your time and your interest. May the Lord hear the cry of your heart and may Jesus be glorified in your life. To stay connected with me via social media, including Facebook, Twitter, and YouTube, just go to my website, AskDrBrown.org, and be sure to avail yourself of the hundreds of free resources in the Digital Library. Forward!

This book is dedicated to my precious mother, Rose, the model of unselfish love and the epitome of a Jewish mom so proud of her son. She passed away during the final editing stages of the book. We all miss you!

PART ONE

———

How Sick Are We?

INTRODUCTION

——

THE SICKLY STATE OF THE UNION

It is not the healthy who need a doctor, but the sick.
—LUKE 5:31 NIV

IT'S BEEN A BEAUTIFUL SPRING DAY IN THE SUBURBS OF Pennsylvania on this Thursday, June 7, 1961. You just got home from work and your wife is almost finished preparing one of her typically delicious dinners. Your kids, a boy and two girls, aged fifteen, thirteen, and nine, have been out all day riding their bikes around the neighborhood and playing with friends. Now everybody's hungry and ready to sit down for the family meal.

Last night was game night, and you barely emerged with a victory in Monopoly. Your kids are getting good, and your wife, normally the more savvy player, had some bad luck. Tonight is TV night, and everyone is ready to enjoy *Ozzie and Harriet* and *Leave It to Beaver*. (The younger ones get to stay up a little later on TV night, and you know they're not going to miss a minute of the shows.)

Of course a live, in-person show is incredible—who could forget your family outing two weeks ago when you all drove into Manhattan and saw *My Fair Lady* on Broadway? But TV has its own unique appeal, especially with shows like *Lassie* and *Andy Griffith* and *Walt Disney's Wonderful World of Color* and *Father Knows Best* and *The Flintstones*. And they're all on at night so the whole family can enjoy them together.

Well, on this lovely spring night, you're a bit more tired than you realized, fighting to stay awake through the current *Beaver* episode, even

3

though it's a bit more suspenseful than normal. In this show Beaver loses his haircut money and is afraid to explain the loss to his parents, Ward and June Cleaver. So he gives himself a ragged haircut with his brother Wally's help—and the two wear stocking caps to dinner, saying the caps are part of a secret club initiation. Later, Ward and June lift Beaver's cap while he sleeps and discover the truth, and the show ends with June explaining to the boys that they have no one but themselves to blame for the deception. As always, there's a good moral conclusion to the show.

But this night, you doze off just before the end of the program, and when you wake up a few minutes later, everything has changed. The TV is still there, except it's gigantic now, flat and hanging on a wall, exploding with colors. And instead of the smiling Cleaver family, it's—no, this can't be real—a nude couple going on their first date together. What is happening?

In a panic, you look for another channel while quickly figuring out how to use the newfangled remote control you now hold in your hands. But your eyes can't believe what you're seeing: two men making out passionately while taking off each other's clothes. This must be a dream—a really bad dream. You hit the button again, and to your relief it's a nice, old-fashioned show with a man and his family—a really big family, with lots of children—and five wives! What?

But wait. You discover that Walt Disney is still here. In fact, there's a whole Disney channel, and it's time for *Good Luck Charlie*—except that the show is celebrating a two-mommy family. Is this meant to be a joke?

You click once more, and this time it's two young moms with their daughters talking about the struggles of life. But the more you listen, the more you realize how young these single moms are—they're both sixteen and unmarried—and their babies were born out of wedlock. This is now on TV? (And though you don't know it, one of these young moms would later release her own sex tape—a term you can't even imagine—in order to stay popular.)

You're now in a cold sweat, frantically switching channels as if some-how you could find a way out of the nightmare. Finally, you come across a show that looks a little like *Bonanza*—at least the people are carrying shot-guns like they did in the old Westerns. But who are they shooting? Walking dead! Zombies, with their brains exploding on TV! (Don't switch to the next channel. There you'll see vampires having sex.)

Did I wake up in hell?

But something else is different when you look around the room. You're the only one there.

Your fifteen-year-old son is out with his best friend Robbie—who used to be called Robin back when he was a girl—along with Robbie's seventeen-year-old brother. All three went to see a new movie in the *Hostel* series, where people are tortured to death and mutilated for fun, but hey, at least he's out of the house. It's better than playing *Grand Theft Auto* for six straight hours where your boy simulates raping women and killing cops on his video screen.

As for your wife, she's at the psychologist's office with your thirteen-year-old daughter discussing whether they need to up her antidepressant medication. She's still cutting herself—she's been doing that for the last year, ever since her best friend at school killed herself after the "sexting" scandal when the girl's ex-boyfriend sent out her naked picture to all the kids in middle school. And what's more, your daughter's weight gain is out of control. (She's almost a hundred pounds overweight, and she's barely a teenager.)

Unfortunately, her new best friend at school is also fighting depression. It seems that things fell apart after her stepfather abused her (it was her mom's third marriage), but thankfully, she survived the drug overdose. That was a real scare. And it's a good thing her mom never found out about the abortion. Her mother would not have been happy to find out that her thirteen-year-old daughter and her boyfriend weren't using protection.

As for your youngest girl, still so innocent at nine years old, she's shut up in her room with her headphones on, dancing to Beyoncé's latest hit. She sure is a smooth dancer for such a little kid, although it's probably good that she's too young to know what the bumping and grinding is all about or what those suggestive lyrics actually mean.

But all is well, since she's just down the hallway, safe in her room. The neighborhood just hasn't been the same since two kids were abducted within twelve months, only for their abused bodies to turn up in the woods weeks later. The police still haven't found the sexual predator responsible for these inhuman acts.

Then, suddenly, you wake up with a start. This was all a dream, a very terrible dream, an absolute nightmare. With relief, you look around at your wonderful family, smiling at their dad who fell asleep in the middle of TV night. And you think to yourself, *Thank God this was only a bad dream. There's no way America—or my family—could ever look like that.*

ONE

How Good Were the Good Old Days?

Thus says the LORD: "Stand by the roads, and look, and ask for the ancient paths, where the good way is; and walk in it, and find rest for your souls. But they said, 'We will not walk in it.'"
—JEREMIAH 6:16

AMERICA WAS FAR FROM PERFECT IN THE EARLY 1960S. IN MUCH OF the nation segregation was the law of the land, and women had far fewer opportunities than men, just to mention two of society's inequities. And it's true that the first issue of *Playboy*, featuring Marilyn Monroe in the nude, was published in 1953. At the same time, there's no denying that 1960s America was a far more innocent, family-friendly country than it is today. And so, fifty-five years ago, when we sat together and watched *Leave It to Beaver*, we didn't say to ourselves, "How corny! There's not a family in the nation like the Cleavers." Instead, we found what we saw as normal as it was entertaining.

Americans in the late fifties to early sixties enjoyed watching *Father Knows Best* and *The Andy Griffith Show*; today we enjoy watching *Keeping Up with the Kardashians* and *Secret Diary of a Call Girl*. In the late fifties to early sixties, Annette Funicello was a popular young female star singing songs like "Pineapple Princess"; today it's Miley Cyrus, singing songs like "Wrecking Ball"—in the nude, riding a wrecking ball, in her music video.

Take an old show like *Dennis the Menace*, which aired from 1959 to 1963, and think of some of the things he got in trouble for (after all, he was called a "menace," right?). In the first episode, "Dennis successfully eludes a babysitter (whom he has never met) and sneaks out of the house and goes to a cowboy movie that his parents also go to while [his friend] Joey is left with the babysitter, pretending to be Dennis." In the next episode, "Dennis and [his closest friend] Tommy replace a fallen street signpost but fail to notice they've put it up with the street names facing in the wrong direction."[1] Oh, what a menace!

Today we would be following Dennis's journey on reality TV, waiting for him to get out of the juvenile detention center after robbing an elderly man in broad daylight. Will Dennis ever change, or will he end up dead before his eighteenth birthday? And rather than having his old scruffy hairdo with that shock of blond locks always out of place, Dennis would be sporting a purple Mohawk, earrings, an eyebrow ring, a lip ring, and tattoos galore. (If you think I'm exaggerating, watch some clips from *Beyond Scared Straight*.)

Or consider another early TV series, *I Love Lucy*, where Lucy and her husband slept in separate beds. Could you imagine today's version, where the show would feature partial nudity (but only partial: after all, it's a family show, so there has to be some modesty), mild profanity, constant sexual innuendos, and kids who show not even the slightest respect to their parents? Or compare *Andy Griffith* to *Stalker* or *Hannibal*, or compare *Lawrence Welk* to the annual MTV Music Awards. Or watch an old Elvis movie where he shakes his hips—that was so controversial—and compare that to the latest crotch-grabbing, bootie-shaking music video (those have been around for quite some time now). And be sure to compare the lyrics too!

If you're a young person reading this, and you're not familiar with the older shows, take a few minutes to watch some of the episodes. They're readily available on YouTube, and you'll be amazed by what you see. Watch an episode of *Lassie*, then switch over to *American Horror Story*, or compare *West Side Story* to *Natural Born Killers*. Then go back to *The Flintstones* cartoon show—remember, we would watch this together as a family—and compare it to today's animated shows like *South Park* or *Adult Swim*. (By the way, if you say, "I'd rather pass on watching these newer shows," you won't get an argument from me.)

As Eliot Cohen noted on February 26, 2016:

Ours is an age when young people have become used to getting news, of a sort, from Jon Stewart and Stephen Colbert, when an earlier generation watched Walter Cronkite and David Brinkley. It is the difference between giggling with young, sneering hipsters and listening to serious adults. Go to YouTube and look at old episodes of *Profiles in Courage*, if you can find them—a wildly successful television series based on the book nominally authored by John F. Kennedy, which celebrated an individual's, often a politician's, courage in standing alone against a crowd, even a crowd with whose politics the audience agreed. The show of comparable popularity today is *House of Cards*.[2]

Irwin and Debi Unger painted a graphic picture for us of what America looked like on the day of JFK's inauguration, January 20, 1961:

America, on that blustery inauguration day in January 1961, was still deep in the throes of postwar conformity. Skirts were worn below the knee, dresses were tailored, and women's shoes had high heels and pointy toes. On prime-time TV, the favorite programs were *The Flintstones, Ozzie and Harriet, One Happy Family*, and *The Bob Hope Show*. In film, the 1961 Academy Award for best picture went to a musical fable about feuding New York gangs, but *West Side Story* was monumentally innocent despite its subject matter. On Broadway, *My Fair Lady* was still drawing crowds after 2,300 performances. Elvis had already stirred the rage of parents and moralists with his swiveling hips and suggestive phrasing, but the most popular recording artist in 1961 was Eddie Fisher, the quintessential boy next door. Sexual mores were strict. Illegitimacy was rare in the middle class, and most Americans considered homosexuality a sin, and drove its practitioners deep into the closet. . . . On college campuses, except for a sprinkling of the most "progressive" and cosmopolitan ones, fraternities and sororities, pledge week, pep rallies, dances, and "sandbox" politics were the dominant extracurricular activities.[3]

Even though the 1960s were marked by a dramatic cultural shift, things did not change overnight, and so the Academy Award–winning movies of 1964 and 1965 were *My Fair Lady* and *The Sound of Music*. By 1969 the winner was *Midnight Cowboy*, a flick as different from the 1964 and 1965 winners as day is from night. Here are some selections from the *IMDB Movie Guide* describing *Midnight Cowboy* (taken from a lengthy description of content not fit for children):

> The main character makes a living off of prostitution and is constantly denying he's gay.
>
> Different bits of a scene, in which a man and a woman are interrupted in the back seat of a car, appear several times throughout the movie. Clips show the man fully nude from the rear. It is implied that the men interrupting the couple rape both people. We see the woman running naked into the house. In another clip in this montage, a boy is being spanked on his bare bottom.
>
> A man beats an old man a couple of times with punching and slapping leaving the man's face bloody and knocking his dentures out. He shoves the old man onto a bed and shoves a telephone into his mouth. The scene is cut short before we know the outcome, but there is later dialog that implies he was killed.
>
> There are several flashback montages of the attempted rape of both a man and his girlfriend by a group of men.[4]

I'm aware, of course, that a movie like *Chariots of Fire* won the Best Movie Oscar in 1981 while big hits in 1982 were *Gandhi* and *E.T. the Extra-Terrestrial*. And there are kid-friendly movies that remain super popular to this day. I'm simply pointing out how a culture of relative innocence was quickly replaced by a culture of violence and immorality, and it all happened in a very short period of time. As described by the Ungers, by the end of the sixties, "The Pill, announced with little fanfare in 1960, had ended fear of pregnancy; penicillin had diminished fear of disease. Sex, in any position, in any form, was considered good; denial was bad. The new sexual liberation movement soon spread beyond youthful flower-child dropouts. All through middle-class and working-class America ran a new current of permissiveness."[5]

To highlight the rapidity of these social changes, consider how song titles of the Beatles changed from "I Want to Hold Your Hand" in 1964 to

"Why Don't We Do It in the Road?" in 1968. And to highlight the longer-term contrast, note that Elvis was singing about his "Blue Suede Shoes" in 1956 while Eminem was rapping about impregnating his own mother in 2000 (in the song "I'm Back").

And how about the many contemporary rap songs calling for the killing of cops or describing parts of women's bodies in the most vulgar terms or celebrating various sexual acts in detail? These lyrics alone point to the massive moral decline in our nation over the period of one generation.

Rev. Jesse Peterson relates, "I grew up listening to people like Diana Ross, James Brown, Otis Redding, the Temptations—the whole Motown lineup, for that matter." He notes that they sang songs with lyrics that talked about couples staying together through thick and thin, like Al Green's "Let's Stay Together." He then writes, "A more typical song today is Kanye West's 'Monster,'" which contains lyrics in which Kanye's mother gives him advice about sexually mounting a woman. Peterson also notes that, "There's even a genre of rap songs that critic Melinda Tankard Reist dubs, 'dead-bitches-are-the-best.'"[6] The times certainly have changed.

Psychology professor David G. Myers gives us a more statistical perspective of the changes that took place between 1960 and 2000. Over that forty-year period, America witnessed:

- Doubled divorce rate
- Tripled teen suicide rate
- Quadrupled rate of reported violent crime
- Quintupled prison population
- Sextupled (no pun intended) percent of
  babies born to unmarried parents
- Sevenfold increase in cohabitation (a predictor of future divorce)
- Soaring rate of depression—to ten times the pre–
  World War II level by one estimate[7]

Or consider this one, shocking statistic: "In 1960, only *1 child in every 350* lived with a mother who had never been married! By 2012, *22 out of every 100 kids* lived with a single mom, and only half of those moms had ever been married."[8] This is truly staggering.

To put this discussion on a more personal level, my wife, Nancy, was born in 1954, and her mother was married four times. But this situation was extremely rare in that day. Growing up on Long Island (the suburbs of New York City), Nancy knew hardly any other kids whose parents were divorced once, let alone multiple times. I was born a few months later in 1955, and I don't recall a single one of my friends whose parents were divorced. We just didn't hear about it much in that day, and it's not because all of these couples were covering up horrific marriages. Divorce simply wasn't considered an option, and in most cases the marriages were not falling apart.

Of course there *were* serious problems in many homes, and some couples were anything but happy. But in the days before no-fault divorce, marital vows carried much more weight—couples really did mean "till death do us part," and they worked harder at preserving the marriage—and there had to be valid reasons for the courts to grant a divorce. (There certainly are some valid reasons for divorce.)

Nancy and I grew up during the counterculture revolution of the sixties, and we both got caught up in the spirit of those times with drinking, drugs, and ungodly behavior. Yet neither of us knew anyone who got an abortion then (I recall one girl in my high school who got pregnant and gave up her baby for adoption), and neither of us remember any of our friends either trying to kill themselves or actually killing themselves.

It's different for teenagers today. The vast majority of them know someone who has had an abortion or who has tried to take his or her own life or even succeeded in doing it. As Americans, we have aborted more than fifty-five million babies since 1973. The entire population of Canada is only thirty-five million! As for teen suicide, "among youths 12 to 16 years of age, up to 10% of boys and 20% of girls have considered suicide." And, "suicide is the second leading cause of death—following motor vehicle accidents— among teenagers and young adults."[9] In addition, at least 50 percent of births to first-time mothers in America today are illegitimate.[10] Numerous studies point to the disastrous effects of fatherlessness in the home, as kids raised without a dad make up a disproportionately high percentage of teenagers who have psychological problems, run away from home, commit violent crimes, do not get a good education, and live in poverty. It is a vicious cycle that will only repeat itself until solid families are restored.

But there is something even more striking than the contrast between the America of fifty years ago and the America of today. It is the contrast between America in 1960 and America in the days of our Founding Fathers—or, even more so, in the days of the American colonies. Consider some of the rules of conduct for students at Harvard University (then Harvard College) in the seventeenth century (the school was founded in 1636):

> No student of any class, shall visit any shop or tavern, to eat and drink, unless invited by a parent, guardian, stepparent, or some such relative;
>
> No student shall buy, sell or exchange any thing without the approval of his parents, guardians, or tutors;
>
> All students must refrain from wearing rich and showy clothing, nor must any one go out of the college-yard, unless in his gown, coat or cloak;
>
> No one must, under any pretext, be found in the society of any depraved or dissolute person;
>
> If any student shall, either through willfulness or negligence, violate any law of God or of this college, after being twice admonished, he shall suffer severe punishment, at the discretion of the President or his tutor. But in high-handed offences, no such modified forms of punishment need be expected.[11]

Moreover, to graduate from Harvard with the most basic degree in arts (not theology—that came later), the student had to be able "logically to explain the Holy Scriptures, both of the Old and New Testaments . . . and . . . be blameless in life and character."

As noted by Matthew Spalding in *We Still Hold These Truths: Rediscovering Our Principles, Reclaiming Our Future*, "Colonial America was a highly literate society, despite its overwhelmingly rural population. The two books likely to be found in every home were a well-worn copy of the Bible and a volume of Shakespeare, Milton, or other great literature."[12] In fact, a major reason that children went to school back then was so that they could learn to read their Bibles.[13]

All this discussion leads to an important series of questions as we look back to our country's past and consider how we can work together for a better future:

1. Was America ever a "Christian nation"?
2. If so, does America need to get "back to God"?
3. If America does need to get back to God, what's the difference between seeking to restore a "Christian" America and trying to impose a theocracy?
4. Or could it be that this whole notion of America once being a Christian nation is nothing more than a popular myth, a myth based on a distorted reading of the past, and a myth with dangerous implications for the present?

We'll take up these questions in the next two chapters as we turn back the clock four hundred years rather than fifty. You're in for some surprises.

PART TWO

AMERICA'S BIBLICAL ROOTS

TWO

THE BIBLE IN AMERICAN HISTORY

Whoever is wise, let him understand these things;
whoever is discerning, let him know them; for the
ways of the LORD are right, and the upright walk
in them, but transgressors stumble in them.
—HOSEA 14:9

DID YOU EVER HEAR OF THE OLD DELUDER ACT DATING BACK TO 1647, right here in America? It was a law passed by leaders of the colony of Massachusetts to ensure that children received a proper education *so that they would be able to read the Bible,* thus making them into good citizens. As for the "Old Deluder," that was none other than Satan himself. (The law was actually called "Ye olde deluder Satan Act.")

This is how the text reads:

It being one chief project of that old deluder, Satan, to keep men from the knowledge of the Scriptures, as in former times by keeping them in an unknown tongue, so in these latter times by persuading from the use of tongues, that so that at least the true sense and meaning of the original might be clouded and corrupted with false glosses of saint-seeming deceivers; and to the end that learning may not be buried in the grave of our forefathers, in church and commonwealth, the Lord assisting our endeavors.

It is therefore ordered that every township in this jurisdiction, after the Lord hath increased them to fifty households shall forthwith appoint one within their town to teach all such children as shall resort to him to

17

write and read, whose wages shall be paid either by the parents or masters of such children, or by the inhabitants in general, by way of supply, as the major part of those that order the prudentials of the town shall appoint; provided those that send their children be not oppressed by paying much more than they can have them taught for in other towns.[1]

If anything underscores the Christian roots of America's earliest settlers, this law does.

The Puritans fled from religious persecution in England to start a new life here in America, and it was persecution *by the church* from which they fled. As noted in the opening lines of the Old Deluder Act: "It being one chief project of that old deluder, Satan, to keep men from the knowledge of the Scriptures, *as in former times by keeping them in an unknown tongue*, so in these latter times by persuading from the use of tongues" (my emphasis). Yes, in the past, the organized church had kept the Bible from Christians, not allowing it to be translated into the language of the people, even persecuting and killing those who undertook such work.

This meant that the clergy alone could read and interpret the Scriptures. It also meant that a corrupt clergy could keep the people ignorant and under their power. Thus, knowledge of the Bible was a real threat to the unethical religious establishment. Now that these Christians were in their new country, they wanted to be sure that knowledge of the Scriptures was not suppressed again. And so, as new settlers began to arrive and the population of Massachusetts began to grow, they wanted to make certain that the children were able to read the Bible for themselves. Proper education, therefore, was a must.

Similar sentiments were expressed in the New Haven Code of 1655, which stated that the purpose of education was to equip children to be "able duly to read the Scriptures . . . and in some competent measure to understand the main grounds and principles of Christian Religion necessary to salvation."[2] It was also assumed that this learning was the key to the colony functioning well: citizens who knew their Bibles would make the best citizens.

Can you imagine the Department of Education issuing a statement today that said, "In order to ensure that all American children are able to study the sacred Scriptures, we are shoring up our reading and grammar programs"? Could you picture Congress enacting legislation that said, "In recognition of Satan's wily ways, foremost of which are his manifold attempts to keep people from reading their Bibles, we are calling for mandatory Scripture reading in all schools and in all classes, beginning in kindergarten and continuing through twelfth grade"? To say that scenarios like this are laughable would be a massive understatement.

Today, it is not uncommon to hear reports of administrators forbidding students from forming a Bible club in their schools,[3] while teachers have told students they could not read the Bible in their own classrooms.[4] And in 2016 the Bible was listed as number six in the list of most-objected-to books in public schools and libraries. Other books on the list included the pornographic *Fifty Shades of Grey*; John Green's *Looking for Alaska*, cited for "offensive language" and sexual content; *Two Boys Kissing*; and a transgender picture book. Who would have imagined that the Bible would ever make it onto a school library list as an "objectionable" book?[5]

As for what *is* taught in our children's schools, in 2013 New York City announced an aggressive, comprehensive, and quite graphic curriculum that would consist of one full semester of sex education in sixth or seventh grade (meaning, beginning with kids as young as eleven) and again in ninth and tenth grade.[6] Specifically:

- High school students go to stores and jot down condom brands, prices, and features such as lubrication.
- Teens research a route from school to a clinic that provides birth control and STD tests, and write down its confidentiality policy.
- Kids ages eleven and twelve sort "risk cards" to rate the safety of various activities, including "intercourse using a condom and an oil-based lubricant" and all kinds of explicit sex acts.
- Teens are referred to resources such as Columbia University's website Go Ask Alice, which explores topics like sexual positions, "sadomasochistic sex play," phone sex, and more.[7]

The Old Deluder must be snickering over this list.

In California a law was enacted in 2011 requiring schools to teach LGBT American history, meaning that every school must celebrate the "contributions of lesbian, gay, bisexual and transgender Americans."[8] The law is quite comprehensive in its scope, applying to all public schools, grades K–12, with no exemptions allowed. This means that parents cannot choose to have their kids opt out of these lesson units, and teachers cannot opt out from teaching, regardless of religious or moral convictions. Instead, every child must learn about influential gay icons and cross-dressing individuals of the past who (allegedly) helped shape our history.

Is it possible, though, that this Old Deluder Act from 1647 was an aberration in American history, an extreme example of Puritan ideology being forced on the population at large? Not at all. The Bible played a major role in American education for several centuries, even though as America diversified, even within its Christian expressions, the Bible was not as universally present in our schools, even before the twentieth century.[9] That being said, the centrality of the Scriptures in our educational history cannot be denied, not to mention its subsequent impact on our national culture.[10]

In 1690 the first *New England Primer* was published. The alphabet was taught using Bible verses for each letter, and the primer contained questions on the moral teachings of the Scriptures, children's prayers, the Lord's Prayer, the Ten Commandments, the Shorter Catechism, and questions on the Bible by John Cotton. *The New England Primer* continued to be widely used in American schools of all types—public, private, home, or parochial—for the next two hundred years.[11]

To read this text for myself, I downloaded the 1777 edition of the *Primer*,[12] meaning the edition that would have been used widely at the time our nation was birthed. On the opening page is an Isaac Watts hymn titled, "A Divine Song of Praise to GOD, for a Child," followed by morning and evening prayers written by Dr. Watts for children.

After listing the pronunciation of letters and words, the first lesson begins with, "Pray to God. Call no ill names. Love God. Use no ill words. Fear God. Tell no lies. Serve God. Hate Lies. Take not God's Name in vain. Speak the Truth. Spend your Time well. Do not Swear. Love your School. Do not Steal. Mind your Book. Cheat not in your play. Strive to learn. Play not with bad boys. Be not a Dunce." Sounds just like one of our kid's textbooks today! (Sarcasm fully intended.)

Next come the ABCs, put in poetic form to make them more easily memorized, with important biblical truths taught at the same time. To repeat, this is how countless American children learned to read in the late seventeen hundreds and beyond:

A
In ADAM'S Fall
We sinned all.

B
Heaven to find;
The Bible Mind.

C
Christ crucify'd
For sinners dy'd.

And on and on it goes through the alphabet, with references to biblical characters like David, Elijah, Esther, Felix, Job, Josiah, Korah, Lot, Moses, Noah, Obadiah, Peter, Ruth, Samuel, Timothy, Vashti, Xerxes, and Zacchaeus. Today many adult Christians could not identify every name on this list. A little more than two centuries ago, familiarity with these biblical characters and the stories associated with them was part of a child's first reading experience.

The primer continues with biblically based questions such as "Who was the first man?" (Adam), and "Who saves lost men?" (Jesus Christ), and "Who is Jesus Christ?" (the Son of God). Then, after including a prayer before meals for children, another exercise follows, called "An Alphabet of Lessons for Youth." It begins:

A wise son maketh a glad father, but a foolish son is the heaviness of his mother.

Better is a little with the fear of the Lord, than great treasure & trouble therewith.

Come unto Christ all ye that labor and are heavy laden and he will give you rest.

Do not the abominable thing which I hate saith the Lord.

What comes next? The Lord's Prayer. And after that? The Apostles' Creed. And then? Dr. Watts's Cradle Hymn.

There is also a series of short moral and ethical exhortations, some of which are quite sober (including lessons from the cemetery). Most of these contain clear biblical teaching, such as "Good children must, Fear God all day, Love Christ alway, Parents obey, In secret pray, No false thing say, Mind little play, By no sin stray, Make no delay, In doing good." And on and on it goes, with the complete text of the Westminster Shorter Catechism and some very serious questions and answers—all biblically based—by Mr. Cotton.

Over time, this primer was displaced by Noah Webster's *Blue Back Speller*, first published in 1783, "with its opening sentence declaring: 'No man may put off the law of God.' This speller [was] widely used in American schools and [was] peppered throughout with Bible verses. Later versions stated, 'Noah Webster who taught millions to read but not one to sin.'"[13] Generations of American children learned to read and write with this book, a sign of the high esteem with which the Bible was held in the culture, even by many nonbelievers.

The facsimile edition of the 1824 printing offers some "lessons of easy words, to teach children to read, and to know their duty." Lesson one says:

> No man may put off the law of God:
> My joy is in his law all the day.
> O may I not go the way of sin!
> Let me not go the way of ill men![14]

The last lesson states, "As for those boys and girls that mind not their books, and love not the church and the school, but play with such as tell tales, tell lies, curse, swear, and steal, they will come to some bad end, and must be whipt till they mend their ways."[15]

Now, to be clear, I'm not advocating corporal punishment in our schools. But I am saying that I prefer the atmosphere of American schools in the nineteenth century to the atmosphere today where, in some school districts, teachers fear acts of violence from their students, metal detectors are required to keep weapons out, and police are on duty to discourage fights

22

(and more). What a far cry this is from the days when Webster's reader was used throughout the land, containing pages of moral warnings (see, e.g., pp. 49–51), exhortations based on Proverbs (pp. 62, 64–65), passages from Jesus' Sermon on the Mount (pp. 72–73), a short recap of the history of creation (pp. 103–04), and a closing moral catechism (pp. 156–68) that would challenge mature Christian readers today.

Just contrast a modern school lesson in which children are taught to buy and use condoms (girls practice putting condoms on boys' fingers),[16] with these words from Webster's reader: "Art thou a young man, seeking for a partner for life? [Notice it does not say "seeking a sex partner."] Obey the ordinance of God, and become a useful member of society. But be not in haste to marry, and let thy choice be directed by wisdom."[17]

In 1836 the first McGuffey Reader was "published which [taught] the ABC's along with Bible verses. This reader [was] looked at as an 'eclectic reader' which combine[d] instructive axioms and proverbs, fundamentals of grammar and selections of the finest English literature."[18] Interestingly, by the late eighteen hundreds the Bible's central place in American education had been greatly eroded, as can be seen by reading subsequent editions of the McGuffey Reader.[19] Nonetheless, the Bible had been so central in American education for so many years that, in 1892, the Kansas Teachers' Union declared that

> if the study of the Bible is to be excluded from all State schools, if the inculcation of the principles of Christianity is to have no place in the daily programme, if the worship of God is to form no part of the general exercises of these public elementary schools, then the good of the State would be better served by restoring all schools to church control.[20]

When it came to higher education, the pattern continued, and "Of the first 108 colleges and universities founded in America, 106 were founded as Christian schools. Of the first 126 colleges, 123 were Christian."[21] And so, just as Christians pioneered education for America's younger children, Christians also pioneered education for America's older children and young adults, establishing colleges and universities to train ministers and then, more widely, to educate others for secular professions.

Consider the origins of several of our nation's most prestigious schools, beginning with Harvard.

- Harvard University was founded in 1636 as Harvard College with the motto "Truth" (Veritas). Its purpose was "to train a literate clergy." Among the "Rules and Precepts" to be observed by the students were these: "Let every Student be plainly instructed, and earnestly pressed to consider well, the main end of his life and studies is, to know God and Jesus Christ which is eternal life"; and, "Every one shall so exercise himself in reading the Scriptures twice a day, that he shall be ready to give such an account of his proficiency therein, both in Theoretical observations of Language and Logic, and in practical and spiritual truths."[22]
- Princeton University was founded in 1746 as the College of New Jersey. The school's motto was "Under God's Power She Flourishes,"[23] and until 1902 every president of Princeton was a minister. Although seminary training was the school's first goal, its founding purpose went beyond that: "Though our great Intention was to erect a seminary for educating Ministers of the Gospel, yet we hope it will be useful in other learned professions— Ornaments of the State as Well as the Church."[24]
- Columbia University, which was founded as King's College in 1754 by a royal charter of King George II, had as its goals to "enlarge the Mind, improve the Understanding, polish the whole Man, and qualify them to support the brightest Characters in all the elevated stations in life."[25] The college was distinctly non-denominational: "The first advertisement of the college disclaims any intention of imposing 'on the scholars the peculiar Tenants of any particular Sect of Christians; but to inculcate upon their tender minds, the great Principles of Christianity and Morality, in which true Christians of each Denomination are generally agreed.'"[26]
- The motto of Boston University was "Learning, Virtue, and Piety." It was founded as a Methodist seminary in Vermont in 1839 before its eventual transfer to Boston in 1867. Until 1967—meaning just

two years before Woodstock—all of its presidents were Methodist ministers. (The university's first non-Methodist minister president, Arland F. Christ-Janer, was still a graduate of Yale Divinity School.)[27]

- The motto of the University of Pennsylvania, founded in 1740 but not opened until 1751, was "Laws without morals are useless" (*Leges sine moribus vanae*).[28]
- The motto of Brown University, founded in 1764 as Rhode Island College, was "In God we hope" (*In Deo speramus*).[29]
- Rutgers University, founded in 1766 as Queen's College, had as its motto "Sun of righteousness, shine upon the West also" (*Sol iustitiae et occidentem illustra*).[30] Its founding purpose was "for the education of the youth of the said province and the neighboring colonies in true religion and useful learning and particularly for providing an able and learned protestant ministry."[31]

To get further perspective on the strong Christian foundation of some of our leading universities, let's focus on one of the oldest institutions in our nation, Yale University, which for many years stood out as one of the most deeply religious schools in the land. Today, Yale remains one of the finest institutions of higher learning in the world, an elite school among elite schools. Among its illustrious list of alumni are presidents of the United States, Supreme Court justices, and Nobel Prize winners, to name just a few. Yale's prestigious accomplishments were showcased in the 2004 elections, in which both presidential candidates (George W. Bush and John Kerry), along with one of the two vice presidential candidates (John Edwards), were Yale graduates. How many other schools can make this claim?

Founded in 1701, Yale's purpose was "to plant and under ye Divine blessing to propagate in this Wilderness, the blessed Reformed, Protestant Religion, in ye purity of its Order and Worship." In keeping with this goal, until the turn of the twentieth century, every president of Yale was also a Christian minister. And during the tenures of several presidents in the eighteenth and nineteenth centuries, Yale experienced a series of spiritual revivals, bringing revitalization and renewal to the student body. To this day, Timothy Dwight Chapel stands as a memorial of Yale's rich spiritual history. Inscribed in front of the chapel are these words: "Christ is the only, the true, the living way of access to God. Give up yourselves therefore to him, with a cordial confidence, and the great work of life is done."[32] (Yes, this inscription is still at Yale.)

One of Yale's precepts was,

> All scholars [i.e., students] shall live religious, godly and blameless lives according to the rules of God's Word, diligently reading the Holy Scriptures, the fountain of light and truth; and constantly attend upon all the duties of religion, both in public and secret. Seeing God is the giver of all wisdom, every scholar, besides private or secret prayer, where all we are bound to ask wisdom shall be present morning and evening at public prayer in the hall at the accustomed hour.[33]

Did you catch that? All students were required to attend public prayer meetings every morning and every evening. *Compulsory chapel attendance at Yale was not abolished until 1928.*[34] Anyone who has attended Yale in recent decades might think this entire account is fabricated, so radically have things changed. Conversely, in their wildest dreams, students at Yale in the early seventeen hundreds could not have countenanced the atmosphere at Yale today.

America in the seventeenth, eighteenth, and even much of the nineteenth century was a dramatically different country than the America of today. The truth is that Christian values and Christian mission played a major role in our educational system, and the Bible was held as an important text to be read in our schools. And these same values caused our Founding Fathers to write, "We hold these truths to be self-evident, that all men are created equal, that they are endowed by their Creator with certain unalienable Rights, that among these are Life, Liberty and the pursuit of Happiness." These truths were "self-evident" only to the extent that there was a benevolent and just Creator. Without him, this entire sentence, which forms the philosophical linchpin of the Declaration of Independence, would disappear.[35] Founding Father Samuel Adams went as far as claiming that the rights of the colonists "may be best understood by reading and carefully studying the institutes of the great Law-giver and head of the Christian

Church [Jesus], which are to be found clearly written and promulgated in the New Testament."[36]

It is easy, of course, to point to our major failings as a nation, including the practice of slavery and our treatment of the Native Americans. Those failings are undeniable and cannot be minimized; they represent horrible blind spots in the lives of some of our forefathers, albeit blind spots largely inherited from their British way of life. And there were certainly extreme and destructive acts carried out in the name of Christianity, most notably the much maligned (and highly exaggerated) Salem witch trials.[37]

At the same time, it cannot be denied that there was a steady Christian witness against slavery in our national history, ultimately leading to its abolition, while there was a constant attempt by Christians to live peaceably with the native population, reaching out to them with the gospel as well. And it was the biblical, Christian ethic that infused our society with the very principles that made us great. Moreover, despite a very real, often dominant, "worldly" aspect to our society, found as early as the seventeen hundreds, and despite times of spiritual backsliding in the church, requiring fresh awakenings and revivals, there can be no question that the Christian faith has played a major role in our history with the Bible at the center of that history.

Simply stated, the ideas that made America exceptional, the ideas that truly enabled us to become "the land of the free and the home of the brave," were ideas based on biblical principles and Christian values. The very concept that freedom and equality are "entitlements" based on "the Laws of Nature and of Nature's God" says it all with precision and clarity. That's why our founders appealed "to the Supreme Judge of the world for the rectitude of our intentions," and that's why they expressed "a firm reliance on the protection of Divine Providence."[38]

Take away these biblical principles and this sense of God-consciousness, and you take away the moral foundations of our nation. In their absence America will only spiral toward self-destruction, and today we find ourselves in that spiral. Conversely, the recovery of these principles is the path to the recovery of what is best about America, and it is our nation's only hope. As Samuel Adams wrote, "A general dissolution of principles and manners will more surely overthrow the liberties of America than the whole force of the common enemy. While the people are virtuous they can not be subdued; but when once they lose their virtue they will be ready to surrender their liberties to the first external or internal invader."[39]

Before, however, we begin to address these principles and their application to our lives today, we need to address the question of a theocracy and explain why we must categorically reject attempts to establish a theocracy in America (or any nation) today. There is a world of difference between advocating for the transformational power of living by biblical principles and seeking to establish a theocracy, defined as a "form of government in which God or a deity is recognized as the supreme civil ruler, the God's or deity's laws being interpreted by the ecclesiastical authorities" and then enforced on the masses.[40]

We'll take up that difference in the next chapter.

THREE

The Bible, Not a Theocracy, Is the Answer

Your word is a lamp to my feet and a light to my path.
—PSALM 119:105

IN MAY 2012 THE FAMED EVANGELIST REV. BILLY GRAHAM, THEN ninety-three years old, took out full-page ads in newspapers throughout North Carolina addressing the upcoming vote on the definition of marriage. The ads featured a large picture of Rev. Graham and carried his own words: "At 93, I never thought we would have to debate the definition of marriage. The Bible is clear—God's definition of marriage is between a man and a woman. I want to urge my fellow North Carolinians to vote FOR the marriage amendment on Tuesday, May 8. God bless you as you vote."

Wayne Besen, an outspoken gay activist, took strong exception to these ads, writing:

I'm a little confused here, because I thought we lived in America. Yet Graham is now trying to jam his own church's rules and doctrine down my throat. The last time I checked, I never signed up for the Billy Graham Evangelistic Association (BGEA). I don't even like his church, yet he thinks I should be forced against my will to live by its rules.

Do we now make our civil laws based upon Christian Sharia? Do we all have to follow his version of the Bible or be punished by government? And if this is the case, are we really a free country? Are we really much different than Iran, or is it only by a matter of degrees or a matter of time until these so-called "Christian Supremacists" get their paws on all of our laws?[1]

Christian Sharia? Christian Supremacists? Isn't this a little extreme?

Actually, Besen is not the only one to react in this way. Already in May 2005, John McCandlish Phillips, formerly a Pulitzer Prize–winning *New York Times* reporter, pointed out how newspapers like the *Washington Post* and the *Times* told their readers that evangelicals and traditional Catholics were engaging in a "jihad" against America. Phillips noted that, days before his article was published,

> Frank Rich, an often acute, broadly knowledgeable and witty cultural observer, sweepingly informed us that, under the effects of "the God racket" as now pursued in Washington, "government, culture, science, medicine and the rule of law are all under threat from an emboldened religious minority out to remake America according to its dogma."[2]

He went on to tell *Times* readers that GOP zealots in Congress and the White House have edged our country over into "a full-scale jihad."

By 2010, Markos Moulitsas, founder of the radically leftist DailyKos.com, had written an entire book on the subject. The title says it all: *American Taliban: How War, Sex, Sin, and Power Bind Jihadists and the Radical Right.*

In the introduction to his book, Moulitsas claimed that "the Republican Party, and the entire modern conservative movement is, in fact, very much like the Taliban. In their tactics and on the issues, our homegrown American Taliban are almost indistinguishable from the Afghan Taliban."[3] And remember, this writing was not meant to be satire. Moulitsas was dead serious, as are many of his readers who share his views.

During the 2012 presidential debates, MSNBC's Chris Matthews launched a tirade against vice presidential candidate Paul Ryan, calling Ryan's pro-life position "extremism" and claiming it was "almost like Sharia." He opined, "You're saying to the country, we're going to operate under a religious theory, a religious belief. We're gonna run our country this way, to the point of making a woman's decision to have an abortion, her reproductive rights, as criminal, perhaps murderous."[4]

This claim of Matthews, which raised quite a few eyebrows in 2012, now seems tame when compared to the latest rhetoric launched against conservative Christians. In fact, it's not enough to compare us to the Taliban. We are now being likened to ISIS.

I gave some anecdotal evidence of this in an article published on September 13, 2012, titled, "When Committed Christians Are Compared to ISIS."[5] In the article, I noted that a few days earlier "Dixie" had posted "You are just as ugly as ISIS!" on my Facebook page. I asked in response, "Because we want to protect innocent babies in the womb? Because we care about marriage and family? Because we feed the poor and needy around the world? Because we want the whole world to know how wonderful Jesus is? Please be kind enough to explain your views." Dixie didn't respond.

Just a few days before that, "Jeromeno" posted this on my YouTube page: "Kim Davis [the county clerk who went to jail rather than issue same-sex marriage certificates] is an ISIS infiltrator in America with a mission to spread. The most radical interpretation of Sharia Law. ISIS needed a hero a Jeanne d'Arc and they found one in KIM DAVIS."

His post was followed by "Charlie," who commented:

Kim Davis, by Virtue of defying the Constitution and the Supreme Court is NO BETTER than those men who conceived, executed, and plotted those attacks on the World Trade Center and the pentagon on September 11. Granted, there haven't been any lives lost in the wake of Mrs. Davis' shenanigans, the ideology of using her religious beliefs as justification to defile the Supreme Court and the Constitution make her a religious terrorist along the order of Osama bin Laden and ISIS.

I remind you that these people really believe what they're posting, as hard as it is to believe. In response to these comments, I wrote (in the article):

So, ISIS is beheading Christians who refuse to convert to Islam and crucifying Muslims who are not radical enough. ISIS is burying little children alive, burning prisoners alive, drowning them in cages, raping teenage girls and selling them into slavery, and throwing gays off buildings. Yet when we say, "Gays are free to live how they please and enter into the relationships of their choosing—that's between them and God—and if they want a minister or judge to sanction their 'marriage,' they can do that, just don't force us to participate in their ceremony"—we are now like ISIS.

But it is not only random, virtually unknown individuals posting these things online. Well-known media personalities like Montel Williams have compared supporters of natural, male–female marriage to ISIS.[6] Perhaps it would be worthwhile if some wealthy benefactor could pay for Chris Matthews, Wayne Besen, Markos Moulitsas, Frank Rich, Montel Williams, and their ilk to spend six months, all expenses paid, living in a country like Afghanistan or Saudi Arabia, where the hanging of gays and the beheading of adulterers is commonly practiced (and fully sanctioned) under Sharia law, and where conversion from Islam to another religion is punishable by death.

Had these men experienced Sharia law firsthand, they would have witnessed barbaric practices like this one, reported in an August 2015 headline: "An eye for an eye: Iran sentences 27-year-old to have eyes GOUGED OUT after damaging sight of another man in street brawl."[7] This is what happens in an Islamic theocracy, where religious law, as established by radical Muslim leaders, is enforced on the entire nation. That means that both Muslims and non-Muslims, devout believers and nonbelievers, must live by Islamic law. Allah is the ultimate ruler, and the religious officials (in Iran, the ayatollahs) are the supreme leaders of the nation. The president, an elected official, is subservient to them.

In similar fashion, wherever ISIS extends its rule, it establishes a theocracy, meaning that nominal Muslims will be punished for nonconformity to Sharia law (in particular, to the extreme interpretation of Sharia by ISIS) and that Christians and other non-Muslims will have to convert to Islam or at best be treated like second-class citizens (if, in fact, they are not simply killed in cold blood). It is ludicrous, then, to say that Billy Graham's urging North Carolinians to cast their votes for the biblical and historic definition of marriage is comparable to Sharia law. Had America been under a Christian equivalent of Sharia law—which does not exist—Rev. Graham would have been part of a ruling class of clergy enforcing biblical standards on the society as a whole, and dissenters would have been decisively punished.

So, to be absolutely clear, I do not in any way advocate some kind of Christian theocracy here in the States. I do advocate a return to the biblical principles on which this nation was founded, principles that would have a life-giving effect on the entire country, principles that ideally would be lived out by more and more Americans and even would be enacted democratically by the consensus of the people. Practically speaking, I am urging that (1) we look back to our roots to understand what made America great; (2) we recognize that the separation of church and state, as originally intended, guaranteed freedom *of* religion, not freedom *from* religion; (3) we demonstrate in the private sector—our own lives and families and communities—that God's ways are best; (4) we make a positive impact on the society as a whole by living out these divine principles; and (5) we advocate for these principles in the public square through the democratic process. Anyone branding this as "Christian Sharia" or likening committed followers of Jesus to the Taliban or ISIS is not dealing with reality.

So a theocracy, which comes from the Greek words *theos*, meaning "god," and *kratia*, "rule," is quite different from a democracy, which comes from the Greek words *dēmos*, "people," and *kratia*, "rule." Accordingly, I am advocating for the powerful influence of the gospel on our country, a democratic republic under God, which is in keeping with our roots and our history. So, to continue our journey forward, let's look back once again.

Colonial Williamsburg

Have you ever visited Colonial Williamsburg in Virginia? It's a throwback to the past, a re-creation of a world gone by—houses, businesses, inns, and taverns look exactly as they did in the mid-seventeen hundreds in America. In addition, it is staffed by workers who all play the part, wearing the clothes of that era, giving presentations about daily life, and answering tourists' questions as if they actually lived at that time.

While visiting there once with my family, I began talking with one of the workers about George Whitefield (1714–70), the powerful British evangelist who preached many times in the colonies, serving as a leading voice during the first Great Awakening. When the population of Boston was twelve thousand, it was said that Whitefield could draw a crowd of fourteen thousand, and historians believe that a great majority of the colonists heard Whitefield preach at least once in their lifetime.

I was curious to see how much this worker knew about Whitefield since, after all, he was playing the part of a contemporary of this great preacher. I was not disappointed! With a twinkle in his eye, the man began to recount the power of Whitefield's preaching and the breadth of his impact, just as if he had been there himself. The fact is, Whitefield was often the biggest show in town, famed for his dramatic, moving preaching and the massive crowds he drew. He was also famous for his booming voice, though he had nothing more than a hanging sounding board to amplify him. Yet according to Benjamin Franklin's calculations as he walked backward away from the crowds until he could hear him no more, Whitefield's voice carried as far as *one mile away.*

A famous account from the year 1740 paints a graphic picture of what happened when Whitefield came to town. It is narrated by Nathan Cole, a farmer who lived twelve miles from Middletown, Connecticut. While a Christian in name only, not reality, he was religiously interested, and he had heard that Whitefield would soon be preaching in his area. He didn't want to miss the opportunity of hearing him speak. Biographer John Pollock related the story:

> Shortly before nine in the morning of October 23, 1740, Nathan Cole was working in his fields when a horseman galloped by, calling out that "Mr. Whitefield is to preach at Middletown." Cole dropped his tool, ran home to his wife to tell her to get ready, "then ran to my pasture for my horse with all my might, fearing I would be too late."

And the only "advertising" that Cole received was the single sentence of a single horseman speeding by.

> He put his wife on the horse with him "and pressed forward as fast as the horse could manage." Whenever it labored too hard he jumped off, eased his wife into the saddle and told her not to stop or slack for him while he ran beside her. He would run until too out of breath, then mount again.

They rode as if "fleeing for our lives, all the while fearing we should be too late to hear the sermon."

Remember, there were no famous music groups, no special youth activities, no promises of miracles and healings to draw the crowds. What drew the people was the power of God's Word and the reputation of Whitefield. Can you feel the intensity of this account, how the reality of divine truths pervaded the atmosphere?

The fields were deserted; every man and woman must be gone to Middletown. When the Coles reached the high ground overlooking the road which runs from Hartford and Stepney they saw it covered with what looked like a fog. At first Cole thought that it was morning mist drifting from the broad Connecticut River, but as they drew nearer they heard a rumble like thunder and soon found that the cloud was of dust made by horses cantering down the road.

    Cole slipped his horse into a vacant space and when Mrs. Cole looked at the dust-coated riders, their hats and clothes all of a color with their horses, she cried, "Law, our clothes will all be spoiled, see how they look!"

What a scene!

On they rode, no one speaking a word [for three miles], "but everyone pressing forward in great haste," until the cavalcade cantered into Middletown and Cole saw the space in front of the old meeting-house on the edge of the town jammed with bodies. The Coles were in time: the ministers, a phalanx of black, were moving across to the hastily erected scaffold platform where Whitefield would preach. As Cole dismounted and shook off the dust, "I looked towards the river and saw the ferry boats running swift backward and forward bringing over loads of people, and the oars rowed nimble and quick. Everything, men, horses and boats seemed to be struggling for life. The land and banks over the river looked black with people and horses."

    Whitefield came forward on the platform. He looks almost angelical, thought Cole: "a young, slim, slender youth before some thousands of people with a bold, undaunted countenance. And my hearing how God was with him everywhere as he came along, it solemnized my mind and put me into a trembling fear before he began to preach, for he looked as if he was clothed with authority from the Great God . . . and my hearing him preach gave me a heart wound and by God's blessing my old foundation was broken up and I saw my righteousness would not save me."

The divine arrows so penetrated Cole's heart that although he had previously believed that he could be saved by his own good works, an intense conviction of sin came upon him and *lasted for two years*, after which time he experienced a wonderful spiritual rebirth, living the rest of his life as a devoted Christian.[8]

Today pastors are glad if their sermons stick with the congregants for a few days. Whitefield's sermons stuck with people for years, if not for life. As for the young preacher, who was only twenty-five at the time, this was just another day of effective ministry. He wrote in his journal, "Preached to about four thousand people at eleven o'clock, and again, in the afternoon at Wallingford, fourteen miles from Middletown."[9]

Think of something like this happening today, if the big, work-stopping, traffic-causing, crowd-drawing event in your city were a visit from a traveling evangelist. How incredible that would be, and in the eyes of most, how far-fetched. Without a doubt, America back then was very different from America today.

It is true, of course, that there were not a lot of other forms of entertainment in 1740 in the colonies. But it is also true that there was a great respect for the gospel; that Christian values were quite mainstream; and that, generally speaking, there was a reverence for God in the culture. When you add to all this the magnetism of Whitefield's preaching in the midst of a powerful spiritual awakening, it's easy to understand how a Whitefield meeting was something to be experienced, and how the crowds flocked to hear his words and to be transformed.

You might say, "Well, we don't live in the 1740s, so what's the point?"

The point is that our nation has deep Christian roots, and it is only because of, not despite, the godly Christian origins of this country that America became a great nation and that our daring national experiment succeeded as wildly as it did. After all, in the beginning we were just a bunch of struggling, fragmented colonies, and it seemed like the height of folly to take on the might of the British homeland. How then did we become the greatest global superpower in world history? Our biblically based foundations paved the way, and to the extent we have cast those off, we have deteriorated.

Consider the original charters of our first colonies. Were you aware that they had such a strong Christian base? Stephen McDowell cites these representative examples:

- The First Charter of Massachusetts (1629) states the desire that all the inhabitants would "be so religiously, peaceably, and civilly governed, as their good life and orderly conversation may win and incite the natives of country to the knowledge and obedience of the only true God and Savior of mankind, and the Christian faith, which in Our royal intention and the adventurers' free profession, is the principal end of this plantation."
- Adopted January 14, 1639, the Fundamental Orders of Connecticut began with the inhabitants covenanting together under God "to maintain and preserve the liberty and purity of the gospel of our Lord Jesus which we now profess."
- The Charter of Rhode Island (1663) mentioned their intentions of "godlie edifieing themselves, and one another, in the holie Christian ffaith and worshipp" and their desire for the "conversione of the poore ignorant Indian natives."
- In 1682 the Great Law of Pennsylvania was enacted, revealing the desire of Penn and the inhabitants of the colony to establish "laws as shall best preserve true Christian and civil liberty, in opposition to all unchristian, licentious, and unjust practices, (whereby God may have his due, Caesar his due, and the people their due)."[10]

In some of these colonies, Sabbath (Sunday) laws were enforced, church attendance was mandatory, and biblical morality was required. And while the penalties were not nearly as severe as in ancient Israel—a nation that God supernaturally delivered from Egypt and to which he personally appeared, hence the high standards and stiff penalties—without question there were repercussions for not living "by the book" (meaning, the Bible).

Obviously, we cannot return to those days because America today is greatly diversified, and even among professing Christians we are far from totally unified. And we cannot expect tens of millions of non-Christians and unbelievers to practice some form of Christianity. Frankly, it would be dangerous to think that, by passing certain laws, we could turn twenty-first-century America into eighteenth-century America. Certainly not. That would be the equivalent of trying to make America into a Christian theocracy, the very thing I continue to speak against and reject. But that doesn't mean we cannot recover much of the spirit and ethic of our earliest founders. And it certainly doesn't mean that followers of Jesus cannot live as followers of Jesus. To the contrary, given the unique history and Constitution of our country, our nation depends on it, and without a thriving church, America cannot be truly great.

So, as the colonies developed and the United States of America was born, as the population grew and diversified, changes had to come, and they most certainly did. There were greater divergences in Christian expression along with an ever-increasing secularism. But as we have seen, the Bible remained prominent in American thinking—and, quite certainly, the nation identified as Christian and was, broadly speaking, a God-fearing country.[11]

It is also true that there were seasons of spiritual declension, even as early as the first decades of the seventeen hundreds, when some leaders bemoaned the pitiful state of religion in America. But the Great Awakening set things right again, meaning that even as the nation expanded and drifted further away from a "Christian only" mind-set, it did not become totally godless or secular or "pagan."

That America's Christian identity remained strong is reflected by the observations of the French philosopher and historian Alexis de Tocqueville during his celebrated visit to America in the 1830s. As he famously remarked,

On my arrival in the United States, it was the religious atmosphere which first struck me. As I extended my stay, I could observe the political consequences which flowed from this novel situation. In France I had seen the spirit of religion moving in the opposite direction to that of the spirit of freedom. In America, I found them intimately linked together in joint reign over the same land.[12]

Tocqueville noticed how bookseller shops contained "an enormous quantity of religious books; Bibles, sermons, holy stories, religious quarrels, reports of charitable trusts." He also spoke of visiting people who lived in log cabins and whose only book was the Bible.[13] So despite the diversity of the United States in the 1830s, the biblical principles on which the nation was founded continued to have a profound influence.

Now, there is a widely circulated, powerful quote attributed to Tocqueville, a quote that scholars agree does not originate with him. But regardless of who first uttered these words—if not Tocqueville, then one of his contemporaries—I wholeheartedly affirm the sentiments they reflect: "America is great because America is good, and if America ever ceases to be good, America will cease to be great."[14]

These words underlie the central argument of this book: *America can be great only to the extent that America is good, and for America to be good, it must recapture its biblical heritage.* Stated another way, a theocracy is not the answer; returning to God's Word is the answer. As Tocqueville also noted:

> The safeguard of morality is religion, and morality is the best security of law as well as the surest pledge of freedom.
>
> Americans so completely identify the spirit of Christianity with freedom in their minds that it is almost impossible to get them to conceive the one without the other; and this is not one of those sterile ideas bequeathed by the past to the present nor one which seems to vegetate in the soul rather than to live.[15]

If we cease to honor the ways of God, we cease to be free, and if we lose our morality, we lose our liberty. As our first president George Washington said in his Farewell Address, "religion and morality" are the "firmest props of the duties of men and citizens" and therefore are "indispensable supports" of "the dispositions and habits which lead to political prosperity."

And, he added, "Reason and experience both forbid us to expect that national morality can prevail in exclusion of religious principle."[16] As noted by Carson Holloway, associate professor of political science at the University of Omaha, according to Washington, "Religion . . . is necessary to the preservation of 'free government.'" And so, the founders "intended to institute a secular government but insisted that it required a religious foundation."[17]

This, then, is the difference between a God-fearing, Bible-honoring democratic republic and a theocracy. The former is shaped by the consensus of the people through a democratic process as the citizens of that country advocate for their various views in the public and private square. Most of those citizens are Christian in their faith, and the foundations of that nation are built on godly principles. The latter is shaped by the decree of the nonelected religious leaders, ruling over the people by force.

So I am absolutely not advocating for a "Christian" theocracy in America, but I *am* advocating for Christians in America to rediscover the power and beauty and life-giving wisdom of God's Word and to become biblically literate again. I *am* advocating for pastors and teachers to throw out their entertainment-oriented, motivational pep talks and get back to preaching the Scriptures with force and conviction and power. I *am* advocating for believers to start living like they really believe, conducting themselves as citizens of heaven while here on this earth (see Phil. 1:27), meaning that they lift the culture around them rather than get dragged down with the culture. I *am* advocating for a holy counterculture movement that will turn society right side up, for a gospel revolution—a revolution of ideas, of attitudes, of actions—that will have a transformational effect on the nation.

In the words of Christian thinker Os Guinness,

> If Christians are living as "salt and light" in any society, and they reach a critical mass where they are more than a small counterculture, then the "Christianness" or otherwise of that society (the degree to which that society reflects the way of Jesus) is a test of the degree to which Christians are living out the way of Jesus in obedience.[18]

In sum, I'm advocating for the followers of Jesus to become so devoted to their Master and so committed to doing his will that there will be a revival in the church that will lead to an awakening in the society at large. What is impossible with people is possible with God.

FOUR

THE BIBLE IS STILL RELEVANT IN AMERICA

[God's wisdom] is like a tree of life to those who obtain her,
and everyone who grasps hold of her will be blessed.
—PROVERBS 3:18, NET

HERE IN AMERICA, ATHEISTS CAN ADVOCATE FOR THEIR WORLDVIEW without fear of persecution. Presidential candidates can range from deeply devout to totally nonreligious, and the populace can vote accordingly. That is the beauty (and danger) of democracy. Most of the people, or at least the people who become the most influential, will determine the direction of the nation.

Will marijuana be legalized throughout America? What about physician-assisted suicide? Will no-fault divorce continue to be the law of the land? Will *Roe v. Wade* be overturned? What about polygamy? Will that ever become legal again?

In a theocracy, religious leaders would answer these questions based on their interpretation of their holy books, and everyone would have to live by their laws, like it or not. In a democracy, we get to vote on many of our laws, and the losers have to accept the final outcome or work hard to overturn it, all while we live side by side in the midst of our differences.

We must remember, though, that the same men who wrote our foundational documents presupposed that America would be a moral and religious society.[1] Otherwise, they realized, the democratic principles on which the country was founded would quickly crumble because we can enjoy freedom only with responsibility, and at base, responsibility requires morality. As Dennis Prager observed, "The Founders of America based their entire view of America on this belief—that God wants us to be free. That is why the most iconic symbol of the American Revolution, the Liberty Bell, has only one sentence inscribed on it—a verse from the Hebrew Bible: 'Proclaim LIBERTY throughout all the Land unto all the Inhabitants thereof.'"[2]

Most of our founders presupposed that the Bible would play a major role in American life and thought. They never would have envisaged a nation in which public Bible reading would be banned from the schools (as decreed by the Supreme Court in 1962, without legal precedent). In the oft-quoted words of Benjamin Rush, a signer of the Declaration of Independence (as well as a staunch opponent of slavery), "The great enemy of the salvation of man, in my opinion, never invented a more effectual means of extirpating Christianity from the world than by persuading mankind that it was improper to read the Bible at schools."[3]

Today we hear about how irreligious the founders were—deists and free thinkers and nominal Christians—but it is a wildly exaggerated picture that tries to correct another exaggerated picture; namely, that the Founding Fathers were all "born again" evangelical Christians who carried a Bible wherever they went. Undeniably, though, the Bible played a major role in their thinking, even among the least religious of the founders. As Matthew Spalding noted in his book, *We Still Hold These Truths*:

> In 1984, two professors studied the sources cited by the founding generation in their major writings between 1760 and 1805. Their findings are revealing, to say the least. The most-referenced work by far was the Bible, accounting for 34 percent of all citations. The next grouping, making up 22 percent of the citations, was dominated by three writers associated with the moderate Enlightenment: John Locke . . . Baron de Montesquieu . . . and William Blackstone.[4]

According to Stephen McDowell,

> Political Science Professor Donald Lutz conducted an exhaustive ten-year research of about 15,000 political documents of the Founders' Era

(1760–1805). From 916 of these items he recorded every reference our Founders made to other sources. This list of 3154 citations reveals those writings and men that most shaped the political ideas of our Founders. By far, the most quoted source of their political ideas was the Bible, 34% of citations. The next most quoted sources were individuals who had a Christian view of law—Montesquieu (8.3%), Blackstone (7.9%), and Locke (2.9%). In fact, over 80% of all the citations were from the Bible or biblical thinkers.[5]

Ironically, the biblically inspired form of government that we enjoy gives us the liberty to be godless, irreverent, materialistic, and narcissistic, but we do this at our own risk. Only free people can govern freely, and true freedom is ultimately found in God. That's why the more we stray from God and his ways, the more enslaved we become—to financial debt, to fleshly passions, to destructive habits. Has there ever been a time when more Americans were more addicted than today? In our rejection of the Lord and his ways, in our scorning of the Scriptures, in our quest for personal "freedom," we have become totally bound.

Our founders understood this, but today we probably need a reintroduction to the Book they revered. It is popular these days to attack the Bible as an evil book and to malign the God of the Bible as an evil god. We are told that the Scriptures are outdated, outmoded, out of touch, and outlandish. Internet mockers and atheistic authors assure us that "the Bible [specifically, the Old Testament] was written by a bunch of Bronze Age goat herders" or penned by "Bronze Age desert tribesmen,"[6] and so it is as irrelevant socially and morally as it is scientifically. What kind of enlightened person would pay attention to such antiquated myths, let alone consider them sacred, inspired, and binding? As someone posted on my Facebook page, "I like how you think your outdated bronze-age mythology is relevant. That's too cute."[7]

We are even told that the Bible is downright dangerous: the website EvilBible.com claims that it "is designed to spread the vicious truth about the Bible." Yes, "for far too long priests and preachers have completely ignored the vicious criminal acts that the Bible promotes. The so called God of the Bible," the website claims, "makes Osama bin Laden look like a Boy

Scout. This God, according to the Bible, is directly responsible for many mass-murders, rapes, pillage, plunder, slavery, child abuse and killing, not to mention the killing of unborn children."[8]

In harmony with this assessment is the famous statement of atheist Richard Dawkins:

> The God of the Old Testament is arguably the most unpleasant character in all fiction: jealous and proud of it; a petty, unjust, unforgiving control-freak; a vindictive, bloodthirsty ethnic cleanser; a misogynistic, homophobic, racist, infanticidal, genocidal, filicidal, pestilential, megalomaniacal, sadomasochistic, capriciously malevolent bully.[9]

The reality, as expressed by Jewish scholar Gabriel Sivan, is that

> Ever since Sinai, the moral imperatives of the Five Books of Moses, reinforced by the thunderous indignation of the Prophets, have provided one of the greatest inspirations for social reformers and religious idealists, motivating their perennial concern for man's physical and spiritual welfare and for the evolution of a more just and humane society. . . .
>
> It is no exaggeration that the Decalogue [the Ten Commandments] has had a greater impact on man's moral thinking and endeavor than all other ethical formulations known to humanity.[10]

Writing to a friend in 1809, John Adams stated that, despite contrary views of men like Voltaire,

> I will insist that the Hebrews have done more to civilize men than any other nation. If I were an atheist, and believed in blind eternal fate, I should still believe that fate had ordained the Jews to be the most essential instrument for civilizing nations. If I were an atheist of the other sect, who believe, or pretend to believe, that all is ordered by chance, I should believe that chance had ordered the Jews to preserve and propagate to all mankind the doctrine of a supreme, intelligent, wise, almighty Sovereign of the universe, which I believe to be the great essential principle of all morality, and consequently of all civilization.[11]

And how, exactly, did the Jewish people accomplish this extraordinary feat? It was through their sacred, inspired writings—the Law, the Prophets, the Psalms, and more—what we call today the Old Testament. In the words of the eighteenth-century German philosopher Immanuel Kant, "I believe that the existence of the Bible is the greatest benefit to the human race. Any attempt to belittle it, I believe, is a crime against humanity."[12]

Through the teachings of the Scriptures, put into practice by the early Christians, the horrible practice of infanticide was eradicated from Roman society. Before this, unwanted babies were commonly and heartlessly abandoned to die at the hands of the elements or wild animals.

Through the teachings of the Scriptures, gladiatorial combat was also eradicated from that society. As the church grew in influence, this barbaric practice, where gladiators competed to the death to the thrill of the fans, came to an end.

Through the teachings of the Scriptures, William Wilberforce eradicated slavery from the British Empire; and through the teachings of the Scriptures, Christian abolitionists eradicated slavery from the United States of America.[13] More recently, also through the teachings of the Scriptures, Christian civil rights leaders brought justice to America for black Americans.

In a chapter of the book *The Bible and Social Reform*, Peter J. Paris explained:

> The prophetic strand of the black Christian tradition is rooted in antebellum [pre–Civil War] opposition to slavery that predates the abolitionist organizations. Soon after the birth of the independent black churches in the early nineteenth century, blacks began to protest slavery through moral suasion. The prophetic strand is the locus of some of the finest rhetoric in American history and the source of some of the most persuasive arguments against human enslavement and oppression.[14]

More broadly, and as summarized by Gabriel Sivan (with emphasis on the Old Testament), "Millions of underprivileged persons in country after country have been rescued from squalor and misery thanks to the humanitarian instincts and philanthropic work of great idealists for whom the reforming spirit of the Hebrew Bible was a lasting inspiration."[15] We can say without exaggeration that the Bible is the most revolutionary book ever written, and its positive fruit is unparalleled throughout world history.

Consider what John Adams had to say about the potential impact of the Scriptures:

> Suppose a nation in some distant region should take the Bible for their only law book, and every member should regulate his conduct by the precepts there exhibited. Every member would be obliged in conscience to temperance and frugality and industry, to justice and kindness and charity towards his fellow men, and to piety and love, and reverence towards Almighty God. In this commonwealth, no man would impair his health by gluttony, drunkenness, or lust—no man would sacrifice his most precious time to cards, or any other trifling and mean amusement—no man would steal or rile or any way defraud his neighbor, but would live in peace and good will with all men—no man would blaspheme his maker or profane his worship, but a rational and manly, a sincere and unaffected piety and devotion would reign in all hearts. What a utopia, what a paradise would this region be.[16]

This is from one of our Founding Fathers. But Adams was not just dreaming. To the extent people have lived by the Scriptures, society has been positively changed.

Os Guinness quoted the Danish theologian Søren Kierkegaard's observation that "the thought of Christianity was to want to change everything. Twelve men united on being Christians have recreated the face of the world." Guinness continued, "Indeed, that transforming power is at the heart of the genius of the West, and a direct gift of the gospel with its emphasis on life change."[17]

Sociologist Rodney Stark pointed out that "amidst contemporary denunciations of Christianity as patriarchal and sexist, it is easily forgotten that the church was so especially attractive to women that in 370 the emperor Valentinian issued a written order to Pope Damascus I requiring that Christian missionaries cease calling at the homes of pagan women."[18]

He also explained that "Christian women did indeed enjoy considerably greater status and power than did pagan women."[19] How so? "First of all,"

Stark wrote, "a major aspect of women's improved status in the Christian subculture is that Christians did not condone female infanticide," which was another revolutionary breakthrough brought about by the new faith in accordance with the teachings of the Scriptures.[20]

Stark noted that males clearly outnumbered females in the ancient Greco-Roman world, meaning that human life was being tampered with: "Exposure of unwanted female infants and deformed male infants was legal, morally accepted, and widely practiced by all social classes in the Greco-Roman world."[21] To illustrate the point, Stark cited a famous letter from the year 1 B.C. written by a man named Hilarion to his pregnant wife, Alis:

> Know that I am still in Alexandria. And do not worry if they all come back and I remain in Alexandria. I ask and beg you to take good care of our baby son, and as soon as I receive payment I shall send it up to you. If you are delivered for a child [before I come home], if it is a boy keep it, if a girl discard it. You have sent me word, "Don't forget me." How can I forget you. I beg you not to worry.[22]

How extraordinary! The Jesus movement changed that mind-set dramatically, and, as noted, infanticide was largely obliterated by the Christian faith as it spread, which was of special benefit to females. And all this came about through the practical application of scriptural principles, including the principle that all life is sacred (see chapter 5).

Stark also noted that "the more favorable Christian view of women is also demonstrated in their condemnation of divorce, incest, marital infidelity, and polygamy. . . . Like pagans, early Christians prized female chastity, but unlike pagans they rejected the double standard that gave pagan men so much sexual license."[23] So the double standard that required sexual purity for women but not for men was also obliterated by the teaching of the Bible. Stark also added, "Should they be widowed, Christian women also enjoyed very substantial advantages," noting that "close examination of Roman persecutions also suggests that women held positions of power and status within the Christian churches."[24]

These changes, which were completely radical in the ancient world, were the natural result of Christians living out the teachings of Moses and the prophets and Jesus and the apostles. These teachings brought life, not death; progress, not regress; freedom, not bondage. We must recover the revolutionary power of the Scriptures once again in our day.

Similar examples could be given throughout history, but the story remains the same: where knowledge of the Bible spreads among a people, it has a liberating, transforming effect. Historian John Richard Green explained the Bible's effect during the reign of Queen Elizabeth I (1558–1603):

> Elizabeth might silence or tune the pulpits, but it was impossible for her to silence or tune the great preachers of justice, and mercy, and truth, who spoke from the Book with the Lord again opened to the people [by means of it being translated into English]. The effect of the Bible in this way was simply amazing. *The whole temper of the nation was changed.* A new conception of life and man superseded the old. A new moral and religious impulse spread through every class.[25]

I'm quite aware that Bible believers today are accused of being anti-education, anti-science, and anti-progress. The reality is that the Bible played a foundational role in Western education—not the least in American education (see chapter 2)—and Christians often led the way in medical and scientific advance through the centuries. In the best sense of the word *progressive*, nothing contributes more to human progress than adhering to the wisdom of the Word.

C. Ben Mitchell, provost and vice president for Academic Affairs and Graves Professor of Moral Philosophy at Union University, pointed out that "Christians have been leaders in medicine and the building of hospitals because their founder, Jesus of Nazareth, healed the sick during his ministry on earth (see Matt. 9; 10:8; 25:24–26). The early church not only endorsed medicine, but championed care for the sick."[26] As stated by the respected medical historian H. E. Sigerist,

> It remained for Christianity to introduce the most revolutionary and decisive change in the attitude of society toward the sick. Christianity

came into the world as the religion of healing, as the joyful Gospel of the Redeemer and of Redemption. It addressed itself to the disinherited, to the sick and afflicted and promised them healing, a restoration both spiritual and physical. [Thus,] It became the duty of the Christian to attend to the poor and the sick of the community.[27]

Mitchell quoted Albert R. Jonsen, a historian of medicine from the University of Washington, who stated that from the fourth to the fourteenth centuries,

the Christian faith . . . permeated all aspects of life in the West. The very conception of medicine, as well as its practice, was deeply touched by the doctrine and discipline of the Church. This theological and ecclesiastical influence manifestly shaped the ethics of medicine, but it even indirectly affected its science since, as its missionaries evangelized the peoples of Western and Northern Europe, the Church found itself in a constant battle against the use of magic and superstition in the work of healing. It championed rational medicine, along with prayer, to counter superstition.[28]

Mitchell also cited Charles E. Rosenberg, another medical historian, who demonstrated that "the modern hospital owes its origins to Judeo-Christian compassion. Evidence of the vast expansion of faith-based hospitals is seen in the legacy of their names: St. Vincent's, St. Luke's, Mt. Sinai, Presbyterian, Mercy, and Beth Israel. These were all charitable hospitals, some of which began as foundling hospitals to care for abandoned children."[29] This pattern continues around the world today as Christian missionaries build schools and hospitals to serve the poor and needy, educate the illiterate, and relieve suffering, all as a natural outgrowth of their biblical faith. The Bible is a book of healing, restoration, and life (see chapter 6). It is also eminently practical.

Jonsen had noted that the church "championed rational medicine, along with prayer, to counter superstition." And Rodney Stark, in his most recent work *The Triumph of Faith*, has pointed out that in European countries where church attendance is especially low, Christian faith has not been replaced by secularism. It has been replaced by superstition.

For example, in Sweden, which

is almost always presented as exhibit A in the case for the triumph of secularization . . . more than 20 percent of Swedes say they believe in reincarnation; half believe in mental telepathy; and nearly one in five believes in the power of lucky charms. A third believe in New Age medicine such as "healing Crystals"; 20 percent would consider purchasing their personal horoscope; 10 percent would consult a medium; and nearly two out of five believe in ghosts.[30]

In Russia, despite decades of the systematic teaching of atheism, only 6.6 percent of the population identifies as atheist, yet church attendance remains relatively low. But that tells only part of the story:

Two-thirds of Russians believe in "supernatural forces." So did many of those employed in the Soviet regime as instructors in atheism or in the Communist Party's inner circle. It was common for Soviet leaders to consult psychics and fortune tellers, and most of them visited occult healers. Leonid Brezhnev, who ruled the USSR from 1964 to 1982, had a personal healer. A 2006 report from the Russian Academy of Sciences acknowledged that there were more occult healers than conventional medical doctors practicing in Russia, and according to one news account, "Russian newspapers are full of ads for all manner of urban witches and wizards." The scholar Holly DeNio Stephens reports, "Healers and psychics frequently appear on morning and evening talk shows and recount their visions and paranormal experiences." In 2008 a national survey of Russia found that 52 percent believed in faith healers and another 20 percent weren't sure.[31]

What about Iceland, considered by many sociologists of religion to be one of the most secularized nations in the world, a nation in which less than half claim they are religious and more than 40 percent of young Icelanders identify as atheist?[32] This secular nation is thoroughly superstitious, as Stark pointed out:

34 percent of Icelanders believe in reincarnation and another 16 percent aren't sure about it. Moreover, a national survey found that 55 percent of

Icelanders believe in the existence of *huldufolk*, or hidden people, such as elves, trolls, gnomes, and fairies. Consequently, planned highways are sometimes rerouted so as not to disturb various hills and large rocks wherein *huldufolk* may dwell, and Icelanders planning to build a new house often hire "elf spotters" to ensure that their site does not encroach on *huldufolk* settlements. In addition, half of Icelanders have visited a fortune teller, and spiritualism is very widely practiced; it is popular even among intellectuals and academics. According to a Reuters dispatch (February 2, 2015), a rapidly growing group of Icelandic neopagans broke ground for a temple dedicated to worship of the old Norse gods.[33]

Here in America, "studies find that in the United States the irreligious are far more likely than the religious to believe in a whole array of occult beliefs such as Atlantis, Bigfoot, the Loch Ness Monster, astrology, UFOs, haunted houses, and ghosts."[34] So it is not those following the Scriptures who believe in fairy tales and superstitious myths. It is those who reject God's Word who are more likely to do this. In the oft-quoted words of G. K. Chesterton, "When people stop believing in God, they don't believe in nothing—they believe in anything."[35]

On October 14, 1941, Adolph Hitler commented:

So it's not opportune to hurl ourselves now into a struggle with the Churches. The best thing is to let Christianity die a natural death. A slow death has something comforting about it. The dogma of Christianity gets worn away before the advances of science. Religion will have to make more and more concessions. Gradually the myths crumble. All that's left is to prove that in nature there is no frontier between the organic and the inorganic. When understanding of the universe has become widespread, when the majority of men know that the stars are not sources of light but worlds, perhaps inhabited worlds like ours, then the Christian doctrine will be convicted of absurdity.[36]

Today we can say that it was not Christianity that died a natural death. To the contrary, it was Nazism that died a violent, ignominious death while the Christian faith, despite setbacks in the West, is thriving worldwide like never before. Nazism, for its part, has been "convicted of absurdity"—and far worse.

More than twenty-five hundred years ago, the prophet Isaiah, speaking for the Lord, declared, "The grass withers, the flower fades when the breath of the LORD blows on it; surely the people are grass. The grass withers, the flower fades, but the word of our God will stand forever" (Isa. 40:7–8). Empires have come and gone, including the mighty Roman empire, but God's Word still stands, including the letters of Paul. As for the words of Jesus, he said almost two thousand years ago, "Heaven and earth will pass away, but my words will not pass away" (Matt. 24:35). So far, the words of this Jewish carpenter who never once left his home country and who died a criminal's death around the age of thirty-three have proven absolutely true. There is something utterly unique about the Scriptures. Read through the books of sacred literature from other world religions and see for yourself if anything truly compares with the Bible in majesty, practicality, wisdom, and relevance.

When our daughters were in their teen years, I read a passage from Proverbs to them about the dangerous effects of getting drunk, wanting them to realize how applicable the Scriptures were to their lives. The text said:

Who has anguish? Who has sorrow? Who is always fighting? Who is always complaining? Who has unnecessary bruises? Who has bloodshot eyes? It is the one who spends long hours in the taverns, trying out new drinks. Don't gaze at the wine, seeing how red it is, how it sparkles in the cup, how smoothly it goes down. For in the end it bites like a poison-ous snake; it stings like a viper. You will see hallucinations, and you will say crazy things. You will stagger like a sailor tossed at sea, clinging to a swaying mast. And you will say, "They hit me, but I didn't feel it. I didn't even know it when they beat me up. When will I wake up so I can look for another drink?" (Prov. 23:29–35 NLT)

This got their attention, driving home the point that the Bible was any-thing but an irrelevant, ancient religious textbook. It is the living Word of the living God, speaking as clearly to us today as it did two or three thousand years ago. No other book is like it, and no other book has had the positive world impact that the Bible has when rightly taken to heart and applied.

Leonard Ravenhill, a fiery revivalist and author, once said, "One of these days some simple soul will pick up the Book of God, read it, and believe it. Then the rest of us will be embarrassed." I want to be that "simple soul." How about you? You may have heard Chesterton's famous statement, "The Christian ideal has not been tried and found wanting. It has been found difficult; and left untried." I think it's high time that we said to God, "No matter the cost or the consequences, by your help and grace, we want to live this out. We want to follow your Word. We want to prove to the world that your ways are ways of life. While we have breath and strength, we want to go for it!"

If we do, I believe God himself will back us. Are you ready to take the plunge?

PART THREE

———

How to Rebuild America

FIVE

CREATED IN THE IMAGE OF GOD

So God created man in His own image;
He created him in the image of God;
He created them male and female.
—GENESIS 1:27 HCSB

WHEN WE ASK THE QUESTION, "WHAT HAS HAPPENED TO AMERICA?" we are really asking, "What has happened to us as human beings?" In other words, the question is not just, "How did our nation fall so far?" but, "How have we, the people of America, fallen so far?" It's as if we have lost our humanity, lost our souls, lost our human dignity. Once again God's Word shows us the way of restoration, and to show the beauty of the solution, let me highlight the ugliness of the problem.

I've been doing live talk radio five days a week, two hours a day, since 2008. In addition to that I've done countless interviews on other live radio shows. As you can imagine, I've heard some of the craziest things and some of the wisest things from callers over the years. But nothing prepared me for what I encountered during an interview for a station in Detroit in 2016.

The host, who had been on the air longer than me, told me about a shocking call he had recently received. The caller, who was a man, felt it was wrong to identify his baby as either male or female. Consequently, he was not going to say a word to his child about its gender identity. The little one would figure it out for himself (or herself; the caller never stated whether it was a boy or girl). But that was not the worst part. The father continued to refer to his child as a "carbon unit." Yes, a carbon unit! That is how a dad talked about his kid.

But on reflection, that viewpoint is not much different from referring to a baby in the womb as a "mass of cells" or comparing it to a tumor to be removed. In fact, it is the very mentality that underlies the pro-abortion movement: That child in the womb, growing and developing and moving and kicking, looking more and more like mom or dad (or both) by the day, is not a human being. It is a fetus, a thing, an appendage to be expelled if not wanted. As expressed by pro-abortion feminist Florence Thomas (speaking of her abortion in France in the mid-1960s), she felt "a relief. An immense relief. This tumor went away, disappeared. I could go back to living."[1]

Really now, if the fetus is nothing more than a mass of cells, a tumor, then the baby (or even the adult) is nothing more than a carbon unit. In keeping with this mentality, the National Abortion Rights Action League (NARAL) took strong exception to a silly Doritos commercial during Super Bowl 50 (2016) in which a pregnant woman is getting an ultrasound of her baby with her husband present. As he mindlessly munches on his Doritos—to his wife's consternation—he then dangles one near her belly, after which we're led to assume that the baby made a premature exit from the womb, eager to grab that Doritos chip.

What was so offensive to NARAL? According to NARAL (via Twitter), Doritos was guilty of gender stereotyping (using "sexist tropes of dads as clueless & moms as uptight"). Worse still, Doritos was guilty of using the "#antichoice tactic of humanizing fetuses." How dare anyone humanize a developing human being in the womb! Not surprisingly, NARAL took a lot of heat for its absurd, even heartless, tweet. But NARAL didn't back down. If the fetus can be humanized, then abortion cannot be justified.

You see, there's a reason that the vast majority of women who see their ultrasounds choose not to abort their babies. There's a reason that expectant moms send out pictures of that ultrasound with the exciting news, "It's a boy!" (or, "It's a girl!") pointing out the little hands and feet and nose and ears. There's a reason the wife grabs her husband's hand and puts it on her stomach as the baby jumps inside so he can experience a little of what she's feeling as that bundle of new life moves around.

Yes, there's a reason many parents pick a name for their child as soon as they hear whether they're having a boy or girl, even though there are a few months to go before the little one makes its appearance. There's a reason some women will mourn for years over a miscarriage, even if it took place in the early months of a pregnancy. And there's a reason that pro-abortionists fight so strenuously against laws requiring abortion clinics to show the mother an ultrasound before going ahead with the murderous act. It's because that fetus is a human being, carefully formed and made, full of life and potential, the unique creation of God and that mother and father. And "humanizing fetuses" is no more an "antichoice tactic" than wanting to humanize Jews during the Holocaust in Germany or wanting to humanize Africans during the slave trade in America.

In the 2016 presidential campaign, Hillary Clinton ignited a firestorm of controversy by stating that "the unborn person does not have constitutional rights." Pro-lifers were critical because Clinton acknowledged the personhood of the fetus yet claimed it had no rights; pro-abortionists were critical because she dared to humanize the fetus (shades of NARAL and Doritos!). In the words of Diana Arellano, community engagement manager for Planned Parenthood of Illinois, "Hillary Clinton further stigmatizes abortion. She calls a fetus an 'unborn child' and calls for later term restrictions."[2] Indeed, "Guidelines issued by the International Planned Parenthood Federation, for instance, discourage the use of terms such as 'baby,' 'dead fetus,' 'unborn baby' and 'unborn child' when discussing abortion, instead recommending 'embryo,' 'fetus' and 'the pregnancy.'"[3] At all costs, avoid recognizing the humanity of that child in the womb.

Tennessee Rep. Marsha Blackburn, a strong pro-life advocate who chairs the Select Investigative Panel on Infant Lives, rightly stated, "The analytical coldness with which [Clinton] dismissed rights of unborn children reveals a type of hardened core that shocks the conscience."[4] Further evidence of this "hardened core that shocks the conscience" is the "Shout Your Abortion" movement, where women are encouraged to get on social media and proclaim without shame, "I had an abortion and I'm proud of it!"[5]

It would be one thing if women shared the agony they went through over their decision to abort their babies. It would be one thing if they said, "Don't be so quick to condemn me. You don't know the challenges I faced and the trauma I endured." It is another thing entirely when they celebrate their decision to abort. Surely that represents the deadening of the soul and the searing of the conscience.

Vishal Mangalwadi, a Christian scholar from India who has worked with his nation's poor for decades, saw how this dehumanizing mentality could be applied to children outside the womb as much as children inside the womb. His wife and he had intervened on behalf of a dying child in a poor village, "a girl named Sheela. In the middle of a windowless, dingy room, an eighteen-month-old living skeleton was lying on a bare string cot, pus oozing from sores covering her body and head, with flies swarming over her because she could not raise her hand to chase them away. Her thighs were only as thick as an adult's thumb. Sheela was so weak that she could not even cry. She only sighed."[6]

The child's parents resisted all attempts to help the baby, despite the Mangalwadis' willingness to meet whatever need arose in nurturing the child back to health. Finally, the Mangalwadis took matters into their own hands, getting a legal injunction to help Sheela, bringing her to the hospital, caring for her in their own home, then returning the healthy, happy child to her mother and father after the mother pressured them to give her back. Within a few weeks, to their horror, they discovered that Sheela was as sick as before.

So they repeated the process, brought Sheela back to the hospital, cared for her in their home, then returned her to her mother once again, thinking the mother had learned her lesson. Soon Sheela was dead, starved to death by her own parents. Mangalwadi explained:

Sheela's parents starved her to death because they saw her as a liability. They already had a daughter to babysit their sons and to clean and cook for the family. A second girl was an unnecessary burden. They would have to feed her for ten to twelve years. Then they would need to go into debt to find a dowry to marry her off. Her in-laws might torture her to extract more money from them. In those days, according to our national press, every year in-laws were killing around three hundred young brides in our nation's capital, in efforts to extract more dowry from their parents. But a dowry is not the end of costs. The daughter would return to her parents' home to deliver her children. Why should they take on this lifelong burden, even if someone was offering free medical care and milk for a few weeks?[7]

This is what happens when human beings are dehumanized. This is what happens when every life is not considered worthy of dignity and honor. This is what happens when the ultimate arbiter of right and wrong is survival—survival of the fittest. This is the result of naturalism, "a philosophical viewpoint according to which everything arises from natural properties and causes, and supernatural or spiritual explanations are excluded or discounted."[8] And it is the book of Genesis that demolishes the naturalistic worldview. It is to that book we turn to begin the journey to heal our nation.

The book of Genesis, the first book of the Bible, is the book of beginnings. Its opening chapter tells the story of the creation of the universe, culminating with the creation of the human race. It is a majestic opening chapter, sublime in its language and massive in its scope, but we often lose sight of the power of this chapter due to the controversy concerning the relationship between science and the Bible.[9] Yet we must recapture the message of Genesis 1 if we are to see America rise again.

The first verse of Genesis 1 tells the whole story in seven Hebrew words: "In the beginning God created the heavens and the earth" (NKJV).[10] This is where everything starts, and the text tells us that the universe had a beginning, in contrast with the view that the universe itself was eternal, as reflected in ancient Greek thought.[11] It is true, of course, that other ancient Near Eastern peoples had their own cosmologies—creation accounts explaining the origin of the universe—but they are crass in comparison to Genesis. These accounts are marked by petty battles between the gods, and deities that are split in half to account for components within creation, and creatures like four-eared and four-eyed giants and "the Viper, the Dragon, and the Sphinx, the Great-Lion, the Mad-Dog, and the Scorpion-Man, Mighty lion-demons, the Dragon-Fly, [and] the Centaur."[12]

In stark contrast to these other accounts,[13] the God of Genesis 1 is transcendent and independent: he works systematically and sovereignly, calling light to come out of darkness and order to come out of chaos. By the simple power of his words ("Let there be light!" "Let the earth sprout vegetation!") *something* is brought out of *nothing,* as each command is executed perfectly and without resistance. Everything he makes is good, and every living thing, be it plant or animal, is designed to carry life within itself, the ability to reproduce. Genesis 1 is a celebration of life, a celebration of God's triumph over hostile forces, a celebration of his majesty and goodness and wisdom.[14]

Ask yourself for a moment: Other than by divine revelation, how would someone gain such an understanding of God in the midst of ancient polytheism? How would a human being conceive of such lofty ideas, not only of a transcendent, independent Lord but of an orderly creation brought about by divine speech? And from a scientific viewpoint, though many dismiss Genesis 1 as unscientific, others, like Orthodox Jewish physicist Gerald Schroeder, find Genesis and science to be in extraordinary harmony.

In 1959, a survey was taken of leading American scientists. Among the many questions asked was, "What is your estimate of the age of the universe?" Now, in 1959, astronomy was popular, but cosmology—the deep physics of understanding the universe—was just developing. The response to that survey was recently republished in *Scientific American*—the most widely read science journal in the world. Two-thirds of the scientists gave the same answer. The answer that two-thirds—an overwhelming majority— of the scientists gave was, "Beginning? There was no beginning. Aristotle and Plato taught us 2400 years ago that the universe is eternal. Oh, we know the Bible says 'In the beginning.' That's a nice story; it helps kids go to bed at night. But we sophisticates know better. There was no beginning."

That was 1959. In 1965, Arno Penzias and Robert Wilson discovered the echo of the Big Bang in the black of the sky at night, and the world paradigm changed from a universe that was eternal to a universe that had a beginning. Science had made an enormous paradigm change in its understanding of the world. Understand the impact. Science said that our universe had a beginning. I can't overestimate the import of that scientific "discovery." Evolution, cave men, these are all trivial problems compared to the fact that we now understand that we had a beginning. Exactly as the Bible had claimed for three millennia.[15]

What's more, as noted on a popular website, even a cursory reading of the first four verses of Genesis 1 points to God's first act of creation—which is light, being preceded by sound. Thus,

> The central tenet of the theory of Acoustic Genesis (www.science provescreation.com) is: sound came first, then light, then matter. This leads to three fundamental premises of the theory: 1) That all matter emits a distinct tone as evidence of creation, 2) that all matter can be manipulated by sound, and 3) that the structure of all matter can be reduced to simple vibration. Science verifies and validates all three assumptions. Once you conceptualize these axioms, then you will begin to unwind the underlying tapestry of "the all."[16]

So, in Genesis 1, God *speaks*, then *light* appears, then *matter*. How would an ancient writer know such things?

To be sure, the Bible uses observational language, speaking of the "ends of the earth" and the "rising and setting" of the sun. And I assume that the ancient Israelites believed the Earth was flat and that rain came down from the clouds when the heavenly windows were opened. At the same time, biblical authors speak of God hanging the world on nothing (see Job 26:7), while the Lord describes himself through the prophet Isaiah as the one "who made all things, who alone stretched out the heavens, who spread out the earth by myself" (Isa. 44:24). Every word of this is without parallel in the ancient world.

Yet the purpose of Genesis 1 is not to teach us about science. It is to teach us about God and to teach us about ourselves. And what we learn about ourselves through this foundational chapter is every bit as revolutionary as what we learn about our Creator. We learn that on the sixth day of creation after the stage has been set and the Earth prepared, with every star in place and every fish and bird and animal already thriving, God spoke these momentous words: "'Let us make man in our image, after our likeness. And let them have dominion over the fish of the sea and over the birds of the heavens and over the livestock and over all the earth and over every creeping thing that creeps on the earth.' So God created man in his own image, in the image of God he created him; male and female he created them" (Gen. 1:26–27). *Human beings are created in the very image of God.*

According to Mangalwadi, this was the concept—that human beings are created in the image and likeness of God—that brought the notions of freedom and nationhood to his home country of India (a concept introduced, interestingly enough, through British Christianity), and this was the concept that produced the best aspects of Western civilization. In short, "The Bible was the very soul of Western civilization."[17]

These may seem like sweeping, even exaggerated claims, but Mangalwadi, who is a respected university professor as well as a servant of the poor, backs his claims both academically and logically. To get the full scope of his intellectual argument, it is necessary to read his important volume and study the many sources he cited, a task that requires some time. But it does not take much time for us to consider the logic of his argument.

In short, if in fact there is a sovereign, eternal, perfect deity and we are created in his image, then it means that we are different from the animals; we are made to rule; we have the ability to create; we are moral and rational; we can love good and hate evil; we have a sense of justice; and we have purpose and destiny—just to name a few. None of this makes sense if we are simply the end-products of a random, unguided evolutionary process, the fittest of the fit to survive so far. None of this makes sense if we are simply "carbon units." None of this makes sense if we are merely material beings and our brains are nothing more than millions of neurons firing. Carbon units cannot grasp the concept of justice, nor can they self-analyze, reflect, or dream of a better world. Carbon units simply exist without consciousness, and carbon units have no purpose or destiny or meaning.

In wrestling with his beliefs when challenged by his professors as a college student, Mangalwadi decided to reread the Bible (having become a Christian a few years before). As he read Genesis 1 through his fresh, inquisitive, and even critical eyes, he had a revelatory experience:

> The biblical words made sense because they were true to what I knew about myself. Machines produce. Human beings create. What's the difference? We create what we choose to create. Freedom, or choice, is the essence of creativity. Determinism explains only a part of me. I eat food

when I am driven by the chemistry of hunger pangs. But I can choose to fast. I can choose to fast unto death or choose to break my fast. At the core of my being, I am free.[18]

And so, while Descartes could say, "I think therefore I am,"[19] Mangalwadi could say (these are my words, not his), "Because I think *the way I do*—with reason; with morality; with freedom—therefore I am *created in the image of God*." And this deduction—this "therefore"—leads to several more critically important deductions, each of which applies to every human being on the planet, from conception until death.

First, if we are made in the image of God, that means that God is the ultimate Creator and we are all creatures dependent on him, not the reverse.[20] And even though we are the pinnacle of his creation, the universe revolves around him, not us. That also means that we can understand the purpose and meaning of our lives only by understanding why God put us here. And so every human being who has ever experienced a sense of destiny, of having a role to play in this world, has to ask himself or herself, "Where do these feelings come from? Why this sense of purpose and calling? Who put this inside of me?"

It also means that, if we have been created in God's image for God's purpose, we are accountable to him as well. That's why the Scriptures consistently point to the Lord as both King and Judge, our Creator and the one to whom we must ultimately report. This infuses our lives with a sense of sobriety: I will have to explain my actions one day to the one who gave me breath. As the ancient Jewish dictum states, "Reflect on three things and you will never come to sin: Know what is above you—a seeing eye, a hearing ear, and all your deeds recorded in a book" (m. Pirkei Avot 2:1).

Second, if we are made in God's image, then our sense of justice and fairness and purity and mercy comes from him, along with our hatred of evil and love for good. These emotions and attitudes and values, at their highest and best, are a reflection of the Lord's image in us. That's why Christian apologist Frank Turek, in his book *Stealing from God*, argued that "atheists steal reason, evidence, science, and other arguments from God in trying to make their case for atheism. . . . Atheists can't make their case without appealing to realities only theism can explain."[21]

C. S. Lewis explained that when he was an atheist, he found himself facing an uncomfortable contradiction:

> My argument against God was that the universe seemed so cruel and unjust. But how had I gotten this idea of just and unjust? A man does not call a line crooked unless he has some idea of a straight line. What was I comparing this universe with when I called it unjust? If the whole show was bad and senseless from A to Z, so to speak, why did I, who was supposed to be part of the show, find myself in such violent reaction against it? A man feels wet when he falls into water, because man is not a water animal: a fish would not feel wet. Of course I could have given up my idea of justice by saying it was nothing but a private idea of my own. But if I did that, then my argument against God collapsed too—for the argument depended on saying that the world was really unjust, not simply that it did not happen to please my private fancies. Thus in the very act of trying to prove that God did not exist—in other words, that the whole of reality was senseless—I found I was forced to assume that one part of reality—namely my idea of justice—was full of sense. Consequently, atheism turns out to be too simple. If the whole universe has no meaning, we should never have found out that it has no meaning: just as, if there were no light in the universe and therefore no creatures with eyes, we should never know it was dark. Dark would be without meaning.[22]

When we leave God out of the picture, we leave out the most essential parts of our very selves.

Only human beings bear his image and likeness, and *that*—not our earthly fame, good looks, or riches, all of which are fleeting and superficial— is the source of our dignity and value. We are special because we are God's agents on earth, God's children who display his characteristics, God's image bearers who can bring healing and hope and transformation.

That doesn't mean that every *human behavior* reflects God's image. To the contrary, many of our actions and attitudes reflect our rebellion against God's image and our determination to cast off his rulership. Many of our words and deeds reflect our fallen nature rather than our divinely given qualities. And if we are candid, we will have to admit that some of the things we find inside ourselves, things found in the core of our beings, are downright evil. Yet our ability to recognize them as evil and work against them reminds us that we are, in fact, created in God's image. One of the main purposes of the Bible, then, is to help us cultivate the potential of that divine image, restored through Jesus, thereby living lives worthy of the Lord (see Eph. 4:1–24).

Third, if we are made in God's image, then every human life is sacred, however fragile that life may be and however unimportant or irrelevant or unneeded or insignificant or unattractive that life may appear to be. That is why, in the book of Genesis, the death penalty is instituted for murder (rather than for killing an animal). As stated in Genesis 9:6, "Whoever sheds man's blood, his blood will be shed by man, for God made man in His image" (HCSB). In other words, because a human life is of such inestimable value—created in the image of the Creator—taking an innocent life is a grave crime. Consequently, if you take a human life unjustly, you forfeit your own.

The offshoot of all this is that God's ways are the ways of life, the ways of health, the ways of blessing. That's why Moses urged his fellow Israelites to "choose life," and that's why Jesus said, "I have come that they may have life, and have it to the full" (Deut. 30:19; John 10:10 NIV).

If the downward spiral of our nation is to be reversed, it is imperative that we recover a culture of life. The good news is that we are not alone in this struggle. As Mangalwadi pointed out, "The Renaissance writers did not derive their high view of man from only one verse of the Bible that describes the creation of man. They found human dignity affirmed most supremely in the Bible's teaching on the incarnation of Christ. The New Testament taught that God saw the misery of man and came as a man, Jesus Christ, to make human beings sons and daughters of God."[23]

God has already reached out to us, and through Jesus he continues to reach out. And so, "Far from violating God's dignity, the incarnation was to be the ultimate proof of man's dignity: of the possibility of man's salvation, of a man or a woman becoming a friend and child of God. The incarnation would make human beings of greater worth than the angels."[24] By God coming into our world, he has lifted us up. "God's descent means man's ascent. Misery, helplessness, despondency, and eternal self-conflict are normal for men. They can be resolved because the transcendent can also be immanent—'Emmanuel,' that is, God with us."[25]

This is the hope of America and the hope of the world. In the words of C. S. Lewis, "The Son of God became man to enable men to become the sons of God."[26] America can be transformed because Americans can be transformed.

It truly is an urgent, even desperate time for our nation, but it is certainly not too late.[27]

SIX

From *The Walking Dead* to a Culture of Life

Choose life, so that you and your descendants might live!
—DEUTERONOMY 30:19 NLT

FOR MANY YEARS I HEARD THE CLAIM, BASED ON A 1999 SENATE report, that "an average American child will see 200,000 violent acts and 16,000 murders on TV by age 18."[1] I have never been able to verify those figures, but I do know that since 1999 TV has gotten more violent, not less. A recent study found that "77% of the violent and graphically violent depictions that aired during primetime broadcast[s] on TV-14 rated shows" included scenes with "child molestation, rape, mutilation/disfigurement, dismemberment, graphic killings and/or injuries by gunfire and stabbings, violent abductions, physical torture, cannibalism, burning flesh, suicide, beatings, guns and bladed weapons that were depicted but not used, and dead bodies."[2]

Even programs that don't focus on violent acts often focus on death and corpses and mutilated bodies, and so a child is exposed to a disproportionate and unhealthy emphasis on death during a formative period in his or her life. Added to this are the shows where the heroes are the living dead (vampires) and the shows where the enemies are the undying dead (zombies). And then there are the ultraviolent video games where players get to slaughter both the bad guys and the good guys to their hearts' content.

Shortly after the 2013 release of the mega-popular video game *Grand*

Theft Auto V, James Delingpole, a British columnist and novelist, wrote of his experience playing the game in England:

> Yesterday, in the process of robbing a bank, I beat up an elderly security guard before shooting dead perhaps 15 policemen, exulting in their murders with the flip dismissal: "Shouldn't have been a cop."
>
> After that, I stole a succession of fast cars, evading my pursuers by driving on the wrong side of the road, mowing down passers-by and killing more police by ramming straight into them.
>
> Then I went home for a change of clothes, a nap, a beer and a joint before getting into my stolen vehicle to wreak more mayhem, pausing briefly to enjoy the services of a prostitute.[3]

But he was just getting started (and note that his report said nothing of the profanity-filled dialogues):

> Had I kept going with this spree of orgiastic destruction and drug-fuelled violence, I would have got the chance to use much heavier weaponry, take stronger drugs, and not only murder people but torture them by pulling out their teeth with pliers, waterboarding them with flammable liquid, kneecapping them with a monkey wrench and making them scream with electric shocks.[4]

All this is experienced in vivid, living color and is played by the hour by video-addicted kids and adults. It presents a graphic (and disturbing) picture of today's culture of death: Millions of young people who could be outside enjoying nature or taking an intellectual journey by reading a captivating book instead sit in front of a computer screen (or, worse still, wear virtual reality goggles), shut out from the real world by the blaring sound track in their headphones, immersed in a fantasy world of gushing blood and exploding bodies and headless victims. And when they tire of all this, they can watch a Hannibal Lecter movie (or TV episode from the series that ran for three years), rooting for the diabolical hero and wondering if Lecter is eating animal meat or human meat when he dines.

We can say without exaggeration that America in the second decade of the twenty-first century is a country awash in death and dying, and it is not limited to Hollywood and video games. It is lurking on our streets and breaking into our homes. Just ask this bereaved mother from inner-city Milwaukee:

> Tamiko Holmes, a mother of five, has lost two of her nearly grown children in apparently unrelated shootings in the last eight months. In January, a daughter, 20, was shot to death during a robbery at a birthday party at a Days Inn. Six months later, the authorities called again: Her only son, 19, had been shot in the head in a car—a killing for which the police are still searching for a motive and a suspect.
>
> Ms. Holmes said she recently persuaded her remaining teenage daughters to move away from Milwaukee with her, but not before one of them, 17, was wounded in a shooting while riding in a car.[5]

This is no video game or scene from a movie. This is reality for millions of Americans today. Even suicide is on the rise.[6] How can we replace this culture of death with a vibrant culture of life?

Let's return to the subject of abortion, where the life of our most vulnerable and innocent citizens is violently snuffed out in the one place where they should enjoy ultimate safety: their own mothers' wombs. With good reason Mother Teresa said, "Abortion kills twice. It kills the body of the baby and it kills the conscience of the mother. Abortion is profoundly anti-women. Three quarters of its victims are women: Half the babies and all the mothers."[7]

Could it be that our indifference to the life of the preborn—really, our all-out assault on those precious little lives—has desensitized us on a national level? Could it be that there is a fine line between killing a baby in the womb and killing a baby outside the womb? (The infamous abortion doctor Kermit Gosnell was guilty of both, yet he felt he was doing women a service.) Could it be that we are reaping what we have sown, now that physician-assisted suicide is becoming increasingly acceptable as yet another manifestation of our culture of death?

Camille Paglia is an outspoken journalist and professor. She is also a pro-abortion lesbian, feminist—and an atheist. Yet she wrote:

Although I am an atheist who worships only great nature, I recognize the superior moral beauty of religious doctrine that defends the sanctity of life. The quality of idea and language in the Catechism of the Catholic Church, for example, exceeds anything in grimly utilitarian feminism. In regard to the Commandment "Thou shalt not kill," the Catechism says: "Human life is sacred because from its beginning it involves the creative action of God. . . . God alone is the Lord of life from its beginning until its end: no one can under any circumstance claim for himself the right directly to destroy an innocent human being" (#2258). Or this: "Human life must be respected and protected absolutely from the moment of conception. From the first moment of his existence, a human being must be recognized as having the rights of a person—among which is the inviolable right of every innocent being to life" (#2270).[8]

Mother Teresa, then, was not exaggerating when she said that "the greatest destroyer of love and peace today is abortion," explaining that abortion "is a war against the child, a direct killing of the innocent child, murder by the mother herself." As she explained, "By abortion, the mother does not learn to love, but kills even her own child to solve her problems. . . . Any country that accepts abortion is not teaching its people to love, but to use any violence to get what they want."[9] And she asked, "If we can accept that a mother can kill her own child, how can we tell other people not to kill one another?"[10] How indeed?

In the last chapter we saw that our dignity as human beings is based on our being created in God's image, which means that our social status or ethnicity or fame or wealth do not determine our human dignity or worth. We learn this from the Scriptures, and from these same Scriptures we learn that God's desire was for us to live forever. He is a God of life! That's why Genesis, the first book of the Bible, tells us that in the middle of the garden of Eden was the *tree of life* (Gen. 2:9, emphasis added), and that's why Revelation, the last book of the Bible, tells us that in the middle of the heavenly city called the New Jerusalem—the place where God's people are destined to live eternally—is a *river of life* and a *tree of life* (Rev. 22:1–2, 14, 19, emphasis added). And that's why the closing invitation in Revelation (and therefore the closing invitation in the whole Bible) says, "Let the one who is thirsty come; let the one who desires take the *water of life* without price" (Rev. 22:17, emphasis added).

For good reason Jesus described himself as "the bread of life" and "the resurrection and the life" (John 6:35, 48; 11:24–25), and John tells us that (1) in him was life; (2) whoever believes in him will have eternal life; (3) the water he offers us leads to eternal life; (4) he gives life to whom he wills; (5) those who partake of his body and blood have eternal life; (6) he has the words of life, even eternal life; (7) whoever follows him has the light of life; (8) he came that we might have abundant life; (9) he is the way, the truth, and the life; and (10) to know him and his Father is eternal life.[11]

Significantly, the Greek word for life, *zoē* (pronounced "zoh-ey"), is found thirty-six times in the gospel of John and another thirteen times in 1 John, which is a very short book. So these two books, which focus so closely on Jesus, have a disproportionate emphasis on *life*. As John wrote toward the end of his gospel, "Jesus performed many other signs in the presence of His disciples that are not written in this book. But these are written so that you may believe Jesus is the Messiah, the Son of God, and *by believing you may have life in His name*" (John 20:30–31 HCSB, emphasis added). This idea is echoed in the last chapter of 1 John: "And this is the testimony: God has given us *eternal life*, and *this life* is in his Son. The one who has the Son has *life*. The one who doesn't have the Son of God does not have *life*. I have written these things to you who believe in the name of the Son of God, *so that you may know that you have eternal life*" (5:11–13 HCSB, emphasis added). To quote the words of Jesus once more, "whoever drinks from the water that I will give him will never get thirsty again—ever! In fact, the water I will give him will become a well of water springing up within him *for eternal life*" (John 4:14 HCSB, emphasis added).

This emphasis on life flies in the face of a common (but misguided) representation of the Bible as a book of death and destruction. Instead, it is a book of life—really, *the* book of life—and by following its precepts, we live. As the Lord said through Moses, "You shall therefore keep my statutes and my rules; if a person does them, he shall live by them: I am the LORD" (Lev. 18:5).

Why, then, did God destroy the earth in Noah's day with a flood, wiping out every person on the planet except for Noah and his family? It was because the human race was destroying itself, and if the Lord didn't intervene, we would have wiped ourselves out, bringing about the end of the human race. By saving one of the only men on the planet who had not become corrupt (that alone tells you how bad things were), God was able to save the human race, and Noah's sons and their wives gave birth to a brand-new generation. God's goal was life, not death, and he took extreme measures to preserve life on earth.

And note these striking words from Genesis 6 describing the state of the world before the flood: "The LORD saw that the wickedness of man was great in the earth, and that every intention of the thoughts of his heart was only evil continually. . . . Now the earth was corrupt in God's sight, *and the earth was filled with violence*. And God saw the earth, and behold, it was corrupt, for all flesh had corrupted their way on the earth" (vv. 5, 11–12, emphasis added).[12] Isn't it interesting that, of all the great evils on the earth at that time, the one sin that is specifically mentioned is violence?

Similarly, before the Lord brought judgment on Jerusalem in the sixth century B.C., the prophet Ezekiel asked the angelic messenger if the God of Israel would actually pour out his wrath on his own people and his own city. The angel replied, "The guilt of the house of Israel and Judah is exceedingly great. The land is full of blood, and the city full of injustice" (Ezek. 9:9). As explained in the book of Numbers, "Bloodshed[13] pollutes the land, and atonement cannot be made for the land on which blood has been shed, except by the blood of the one who shed it" (35:33 NIV).

If we understand this, we understand why God brought judgment on Israel and the nations in times past. It was not because he was "a vindictive, bloodthirsty ethnic cleanser" (as claimed by atheist Richard Dawkins; see chapter 4). To the contrary, it was because he was bringing judgment on those who destroyed innocent life, and to bring judgment on the wicked is both just and good. It would be like our military defeating ISIS: while we would mourn the lost estate of these radical Muslims, we would be glad that their terrorist acts were stopped. No more blowing up babies in airports. No more burning captives to death in a cage. No more kidnapping and raping young girls. *The destruction of ISIS would be life-giving and liberating.*

In the same way, we learn from the Scriptures that God hates the shedding of innocent blood because he is a God of life and because human life is precious. And so, if we are to rise above today's culture of death, we must

celebrate and cherish life while viewing death (including gratuitous violence and bloodshed) as an enemy.

Of course, at times we must be confronted with images of the dead and
dying, as in a tragic terrorist attack when the devastating footage stares
us in the face. By all means, we should look at the ugliness and brutality,
and we should mourn with those who mourn. But it is another thing to be
entertained by death, to trivialize death, to fixate on death. We must renew
our minds with the divine principles of life and look to Jesus, the Author of
life and the Giver of life and the very life himself. As stated in the opening
verses of 1 John:

> That which was from the beginning, which we have heard, which we have
> seen with our eyes, which we looked upon and have touched with our
> hands, concerning *the word of life—the life* [speaking of Jesus] was made
> manifest, and we have seen it, and testify to it and proclaim to you *the
> eternal life*. (1:1–2, emphasis added)

John described Jesus as the word of life, the life, eternal life—not only
as the way *to* life but as *life itself*. That is who Jesus is by his very nature, and
by focusing on him we focus on life.

That's why the gospel story doesn't end with the cross. Not at all! When
Jesus rose from the dead, he broke the power of death and now lives forever in victory and triumph. That's why the angels asked the women who
came to the tomb of Jesus after his crucifixion, "Why do you seek the living
among the dead? He is not here, but has risen" (Luke 24:5b–6a). That's why
Peter said seven weeks later to the Jewish crowds in Jerusalem, "God raised
[Jesus] up, loosing the pangs of death, because it was not possible for him to
be held by it" (Acts 2:24).

Death literally could not keep him in the grave, and so our focus is not
on the grave or on death but on a living God and on a living Savior and on
life itself. While this might sound abstract, if we take inventory of our lives
and recognize where we have embraced the spirit of the age—specifically,
the culture of death—turning our attention instead to the God of life and to
eternal life and to the resurrected and living Jesus, we will be amazed to see
how our attitudes change.

So, I give you this little challenge: First, go about your normal daily activities, watching and reading and listening to what you normally watch and read and listen to, but this time take note of how much death is involved. How many images of the dead and dying? How many corpses? How much graphic violence? How much death are you seeing (by choice, not by necessity) over the course of a week?

Second, if you realize that you're being influenced by a culture of death, take a thirty-day break from all forms of death-related media entertainment, be it video games or favorite TV shows or gratuitously violent novels.

Third, immerse yourself in words of life. Read several chapters from Proverbs and the gospel of John each day, noticing the constant emphasis on *life*. As the voice of wisdom says in Proverbs 8, "For whoever finds me *finds life* and obtains favor from the LORD, but he who fails to find me injures himself; all who hate me *love death*" (vv. 35–36, emphasis added).

Fourth, when you spend time in prayer, ask God to flood your heart with his life and to give you his perspective of life, to see the world as he would have you see it.

Fifth, after thirty days ask the Lord how he would have you to live. You might be surprised to see how your perspective has changed. In the words of Paul, "Finally, brothers and sisters, whatever is true, whatever is noble, whatever is right, whatever is pure, whatever is lovely, whatever is admirable—if anything is excellent or praiseworthy—think about such things" (Phil. 4:8 NIV).

Years ago, I received a call on my radio show from a man who had lived a decadent life before he became a follower of Jesus. His life had been filled with drugs and alcohol and immorality, and when he came to faith, he knew he had to give all this up. That was quite obvious to him. But what about the other areas of his life that were not so black and white? What about the other decisions he had to make? He talked with his pastor about it, and that wise leader said to him, "Before you do something, ask yourself this question: Is it light or is it darkness?" As this man said to me on the air, that greatly limited the activities he engaged in, but he found it to be a wonderful way to live. Exactly!

So ask yourself, *Is this light or darkness? The entertainment that I enjoy; the decisions that I make; the way I conduct myself: Is this light or darkness, life or death? Is this edifying or destructive?* Remember always to choose life!

We can also put this idea into practice in some critically important ways. Here are three practical ideas. First, get involved in the pro-life movement and work against abortion on demand in our nation. If Mother Teresa and others are right, this work strikes at a major root of our culture of death, and by joining together as pro-life Christians, we can see the nation impacted.

But how exactly can we do this? My good friends David and Jason Benham were raised in the pro-life movement because their dad, Flip, was a fearless gospel preacher. He would stand in front of abortion clinics sharing the gospel, urging women not to abort their babies, and offering them a better way. Flip was even used by God to lead Norma McCovey to Jesus—she was the Jane Roe in *Roe v. Wade*—and had the privilege of baptizing her.[14]

Over the years the Benham brothers felt the need to establish a pro-life template that could be used in cities across the nation, and that's why they set up Cities 4 Life with the threefold vision of Proclaim, Provide, and Protect. If you visit their website (Cities4Life.org), you'll find ways you can get involved in pro-life work in your own city. Allow me to offer you some suggestions right here. You can volunteer time in a pregnancy crisis center, join with a team that ministers outside an abortion clinic, help to provide baby showers for mothers (or couples) who decide not to abort, donate finances to a pro-life ministry, adopt an unwanted child, educate your local church on pro-life issues, vote for pro-life candidates (and urge your elected officials to vote for life), and pray daily for God's intervention to turn the tide in America. All of us can choose life for those who can't choose it for themselves.

Second, affirm the dignity of every human life by reaching out to the elderly, who are some of the most forgotten and neglected people in our society. In biblical times, older men and women were greatly respected to the point that the law of Moses taught, "You are to rise in the presence of the elderly and honor the old. Fear your God; I am Yahweh" (Lev. 19:32 HCSB). As Proverbs taught, "Gray hair is a crown of glory; it is gained in a righteous life," and "The glory of young men is their strength, but the splendor of old men is their gray hair" (16:31; 20:29). In fact, in biblical times Paul had to urge Timothy not to let anyone despise his youth (1 Tim. 4:12). Today, being a youthful leader is considered cool and chic and cutting edge while being older is equated with being irrelevant and out of touch. Today Paul would have to write to a gray-haired elder, "Don't let anyone despise your old age!" May God help us recover a culture that honors the elderly.

My mom just passed away at ninety-four years old, and she had been living about ten minutes from me in a seniors' facility. She was very frail, but aside from day-to-day forgetfulness, her mind was sharp. She spent her time playing card games on her iPad, doing crossword puzzles, and watching TV. By her choice, she never left her room. I visited her a couple of times per week, checking to see what she needed from the store, getting her laundry, and the highlight of every visit, playing cards with her.

During the last few years of her life, in natural terms, she could not do anything for me or my family. She was not there to provide counsel or wisdom; her income was limited; she couldn't help us with a project; if our grandkids were little, she couldn't babysit for them. I was there for her simply because she was my mom and simply because it gave her great joy to sit and play cards with me. (And she won more times than not!)

The funny thing is that, by nature, I'm a totally driven "achiever."[15] But when it came to visiting my mom, nothing was "achieved" in terms of my normal daily activities, such as writing, doing radio, preaching, teaching, studying, praying, mentoring, answering e-mails. I was simply there to spend time with my mom, and I always thanked God for the privilege of being able to be a blessing in her life after she blessed me by raising me and caring for me.

Of course, contributing to my mother's happiness was certainly an achievement of sorts, but it wasn't measurable like my normal achievements. To the contrary, it took time away from writing or working on a new project or meeting a critical deadline. But because it was my own mother, it was easy for me to shelve the achiever mind-set for a little while, enjoy our time together, and honor my aged parent.

But would I have been at a facility like that if I didn't have a parent there? I seriously doubt it. After all, a million things are calling for my attention, and when it comes to spending time with others, I want to pour it into those who will also be producers for the kingdom of God. Perhaps I need a deeper heart adjustment. Perhaps all of us would learn to value life more by giving ourselves to those who have nothing outward to give. Perhaps this is another way to recognize the dignity of each human being. Perhaps honoring the elders—both the active elders in our midst and the inactive elders whom we have to seek out—would help restore deeper health to our culture. When it's not so much the "rich and famous" who get our attention, then we know we're getting closer to God's heart.

Third, get involved with another group that society discards—namely, the poor and the hurting. Many churches have ministries to the poor and the needy, every city has feeding programs and the like, and for the most part they are greatly understaffed. We celebrate life when we bring meaning and hope into the lives of the hurting. We reaffirm that they too are created in the image of God and therefore are of inestimable value and worth. Caring for the poor is something near and dear to the Lord's heart.

Consider these remarkable verses in Jeremiah, where the prophet rebuked King Jehoiakim, a godless and insecure king who thought that building a bigger palace would make him more of a leader. The prophet contrasted Jehoiakim's mentality with the mentality of his godly father, King Josiah, asking,

> "Does it make you any more of a king that you outstrip everyone else in building with cedar? Just think about your father. He was content that he had food and drink. He did what was just and right. So things went well with him. He upheld the cause of the poor and needy. So things went well for Judah." The LORD says, "That is a good example of what it means to know me." (22:15–16 NET)

Did you get that? God equates knowing him with upholding the cause of the poor and needy. What a statement!

I have older friends in Israel who tirelessly reach out to the outcasts of society there with no hope of any earthly reward. They simply do it to share God's love. They also visit children who have severe handicaps, and in that case the smiles they receive are more than enough reward.

It would do our own kids well to get involved in activities like this too. They can learn to value those who have nothing outward to offer: these people don't look cool; they don't smell good; they have no money; they have no social status; they don't even have any online "friends." This involvement will help your children put compassion above celebrity and service above stardom.

In the late 1970s and early 1980s, during the boat people crisis when refugees fled Vietnam, my family had the privilege of hosting a total of six refugees in our home. The first were a young couple and their baby boy. They lived with us for a period of months (some of the refugees even stayed for more than a year), and they grew up side by side with our two daughters. All of us were enriched by the experience. Years later I heard from another son of that first couple, born to them here in the States. He wanted me to know that when his dad became a US citizen, he chose the name Michael in my honor. I was deeply moved to hear this.

Let us, then, turn away from our obsession with death and instead celebrate life. As people who already enjoy eternal life—the life of the age to come—we can surely radiate that life here in this world. This is exactly what America needs today.[16]

SEVEN

HAVING A MULTIGENERATIONAL MENTALITY

A Key to Rebuilding American Families

*So even to old age and gray hairs, O God, do not
forsake me, until I proclaim your might to another
generation, your power to all those to come.*
—PSALM 71:18

HEZEKIAH WAS ONE OF THE GREATEST KINGS IN THE HISTORY OF Israel and Judah. But at the age of thirty-nine, he became ill and received this devastating news from the prophet Isaiah: "Thus says the LORD, 'Set your house in order, for you shall die; you shall not recover'" (2 Kings 20:1). Hezekiah, you're about to die! So he turned to God in prayer, crying out, "Now, O LORD, please remember how I have walked before you in faithfulness and with a whole heart, and have done what is good in your sight" (v. 3). Then he wept bitterly, and almost instantly God answered his prayer. Hezekiah was healed, and the Lord added fifteen years to his life.

Why did he pray so fervently? What was it that he dreaded so much about dying? Why did he shed so many tears?

On the one hand, he was at the height of his powers, the anointed king of the people of Judah, and not yet forty years old.[1] Who would take such news lightly? He was too young to die. On the other hand, something else was weighing heavily on him. At that point in life, it appears that Hezekiah had no sons—which meant he had no heir, which meant he had no legacy.[2] For an ancient Israelite man, this would be even more devastating than dying at a fairly young age, since your life continued through your offspring, and your legacy lived on through the children who would carry your name.

To put this scene in contemporary terms, everyone knows me today as Michael Brown, which is a very common name. There are lots and lots of Browns and plenty of Michael Browns, like the eighteen-year-old Michael Brown who in 2015 was killed in a confrontation with a policeman in Ferguson, Missouri. But had I lived in biblical times (or, to this day, in some parts of the world), I would have been known as Michael son of Abram (son of Louis).[3] That's quite a difference! I would be directly linked to my father and his father, and they would be directly linked to me. Sometimes in the Bible the links were quite long, as in "Ezra son of Seraiah, the son of Azariah, the son of Hilkiah, the son of Shallum, the son of Zadok, the son of Ahitub, the son of Amariah, the son of Azariah, the son of Meraioth, the son of Zerahiah, the son of Uzzi, the son of Bukki, the son of Abishua, the son of Phinehas, the son of Eleazar, the son of Aaron the chief priest—this Ezra" (Ezra 7:1–6a NIV). That's quite a mouthful!

Coming at this from the opposite angle, in certain parts of the Arab world, when a man has his first son, he changes his own name. So if his firstborn son were named Jamal, the man would become Abu Jamal, meaning "father of Jamal," which means that the man becomes known primarily as his son's father. The generations are deeply intertwined, and you almost literally live on through your children and their children, as if you lived multiple lifetimes. In a sense you do, through your offspring.

Hezekiah understood this principle, proclaiming after he was healed, "Indeed Sheol does not give you thanks; death does not praise you. Those who descend into the Pit do not anticipate your faithfulness. The living person, the living person, he gives you thanks, as I do today. *A father tells his sons about your faithfulness*" (Isa. 38:18–19 NET, emphasis added; we'll have more to say about Hezekiah at the end of this chapter). In contrast, the Scripture records this verse about Absalom, one of David's sons who died after he set himself up as king: "Now Absalom in his lifetime had taken and set up for himself the pillar that is in the King's Valley, for he said, 'I have no son to keep my name in remembrance.' He called the pillar after his own name, and it is called Absalom's monument to this day" (2 Sam. 18:18). His legacy ended with him.[4]

Psalm 78 lays out this multigenerational concept with real clarity. The psalmist said:

> I will sing a song that imparts wisdom; I will make insightful observations about the past. *What we have heard and learned—that which our ancestors have told us—we will not hide from their descendants. We will tell the next generation* about the LORD's praiseworthy acts, about his strength and the amazing things he has done. He established a rule in Jacob; he set up a law in Israel. *He commanded our ancestors to make his deeds known to their descendants, so that the next generation, children yet to be born, might know about them. They will grow up and tell their descendants about them.* Then they will place their confidence in God. They will not forget the works of God, and they will obey his commands. (vv. 78:2–7 NET, emphasis added)

This theme is found throughout the Old Testament, and many laws and customs were instituted for the dual purpose of reminding the current generation about the works of the Lord and informing the next generation about those mighty works. That was the case with the Passover celebration, as Moses explained to the people of Israel on the eve of their exodus from Egypt:

> You shall observe this rite as a statute for you and for your sons forever. And when you come to the land that the LORD will give you, as he has promised, you shall keep this service. And when your children say to you, "What do you mean by this service?" you shall say, "It is the sacrifice of the LORD's Passover, for he passed over the houses of the people of Israel in Egypt, when he struck the Egyptians but spared our houses." (Ex. 12:24–27)

Do this *today* so that your children will carry this out *tomorrow*, passing on the legacy of your faith to the succeeding generations. This idea is something traditional Jews grasp deeply, training their children from their earliest conscious hours, as taught in verses like these in the Psalms: "From generation to generation we will recount your praise. . . . One generation shall commend your works to another, and shall declare your mighty acts" (79:13b; 145:4).

The Ten Commandments even taught that blessing or judgment could be passed on to future generations:

> For I the LORD your God am an impassioned God, visiting the guilt of the parents upon the children, upon the third and upon the fourth generations of those who reject Me, but showing kindness to the thousandth generation of those who love Me and keep My commandments. (Ex. 20:5–6 New Jewish Publication Society Version)[5]

Unfortunately, this multigenerational mentality is often missing in the church today, due largely to a faulty, escapist theology that says, "We're going to be out of here any minute!" With a mind-set like that, how can we plan for the future or have a long-term strategy? How can we compete with those who believe they are here to stay when we are convinced that we won't be staying much longer?

What makes this more insidious is that the worse things get in society, the more prone we are to think, *This must be the end of the world! Jesus is coming any minute.* And so, at the very time that we should be taking a stand against societal decline and working for a better world for our kids and grandkids, we abdicate our responsibilities, thereby clearing the way for our ideological opponents to set the agenda for the coming generations. Even Christians who don't believe in this "we're out of here any moment" theology are often prone to think in the short term since, they reason, "The world will only get worse and heaven is our real home. The best thing we can do is hunker down and get ready for the end to come."

That is an unbalanced, unbiblical, and unfruitful mentality,[6] often leading to apathy (Why bother?) or carnality (Just enjoy yourself!) or pessimism

(Everything's falling apart!). It certainly does not lead to long-term, positive, multigenerational planning and acting.

Life on Earth One Hundred Years from Now?

In February 2016, the Future Timeline website reported that "Hyper-tall sky-scrapers, underwater bubble cities, personal home 'medi-pods' and civilian colonies on the Moon are all likely to be a reality in a hundred years' time, according to a report commissioned by Samsung."[7] The article was titled, "Samsung Predicts the World 100 Years from Now," and it summarized some of the findings of Samsung's eighteen-page "SmartThings Living Report," a report that was meant to be anything but abstract.[8] As James Monighan explained in the foreword:

> Since the dawn of time, we humans have strived to enhance our living and working environments. The environments we live in today are almost unrecognizable from those that existed just a century ago. The Internet is a great example of this. As this technology has spilled over from laptops to smartphones, we've become used to having total knowledge and control in the palm of our hand. The smartphone revolution is now ushering in the smart home revolution, making it possible for anyone to easily monitor, control, and secure their home from anywhere through one simple app.[9]

So, what seemed far-fetched just a few years ago is now a matter of course. What, then, does the future hold? As cities grow in population, how will the large numbers of people be accommodated? Through better technology. Monighan continued:

> If enough homes become greener, we can attain widespread energy conservation and create a greener planet. By being able to better monitor and secure our homes, we can reduce the overall crime rate in cities. By better monitoring the habits of ageing relatives, we help seniors achieve greater independence and a higher quality of life.[10]

Now, some of you will read this and say, "But it's obvious that we're not going to be here a hundred years from now! Can't Mr. Monighan see the signs of the times?"

And that illustrates the very point I am making: while the worlds of technology and business and culture and education continue to think in the long term, we are trapped in the short term. As a result, even if we pour ourselves into our children, we often do it without a long-term vision. Worse still, many of us do not really pour ourselves into our children because we are too consumed with our busy, distracted, day-to-day lives.

Dietrich Bonhoeffer once said, "The ultimate test of a moral society is the kind of world that it leaves to its children,"[11] yet that is a test we often fail to apply to ourselves. What kind of world *are* we leaving to our kids? Many of us do our best to teach and train and instruct our children, but we often fail to think about the world in which they will grow up, let alone the world in which *their* children will grow up. Shouldn't these questions concern us?

Joshua Charles, himself a millennial, has addressed the lack of multi-generational thinking in conservative political circles, writing:

> The abolitionist movement took decades. The women's suffrage movement took decades. The labor movement took decades. The civil rights movement took decades. The homosexual rights movement took decades. Heck, the American Revolution was merely the culmination of 15–20 years of tensions, and it took an additional 15 to get the Constitution, making its initial stages roughly 30–35 years long! And each of these movements changed hearts and minds before they ever obtained the political power with which to do something. . . .
>
> But many modern conservatives don't think in terms of generations, or even decades. They claim to know and understand history but have refused to learn its lessons. They think in terms of every four years. *Maybe* eight. And ironically, virtually the only power many champions of limited government seem to care about is political power.[12]

When I came to faith in late 1971 at the age of sixteen, there was a lot of talk about end-time prophecy. We were told that everything was falling into place and that Jesus would be returning soon . . . very soon . . . possibly any second. And when he returned, he would rapture out his faithful people—we would suddenly disappear—leaving the rest of the world to suffer seven years of hellish tribulation.

If my memory is correct, it was in the fall of 1972 or 1973 on the weekend when we set our clocks back an hour on Saturday night, and I forgot to make the adjustment. Consequently, I showed up for Sunday school one hour early, and there was no one at our church building when I arrived. Oh no! For a moment I thought to myself, *Jesus came back and I missed him!* What a dreadful thought this was, but it illustrates the way we lived back then: at any moment, sooner rather than later, Jesus would return and we would be gone.

The most famous Christian book at that time was Hal Lindsey's *The Late Great Planet Earth*, published in 1970. Based on Lindsey's teachings, it seemed that everything that was happening in the world—from Israel to Europe to America—fit neatly into a prophesied end-time scheme. Surely the end was at hand! And that book, which sold tens of millions of copies, colored the thinking of many Christians during those years, especially evangelical Christians.

In fairness, Lindsey's book did cause many people to realize that the Bible remained relevant to this day, and he was certainly right in stressing the importance of the reestablishment of the modern State of Israel. And it's true that many people came to faith in Jesus as a result of reading *The Late Great Planet Earth*. But Lindsey was forty-one years old when the book was published. He turned eighty-seven in 2016, and I seriously doubt that he thought he would ever see his sixtieth birthday, let alone his eighty-seventh. Surely Jesus would return before then.[13]

By the time this book you are reading is published, my eldest granddaughter will have turned sixteen. I can assure you that, in my early years in the Lord, I did not foresee having a sixteen-year-old grandchild before Jesus returned. Not a chance. I certainly did not have a multigenerational mentality.

What, then, does it look like when we think in terms of multiple generations? What does it mean in our everyday lives? It means that we invest in the next generation at least as much as we invest in the current generation.

It means that we work toward the success and well-being of our children and their children at least as much as we work toward our own success and well-being—and I mean "success and well-being" in the most positive, God-glorifying way. It means that we consider the impact of our actions on those living today and on those who will live tomorrow.

"But," you ask, "doesn't the Bible call us to live in readiness, as if the Lord could come back at any time? And doesn't the New Testament repeatedly tell us that we are pilgrims and strangers here on earth, meaning that we are just passing through?"[14]

You're absolutely right on both counts. We should live in readiness to meet the Lord at his return, just as we live in readiness to meet him in death, since none of us knows the day we will die. We should also long for his return, since that will mean the end of human suffering and the beginning of eternity with him. And we should live as those whose treasures are in heaven, not on the earth. But that doesn't mean that we are the last generation or that we shouldn't think in a multigenerational way, because: (1) every previous generation has died; (2) many of the previous generations believed that they were the last generation, yet none of them were; (3) God's promises remain the same from generation to generation; and (4) the Bible teaches that a fool is shortsighted and selfish while a wise man has long-term vision and thinks of the next generation (see Prov. 13:22).

To be candid, I still hope to see Jesus return in my lifetime, and I still live with a sense that the whole world is about to be shaken. Yet for decades I have poured myself into college-age ministry students, seeking to raise up several generations of gospel workers who in turn are raising up their own spiritual sons and daughters. And I have frequently (and quite joyfully!) invested time in my grandchildren, wanting to make a lasting and positive impact on them, believing that God has a calling on their lives and on the lives of their children to come.

So, we live here on earth with a holy tension, having one foot in this world and one foot in the world to come, but that doesn't mean that we should be shortsighted. Instead, we should live with a sense of urgency and purpose—after all, we have only one life to live—and we should plan as if future generations will follow us. And since we live in the light of eternity, we are not just thinking about one hundred years down the line; we're thinking about one million years down the line. The principles we live by today are principles that will endure through the decades, through the centuries, through the millennia.

Conversely, our ideological opponents—such as those who are pro-abortion or who want to redefine the family in a radical way—purport to be long-term visionaries, but their policies are not built to last. The abortion culture seriously reduces the population (among other things, as we have seen), undermining the foundation of support for the next generation, and the more the family is redefined, the more society will collapse. And so, to paraphrase the title of one of my recent books, if we will follow God's principles—which are the ultimate long-term, visionary principles—we will outlast every worldly revolution.[15] We will do it by recapturing the importance of the family, which is the foundation of today and the building block of tomorrow.

Carle C. Zimmerman was a highly acclaimed Harvard sociologist whose most famous book was *Family and Civilization*, first published in 1947 but reissued with a new introduction by Allan C. Carlson in 2008. That introduction points to the enduring value of this study, which made clear that solid families were the nucleus of healthy societies. Especially interesting, though, is that Zimmerman became increasingly pessimistic of the direction the world was going, not in 2017 or 1987 or even 1967, but already in 1947.[16] He saw the family fragmenting; he saw the rise of individualism; he saw a birth-control culture leading to more, not less abortions; he saw the destructive power of adultery and divorce.

Interestingly, in the years following World War II, when the baby boomer generation gave rise to growing families, it appeared that some of Zimmerman's pessimism was unjustified. But as time has gone on, his predictions have proven to be true. The positive, family-centric burst didn't last.

Today our society is much less stable than it was in 1947, perhaps in ways even beyond what Zimmerman would have predicted: from the ravages of no-fault divorce to the slaughter of tens of millions of babies in the womb, and from the radical redefinition of marriage to the war on gender distinctions. And worldwide, from Russia to Japan to Greece to Spain, there is a dangerously low birth rate, meaning that there are not enough children being born per childbearing woman to sustain future generations.[17] Here in America, where today couples tend to get married later (if at all) and then have only one child (if any), the immigrant population has helped us maintain the minimum birthrate. This, too, does not bode well for the long-term success of a nation.

To be clear, some of those in the body of Christ are called to be single (at least for a season of their lives), and we need to honor them as being just as important as moms and dads. And some singles are not ready to get married at younger ages, let alone ready to have kids. So the last thing we want to do is put unhealthy pressure on people to marry quickly and have big families. I've seen that happen with disastrous effects. Ultimately, you will give account to the Lord, not to me (or anyone else), so I'm not here to play God and tell anyone what to do. I'm simply saying that (1) we do well to have a multigenerational mentality; and (2) healthy families are the key to healthy societies, in particular over the course of several generations.

What happens when the society at large is heading in the wrong direction? That's when a remnant needs to rise up, swimming against the tide of the dominant culture and planting seeds of change for the coming generations. That's why Zimmerman, in his somewhat technical language, spoke of a "familistic remnant" that would become "a vehicular agent in the reappearance of familism." Accordingly, the hope for the future "lay in the making of familism and childbearing the primary social duties of the citizen."[18] In other words (and in terms that everyone can understand), our future will be healthy to the extent that we make strong, large families a priority. Stated even more simply, we should get stoked about getting married and having kids who will follow in our footsteps.[19]

Allow me, then, to share with you six biblical principles for marriage and family that will endure through the generations. They are so simple that you'll be tempted to say, "I've heard all this before!" The problem, though, is that we often fail to live by these principles, and perhaps, by presenting them in a fresh, new context, they will have even more meaning and relevance. So, if we are to recover God's purpose for the family, we need to start here. (I'll spend extra time on this first principle.)

Principle 1: We must regain our appreciation of marriage, family, and children.

What was the first commandment God gave to the human race? It was "be fruitful and multiply," found in Genesis 1:28. And what was the first thing God did after creating Adam and placing him in the garden? He made a suitable companion and helper for him, leading Adam to exclaim when he saw her, "This at last is bone of my bones and flesh of my flesh; she shall be called Woman, because she was taken out of Man." And then this commentary is added: "Therefore a man shall leave his father and his mother and hold fast to his wife, and they shall become one flesh" (Gen. 2:23–24).

When we get to the end of the Bible, in the book of Revelation, we see another marriage celebration, that of Christ and his bride, which is the church (see Rev. 19:6–9). That's why some have pointed out that the Bible starts and ends with a wedding, and why Jesus performed his first miracle at a wedding in Galilee (John 2:1–11). Weddings are wonderful in the Lord's sight!

Again, I recognize that some are called to singleness, at least for an extended season of their lives (think of Jeremiah, Jesus, and Paul), and we relate to God ultimately as individuals, not as couples or families. But marriage is God's plan for the vast majority of human beings because "it is not good for the man to be alone" (Gen. 2:18 NIV), and it is in union with our spouses that we can best fulfill our destinies.[20] A Jewish website explains,

> Marriage is the process of becoming one flesh. Marriage is not two people coming together to form a partnership, nor an agreement to be roommates permanently. It's not a method to get a tax break, or a way to share household chores. The Jewish idea of marriage is two halves becoming one, completing each other.[21]

Well said!

In today's society, marriage has been greatly downgraded. A large number of couples are living together out of wedlock, and many individuals are waiting until much later in life even to get involved in a serious relationship. Once married, couples are waiting longer to have kids. They're also having fewer kids and are more prone to divorce. These new, largely negative attitudes to marriage and family color our thinking more than we realize, and so we must intentionally rebuild a culture that celebrates marriage, that recognizes marriage as the means by which, in most cases, the woman and the man can best fulfill their calling, and that rejoices in having and raising children.

Nancy and I were close friends with a couple that was not able to have children, but after more than twelve years together, their prayers were wonderfully answered. The Lord gave them three terrific kids, fulfilling this promise that the Lord gave to the mother in a very personal way: "He gives the barren woman a home, making her the joyous mother of children. Praise the LORD!" (Ps. 113:9). Praise the Lord indeed!

The great joy of having children was often expressed in the Scriptures:

Sons are indeed a heritage from the LORD, children, a reward. Like arrows in the hand of a warrior are the sons born in one's youth. Happy is the man who has filled his quiver with them. Such men will never be put to shame when they speak with their enemies at the city gate. (Ps. 127:3–5, HCSB)

Your wife will be like a fruitful vine within your house, your sons, like young olive trees around your table. In this very way the man who fears the LORD will be blessed. May the LORD bless you from Zion, so that you will see the prosperity of Jerusalem all the days of your life and will see your children's children! Peace be with Israel. (Ps. 128:3–6, HCSB)

The ideas of radical feminism stand in total contrast with this celebration of marriage and family. They have permeated our society more than we realize, denigrating motherhood and childbirth.[22]

Feminist and historian Linda Gordon once said, "The nuclear family must be destroyed. . . . Whatever its ultimate meaning, the break-up of families now is an objectively revolutionary process."[23] Similarly, Sheila Cronin, former leader of the National Organization for Women (NOW), argued, "Since marriage constitutes slavery for women, it is clear that the women's movement must concentrate on attacking this institution. Freedom for women cannot be won without the abolition of marriage."[24] And Andrea Dworkin, another radical feminist and writer, said, "Marriage as an institution developed from rape as a practice."[25]

Pioneer gay activists shared a similar hostility toward marriage. Carl Wittman, author of the famous *Gay Manifesto*, stated that "marriage is a contract which smothers both people, denies needs, and places impossible demands on both people." And, "Gay people must stop gauging their self-respect by how well they mimic straight marriages. Gay marriages will have the same problems as straight ones except in burlesque."[26] Another pioneer gay activist, Jack Nichols, put it this way:

> Nonprocreative same-sex relationships have a particularly redeeming quality, namely, that they take place between people who are the same and can therefore, theoretically at least, welcome others into affectional relationships that bypass exclusivity. This, conceivably, could promote a maximization of affection through communal contact, replacing today's failing models of exclusive, neurotic, narrow, monogamous duos.[27]

Statements like this from early gay activists could be easily multiplied, meaning that the contemporary push for same-sex "marriage" represents a different direction for gay leaders. Yet even the "pro-marriage" position of gay activists fundamentally revises the very meaning of marriage, while same-sex marriage also challenges normal marital expectations, because gay leaders (especially male) argue for "open marriages," meaning marriages in which the spouses are allowed to have sex with others.[28]

From every angle, then, marriage is under assault (I should also mention that pornography is a growing cause for divorce).[29] And if marriage is less highly esteemed, then having children is less highly esteemed, and so the abortion culture further demeans the value and importance of children. *If, then, we are to see our nation rebuilt, we must start with one wedding at a time, one child at a time, one family at a time.*

An eye-opening chart titled "Will Your Grandchildren Be Jewish?"[30] divides the Jewish world into five categories: Secular (meaning completely nonreligious), Reform (which is quite liberal), Conservative (also liberal, but not as extreme), Centrist Orthodox (this is fairly observant and traditional), and Hasidic/Yeshiva Orthodox (extremely observant and traditional). The chart starts with one hundred Jews in each of the five categories, representing a hypothetical first generation. By the second generation, those numbers are respectively: 41, 46, 66, 163, and 324; by the third generation they are 17, 21, 44, 266, and 1,050; and by the fourth generation the numbers are truly astounding: 7, 10, 29, 434, and 3,401. This is incredible.[31]

The intermarriage rates across these five categories are listed at 49 percent, 46 percent, 32 percent, 6 percent, and 6 percent, so this is one major reason for the vast difference in Jewish identity over the generations. The childbirth rate is also vastly different across the five categories. The average number of children per woman is listed at 1.29, 1.36, 1.74, 3.39, and 6.72, respectively. In sum, the more committed to Judaism these families are, the more children they will have and the more those children will remain true to their heritage. Conversely, the less committed they are to Judaism, the less children they will have and the less those children will remain committed to their heritage.

What does this mean on a societal level? Starting with 100 secular Jews today, their numbers will be reduced to 7 in 4 generations; starting with 100 ultra-Orthodox Jews today, their numbers will rise to 3,401 in 4 generations. Thus, "Based on current intermarriage rates and the average number of children per family, the chances of young, contemporary Jews having Jewish grandchildren and great-grandchildren, with the exception of the Orthodox, are increasingly remote."[32]

If American Christians today begin to celebrate marriage and family, we can be the dominant demographic group within two or three generations.

Principle 2: We must recover the sacredness of our marriage vows.

Although there are some biblical grounds for divorce and although there can certainly be life after divorce,[33] believers need to marry with the mind-set that divorce is not an option. Marriage is for life! The Scriptures teach that God hates divorce (Mal. 2:13–17)[34] and that God gave it as an option to Israel only because of the hardness of their hearts, since it was certainly not his intent from the beginning (Matt. 19:4–8).

Divorce continues to hurt children and families,[35] and as I've said many times before, no-fault divorce in the church has done more to undermine marriage than all gay activists combined. It is essential that we recover the sacredness of the marriage compact, because *you are being joined to your spouse as one flesh for the rest of your life.* It is a solemn and wonderful and glorious commitment. I'm convinced that, in the midst of the most serious marital conflicts, if both the husband and wife will humble themselves and seek God's help, divorce need never occur.

I do understand that divorce is unavoidable sometimes, such as when a spouse commits adultery, abandons the marriage, and initiates the divorce. But when it comes to two believers wanting to follow Jesus, there's no such thing as "irreconcilable differences." If you were married in the Lord, you made a sacred declaration before him—"till death do us part"—and if you live as if divorce is not an option, he'll give you the grace to get through.

In 2017 Nancy and I celebrated forty-one years of marriage, and all the couples on our ministry leadership team have been happily married for decades. Solid marriages are the foundation for multigenerational blessing, and they should be the norm, not the exception, in the body of Christ.

Principle 3: Husbands must love their wives the way Christ loved the church.

Paul didn't say, "Husbands, love your wives if they're lovable." To the contrary, he wrote:

> Husbands, love your wives, as Christ loved the church and gave himself up for her, that he might sanctify her, having cleansed her by the washing of water with the word, so that he might present the church to himself in splendor, without spot or wrinkle or any such thing, that she might be holy and without blemish. In the same way husbands should love their wives as their own bodies. He who loves his wife loves himself. (Eph. 5:25–28)

Husbands, if you will seek to do this, putting your wife first, considering her needs above your own, giving yourself to her and for her, I am sure that you will be richly blessed in return. She will thrive as a result of your care for her, and as you lead well, she will follow.

Despite the tremendous strengths that women have, strengths that often outstrip those of men, there is something to what the Bible says about the woman being the weaker vessel (1 Peter 3:7). How so? I believe that the man is made to be the buck-stops person in the home, and that means bringing security and stability to the household, all based on a solid relationship with the Lord. Accordingly, despite the positive egalitarianism of our society, the great majority of husbands feel the calling to protect and care for their wives more than wives feel the calling to protect and care for their husbands. This is in keeping with how God designed us.

My brother, you do well to make your wife feel like the most special and important person in the world. Lavish your love on her, and you will reap what you sow. Water the plant, and it will flourish and thrive. (In the course of a week, I probably tell Nancy that I love her or that she's beautiful dozens of times—always from my heart.)

When you show love for your wife, when you praise her and encourage her, she will turn out to be everything you could have asked for. (Really now, has doing the opposite really changed anything? Has harping on her and complaining and criticizing helped the relationship?) You can even have the spark of romance return to your relationship years after it went out. God can do it! Husbands, why not serve your wives? Dads, why not give your wives a periodic day off from the kids and household chores?

And notice again what Paul wrote: we are called to love our wives the way Jesus loved the church, and by his laying down his life for us, he made us into something beautiful. He nourishes us and cares for us, and as we do the same for our wives, we will see wonderful results as well. It's also a great example for our kids to witness, especially our sons, who will learn how to treat their wives by watching their dads.

I often joke that the wedding day is the bride's day and from there on, it's the bride's life. But I can say in all seriousness that Nancy has been incredibly loyal to me through thick and thin, that she has made many sacrifices for our ministry work, and that she was often the guiding force in raising our kids as I traveled to speak around the world. She is the strongest woman I know, much stronger than me in many ways. Yet she leans on me to be the head of the house, and she thrives as I'm sensitive to her "love language,"[36] spending quality, focused time with her.

Again, I realize that in some situations the wife turns her back on the Lord and on her husband and her kids, and we cannot control another person's will. But to the extent it depends on us, let us, as husbands, live honorable lives and love our wives as Jesus loved the church, remembering how he loved us when we were lost sinners and how he continues to love us in the midst of our many failures.

Principle 4: Wives must respect their husbands just as they respect the Lord.

Paul did not say, "Wives, respect and submit to your husbands to the extent they are worthy of your respect." No, he wrote, "Wives, submit to your own husbands, as to the Lord. For the husband is the head of the wife even as Christ is the head of the church, his body, and is himself its Savior. Now as the church submits to Christ, so also wives should submit in everything to their husbands" (Eph. 5:22–24).

I can say to you, my dear sister, that your husband will not become the man you want him to be if you badger him and degrade him and criticize him and dishonor him. Instead, *because he is your husband*, you should honor him and submit to him, as long as he doesn't ask you to violate your conscience or disobey God's Word.

I'm aware, of course, that some husbands can be self-centered, domineering, and demanding. Being respectful doesn't mean being silent. Honest communication is essential for a happy marriage, and sometimes marital counseling is called for. By no means am I encouraging a wife to suffer abuse silently, especially when her life or the lives of her children are in danger. I also believe that mutual submission takes place—the husband heeds the wife's words, and she heeds her husband's words as they make decisions together.

In my own marriage, when it comes to practical wisdom, Nancy outshines me greatly, and in day-to-day decisions I rely on her far more than she relies on me. But under God I am the head of the home, and Nancy's respect for me empowers me to carry the spiritual, financial, and emotional burdens. So, wives, I encourage you to take Paul's words seriously here—notice he didn't add a long list of caveats—and as you do, you will watch your husbands become the men you need and desire them to be.

Principle 5: Children must obey their parents.

Yes, I know this is basic stuff, but in today's culture there is far less respect for one's parents and elders than in past generations. Just watch the way kids talked to their parents (or teachers or other people in authority) in TV programs and movies from the fifties and compare that with the way kids talk to their parents and elders in contemporary programs and movies. This has been the pattern for several decades now.

I've ministered overseas on more than one hundred fifty trips, including about forty-five trips to Asia, and in some of these Asian countries, the people give tremendous honor to their elders. That's why arranged marriages are still regularly practiced in countries like India.

I spoke with an Indian colleague a few years back about his arranged marriage. (He and his wife are in their forties now and serve together in ministry.) He told me that he spoke with his prospective wife on the phone a few times before they were married, also meeting her face-to-face one other time, and that was the extent of their contact. When I asked him if he was concerned about their lack of contact before they were married, he told me he was not. Why? It was because he trusted his parents; as he told me, "I observed how they cared for me and made the right decisions for me all my life until then, so I trusted them in choosing my spouse."

My point here is not to advocate for arranged marriage but to advocate for that level of respect. The Hebrew word for *honor* (as in "Honor your father and your mother") is a weighty word (you could say that it literally means to treat them in a weighty way), and God will bless you as you honor and obey your parents. Again, honoring them does not apply only when they make decisions you like and only when they don't get frustrated and upset. It applies in the midst of their human failings. You still honor them as your parents, not just in words and deeds but in attitude.

When I came to faith, I had been a drug-using hippie rock drummer, and although I quickly turned away from my sinful lifestyle, I still had the hippie mentality that scorned formal education. So I made no plans to go to college, despite my father's strong requests. One Sunday when I came home from church, my dad asked me what the sermon was about. Well, it so happened that we had a rare guest speaker that morning, and he spoke on an unusual theme: "Jesus was a teenager!" I can still hear his somewhat thunderous voice as he said with great passion and a big smile, "Think of it! Jesus was a teenager." This guest speaker proceeded to talk about how Jesus honored his father and mother as he grew up, and he urged us to do the same.

When I shared that with my dad, he asked me, "How can you reconcile that sermon with the fact that your mother and I want you to go to college more than anything else, yet you won't do it?" I was immediately convicted in my heart and said, "Then I'll go." Little did I know how momentous that decision would be or that it would lead to a BA in Hebrew and an MA and PhD in Near Eastern Languages and Literatures, degrees that have been greatly used by the Lord in my life. My life has been richly blessed because I obeyed my father and mother.

And notice what Paul said in Ephesians 6: "Children, obey your parents in the Lord, for this is right. 'Honor your father and mother' (this is the first commandment with a promise) 'that it may go well with you and that you may live long in the land'" (vv. 1–3). This is another key to multigenerational blessing; out of the Ten Commandments given by God at Mount Sinai, this is the only one that promises longevity in the promised land. Children, if you want things to go well for you and your descendants, honor your father and mother.

As Dennis Prager pointed out:

> This commandment is so important that it is one of the only commandments in the entire Bible that gives a reason for observing it: "That your days may be long in the land that the LORD your God is giving you."
>
> Many people read that part of the Fifth Commandment as a reward. But while it may be regarded as a reward, the fact remains that it is a reason: if you build a society in which children honor their parents, your society will long survive. And the corollary is: a society in which children do not honor their parents is doomed to self-destruction.[37]

Which kind of society will we build? Let it be a society where parents and elders are honored. If we do that, one family at a time, things will go well for our nation.

Principle 6: Parents must nurture their children.

Shortly before his death, Moses gave the Israelites their final instructions before entering the promised land, calling for complete devotion to Yahweh alone: "Hear, O Israel: The LORD our God, the LORD is one. You shall love the LORD your God with all your heart and with all your soul and with all your might." But look at what follows:

> And these words that I command you today shall be on your heart. *You shall teach them diligently to your children, and shall talk of them when you sit in your house, and when you walk by the way, and when you lie down, and when you rise.* You shall bind them as a sign on your hand, and they shall be as frontlets between your eyes. You shall write them on the doorposts of your house and on your gates. (Deut. 6:4–9, emphasis added)

Love God with all your heart, soul, and strength, and then teach your children to do the same. And note carefully that phrase "teach them diligently," which translates one Hebrew word meaning either "repeat, recite" or "make sharp." So, Moses is either stressing the importance of repeating these truths to our children over and over again, or he is urging us to impress them on our children incisively and clearly.

We are called to drill the words of God into our kids in a life-giving way, remembering this divine principle: "Train up a child in the way he should go; even when he is old he will not depart from it" (Prov. 22:6). We also do well to remember what Spurgeon said on this: "Train up a child in the way he should go—but be sure to go that way yourself." As Paul wrote, "Fathers, do not provoke your children to anger, but bring them up in the discipline and instruction of the Lord" (Eph. 6:4).

Unless you're homeschooling your kids or you have them in a fine Christian school, you must remember that your precious youngsters are getting bombarded with other messages all day long in school, from both teachers and peers (and even kids in homeschool and Christian school can be exposed to all kinds of negative messaging). Outside of school, they are often bombarded with other messages through the media and social media, which are tremendously powerful forces. Seeing that children are the most valuable commodity the Lord has entrusted us with—they are impressionable human beings for whom Jesus died, and they are far more valuable than money or fame—how much time and effort should we put into nurturing their lives? The next time you read through Proverbs, look at how much emphasis is put on the instruction and example of moms and dads. This is how the message is transmitted to the next generation.

WHATEVER HAPPENED TO HEZEKIAH?

After Hezekiah's miraculous healing, envoys from Babylon came to visit him in honor of his recovery. Their motivation, although not recorded explicitly in Isaiah 39, was obvious. They had a common enemy in the nation of Assyria, and they were looking to gain Hezekiah as an ally.

Hezekiah greeted them warmly and "showed them his treasure house—the silver, the gold, the spices, and the precious oil—and all his armory, and everything that was found in his treasuries. There was nothing in his palace and in all his realm that Hezekiah did not show them" (v. 2 HCSB).

After they left, the prophet Isaiah came to the king and asked him about these visitors: "Where did these men come from and what did they say to you?" Hezekiah answered, "They came to me from a distant country, from Babylon."

Isaiah then asked, "What have they seen in your palace?" Hezekiah replied, "They have seen everything in my palace. There isn't anything in my treasuries that I didn't show them" (vv. 3–4).

Isaiah then delivered a devastating, prophetic word to Hezekiah: "'The time will certainly come when everything in your palace and all that your fathers have stored up until this day will be carried off to Babylon; nothing will be left,' says the LORD. 'Some of your descendants who come from you will be taken away, and they will become eunuchs in the palace of the king of Babylon'" (vv. 6–7).

What terrible news! Everything the past generations had worked for would be carried off to Babylon, and even the king's own offspring—his sons or grandsons or great-grandsons—would go into exile. Some of them would even be castrated.

And how did Hezekiah respond to this dreadful word? Did he turn to the Lord and weep, as he did when he was told by the prophet that he was about to die? (See Isaiah 38:1–3.) Did he go to God in desperation, as he did when the Assyrians were threatening to destroy the nation? (See Isaiah 37:1–4.)

No. He responded with these shocking words: "'The word of the LORD that you have spoken is good,' for he thought: There will be peace and security during my lifetime" (Isa. 39:8 HSCB). In other words, "Praise the Lord! As long as I'm going to be alright, it doesn't matter what happens to my kids and grandkids. That's a good word, Isaiah, since there will be *shalom* during my lifetime."

What a shortsighted, self-centered mind-set. It was the polar opposite of the words spoken by Thomas Paine twenty-five hundred years later: "If there must be trouble, let it be in my day, that my child may have peace." (Paine was hardly an orthodox believer either.)

Is it any wonder, then, that Manasseh, the son born to Hezekiah after he was healed, ended up being the wickedest king in Judah's history? Could it be that Hezekiah, a great and godly leader, failed to transmit his values to his son? Could it be that he failed to have a vision for the next generation?

If he did err here, let's not repeat his mistakes. Instead, let's run our race with excellence, either reaching the finish line ourselves (if Jesus returns in our lifetimes) or else passing the baton to the next generation, having done everything we can to help them win their own race. It's a short-term and long-term strategy that works. Our God is a multigenerational God.

EIGHT

RECLAIMING OUR SCHOOLS AND LEARNING HOW TO THINK AGAIN

Wisdom is supreme—so acquire wisdom, and
whatever you acquire, acquire understanding!
—PROVERBS 4:7 NET

The beginning of wisdom is: get wisdom! And
along with all your getting, get insight!
—PROVERBS 4:7 CJB

FOR MORE THAN THREE DECADES, AMERICAN COLLEGES AND UNI-
versities have been leaning more and more to the left, moving steadily from
education to indoctrination and from the free exchange of ideas to the sup-
pressing of viewpoints not conforming to progressive orthodoxy. This trend
has been growing for many years. As Roger Kimball observed in 1998:

> The much-publicized controversy over attempts to enforce "politically cor-
> rect" thinking on American campuses in the name of "diversity" and higher
> virtue, for example, has underscored the extent to which higher education
> has been transformed into a species of ideological indoctrination—
> a continuation of politics by other means. The politics in question are
> the politics of victimhood. Increasingly, academic study is organized not
> around intellectual criteria but simply to cater to the demands of various
> politically approved "marginalized" groups.[1]

This has resulted in books like *Feminism and Geography: The Limits of Geographical Knowledge*, which claims that "geography is masculine" and that "the notion of reason as it developed from the seventeenth century is not gender neutral. On the contrary, it works in tandem with white bourgeois heterosexual masculinities."[2]

Kimball rightly noted:

No one familiar with the kind of thing that passes for scholarship today will be surprised to discover—to take just one example—that the presentation of a paper called "Jane Austen and the Masturbating Girl" at the 1989 meeting of the Modern Language Association was matched by a paper at the 1990 meeting on "The Lesbian Phallus: Or Does Heterosexuality Exist?" and, in 1994, "The Epistemology of the Queer Classroom."[3]

What makes this all the more distressing is that, as we saw previously (chapter 2), many of the greatest universities in our nation were founded by and for Christians, while children's schools were first established in America to be sure that young people could read the Bible for themselves. And so, while America continues to lead the world in higher education, boasting ten of the top fifteen universities in the world,[4] American universities often serve as bastions of radical left ideology where opposing views are suppressed.

At the same time, there has been a consistent dumbing down of children's education in America, as illustrated by a 2012 report from the Council of Foreign Relations, which found that:

- While the USA invests more in K–12 public school education than the rest of the world, our students are not competing well with their peers in other nations.
- More than 25 percent of our students (including an even higher percentage among Hispanic and black students) do not graduate from high school in four years.
- Despite high unemployment rates, American companies are having a hard time finding qualified employees.
- "75% of U.S. citizens ages 17–24 cannot pass military entrance

exams because they are not physically fit, have criminal records, or because they lack critical skills needed in modern warfare, including how to locate on a map military theaters in which the U.S. is fulsomely engaged, such as Afghanistan."

The report also outlines the implications of this study for national well-being, claiming that "the lack of educational preparedness poses threats on five national security fronts: Economic Growth and Competitiveness; Physical Safety; Intellectual Property; U.S. Global Awareness; U.S. Unity and Cohesion."[5] This sounds pretty serious—after all, it doesn't get much more serious than talking about our public safety—and on a practical level, these educational deficiencies are being felt as students graduate from college and enter the workforce, where many are not doing well.

According to a 2013 article posted on Time.com,

employers are facing some hard facts: the entry-level candidates who are on tap to join the ranks of full-time work are clueless about the fundamentals of office life.

A survey by the Workforce Solutions Group at St. Louis Community College finds that more than 60% of employers say applicants lack "communication and interpersonal skills"—a jump of about 10 percentage points in just two years. A wide margin of managers also say today's applicants can't think critically and creatively, solve problems or write well.[6]

Yes, young people are having a harder time thinking critically and creatively. Some even have a hard time sitting down and reading through a book. I've heard this firsthand from educators in the States, and in April 2016, professors from the University of Sheffield in England created an uproar when they made this very claim. As the United Kingdom's *Independent* reported, "Students have reacted to claims from university professors that they struggle to read books from cover to cover by admitting it is true—but insisting it's because universities don't give them enough time to finish them."[7]

I too have noticed that I have to force myself to focus more when studying, the obvious result of years of constant digital communication (and interruption). In many ways, America has become an ADHD nation.[8]

Younger men in particular seem to have been hit hard here, and Samuel D. James asked, "Where have America's young men gone?" He answered:

> According to Erik Hurst, an economist from the University of Chicago, they haven't gone anywhere—they're just plugged in. In a recent interview, Hurst says that his research indicates that young men with less than a four-year degree (according to virtually all data, that's an increasing number) are spending their days unemployed and unmarried, but not unamused. "The hours that they are not working have been replaced almost one-for-one with leisure time," Hurst reports. "Seventy-five percent of this new leisure time falls into one category: video games. The average low-skilled, unemployed man in this group plays video games an average of twelve, and sometimes upwards of thirty hours per week."[9]

But we are not only a nation of hyper-distraction; we have also become a nation of hyper-sensitivity.[10] Our universities are leading the way here as well, now providing "safe spaces" where you can be sure that your feelings won't be hurt or your viewpoints challenged. And so we have gone from the *closing of the American mind* (in the words of philosopher Allan Bloom's 1987 classic, which focused on higher education)[11] to the *coddling of the American mind*, to borrow the title of a 2015 article by Greg Lukianoff and Jonathan Haidt. They wrote, "In the name of emotional well-being, college students are increasingly demanding protection from words and ideas they don't like." And, the authors noted, "that's disastrous for education—and mental health."[12]

How far has this gone? During the 2016 Republican National Convention in Cleveland, Case Western Reserve University, which was located four miles from the convention, provided a "safe space" for students who were upset by the proceedings of the RNC. Yes, "a July 11 statement in *The Daily*, Case Western's internal e-newsletter, informs students—and professors, and administrators—that the private school's Social Justice Institute 'will host a "safe space" in the basement of concrete-laden Crawford Hall for the duration of the convention, which runs from July 18 to July 21.'"[13]

For good reason Karin Agness, founder and president of the Network of Enlightened Women, wrote on Time.com, "There should be no safe spaces from intellectual thought. University administrators should rethink their policies to encourage more intellectual diversity on campuses." She noted:

> Students should not be intellectually bubble-wrapped, shielded from any idea that they might find new or frightening. They shouldn't be retreating to "safe spaces" and worse, our universities themselves shouldn't become intellectually homogenous "safe spaces" where everyone marches to the same tune. The world does not work that way—nor should it—and universities do a disservice to their students by pretending otherwise.[14]

And make no mistake: it is primarily conservative, right-leaning, biblically affirming thought that is being suppressed on our campuses, which now reflect anything but true diversity.

This can be seen, for example, in the high percentage of law professors who are Democrats (outnumbering others five to one)[15] and the low percentage of conservatives who are asked to deliver commencement addresses at leading schools (at the very least, less than 20 percent).[16] When it comes to religious faith, a 2011 survey indicated that although most professors claimed to believe in God, the percentage of those who identified as atheist or agnostic was much higher than in the general population. Specifically, 3 percent of the population identified as atheist and 4.1 as agnostic; the rates among college professors surveyed were 9.8 and 13.1 percent, respectively (so, more than three times higher than the general populace). A whopping 50 percent of psychology professors identified as atheist (no surprise to hear that), while among biology professors "33.3 percent were agnostic and 27.5 percent were atheist" (no surprise to hear that either).[17] You can be assured that many of them are quite aggressive in their nonbelief.[18]

But as disconcerting as it is to see what's happening on the college and university level, what's happening in our children's schools is of even greater concern. We're talking about impressionable little children who are much less able to think for themselves, yet they are getting indoctrinated. There are even educational materials designed to teach *preschool children* (kids as young as three or four) the definitions of words like *gay, bisexual,* and *transgender.*[19] What could these materials possibly mean to a three- or four-year-old? And how in the world did we fall so far from our Bible-based,

Christian educational roots? Can you imagine what our Founding Fathers would have thought of curricula like this?[20] Matthew Spalding noted, "Colonial America was a highly literate society, despite its overwhelmingly rural population. The two books likely to be found in every home were a well-worn copy of the Bible and a volume of Shakespeare, Milton, or other great literature."[21] That's quite a contrast with today!

Again I ask the question: How did we get *here* from the lofty educational vision we embraced for our first two hundred years as colonies and a nation? According to Kraig Beyerlein, now a sociology professor at the University of Notre Dame, much of this antireligious shift can be traced to the National Education Association, dating as far back as the early 1870s. In the years before that, beginning with its founding in 1857, the NEA supported "the teaching of 'common Christianity'—which included, among other things, devotional Bible reading." But by the late 1890s and early 1900s, the NEA supported "educational positions and policies forbidding public schools from engaging in formal religious teachings and expressions." And so, "The leading organization in American public education had become a leading advocate for secularizing public education."[22] Today, it is a leading advocate for radical left ideologies, consistently opposing conservative social positions.[23]

Countless thousands of educators in our country are working tirelessly and sacrificially for our children's good, but there is little doubt that (1) our educational system is getting worse in many ways; (2) when it comes to moral, social, and spiritual issues, the system often indoctrinates more than it educates; (3) having abandoned the concept of absolute truth, schools have embraced the concept of relative truth, and so what's true for you may not be true for me; (4) the same now goes for morality, since everything is relative.

In an environment like this, how can kids learn science and math and history, let alone be encouraged to think critically, let alone be equipped to make sound moral choices? Even reality is relative today, since, we are told, you are whatever you perceive yourself to be. As I've said many times before, if perception is substituted for reality, there is no end to the social madness that follows. You do not just have a man being named Woman of the Year. You do not just have a white woman who identifies as black. Instead, you have a father of seven who identifies as a six-year-old girl. You have a man who identifies as a dog named "Boomer." You have a young lady who believes she is a cat trapped in a woman's body. You have a man who has his ears removed because he identifies as a parrot. And you have a man who changed his identity to female but who has now had "her ears and nose removed to transform into a 'dragon lady' with scales, a forked tongue and a horned skull." But why not? More power to him/her/it! If that's what he/she/it perceives himself/herself/itself to be, why not?[24]

In no way do I want to mock the individuals I mention here. I simply want to point out that, if perception really is reality, then the sky is the limit. Yet this mentality is pervading our schools today, and because of it kids believe they can have *their* realities and *their* truths. So much for education being objective!

In many ways, though, all this is just the tip of the iceberg. Homeschool icon John Taylor Gatto, who was a public school teacher in Manhattan for thirty years, raises some larger, important questions:

> Do we really need school? I don't mean education, just forced schooling: six classes a day, five days a week, nine months a year, for twelve years. Is this deadly routine necessary? And if so, for what? Don't hide behind reading, writing, and arithmetic as a rationale, because a million happy homeschoolers have surely put that banal justification to rest. Even if they hadn't, a considerable number of well-known Americans never went through the twelve-year wringer our kids currently go through, and they turned out all right. George Washington, Benjamin Franklin, Thomas Jefferson, Abraham Lincoln? Someone taught them, to be sure, but they were not products of a school *system*, and not one of them was ever "graduated" from a secondary school.[25]

Our students are not doing as well as they used to, and a radical, liberal bias dominates many of our campuses. This means that we need to become much more serious about getting involved in reforming the educational system if we are to rebuild the nation.

How then do we address the massive problems in this critically important part of our society? The solution is simple and doable, although daunting in scope: (1) we confront the spirit of relativism with absolute truth and morality; (2) we learn to reengage our own minds, and we teach our kids to think;

(3) we get more involved in children's education, becoming school teachers and administrators and librarians and counselors and local school board members (or at least, meet with our kids' teachers and be aware of what's happening in their schools); (4) we prioritize raising up more Christian schools and developing more homeschooling networks; (5) we get more involved in higher education, becoming professors and administrators at secular colleges and universities; (6) we develop more Christian alternatives for undergraduate and graduate studies with the end goal of either influencing current accreditation institutes (which often lean left) or rendering them unimportant.

And this is where we start: *we engage our minds in serious study of the Scriptures.* In doing so, we will be stretched, we will be challenged, we will grow, and we will learn to love God with our hearts *and* minds. Then we teach our kids to do the same.

Do You Really Love God's Word?

Here's a little test you can take to assess your love for the Scriptures. When you're able to get alone in a quiet place, read Psalm 119 out loud, asking yourself as you read, "Do these words reflect my heart, or do I feel like a hypocrite, saying things like, 'I prefer the teaching You proclaimed to thousands of gold and silver pieces' (Ps. 119:72 njv)?" If you realize as you read this psalm that you do not love God's Word as the psalmist did, ask the Lord to give you a fresh love for his teaching, even praying to experience what Jeremiah experienced: "Your words were found, and I ate them, and your words became to me a joy and the delight of my heart, for I am called by your name, O Lord, God of hosts" (Jer. 15:16). How delicious are God's words! And how life-transforming and life-imparting those words are. As expressed in Psalm 1, the one whose "delight is in the law of the Lord," and who "meditates day and night" is given a promise: "in all that he does, he prospers" (vv. 2–3).

This does not mean that everyone is called to be an intellectual who studies day and night or that scholarship is the goal of every American. But it does mean that we make a real effort to sharpen our thinking, that we put our brains to work, that we take in the Word every way we can—be it in writing or in audio or video form or a combination of forms—and that we push ourselves to go deeper, not competing with others but getting intellectually "tuned up" for ourselves, just like a car gets a tune-up to run more efficiently. We must learn to think again, and we must recover the rock-solid foundation of divine absolutes. While society is drowning in a sea of relativism, we stand safe and secure on an immovable Rock.

I have the utmost admiration for homeschooling moms who taught their kids from kindergarten through high school, all while juggling the demands of motherhood and wifehood and personal and community interests, producing a generation of young people far more equipped to deal with the world than so many kids who attended the "best" schools in the country. These moms are a vital part of a revolutionary movement that could literally influence the nation, and we are indebted to them. (We're also indebted to the homeschooling dads for their many important contributions.)

And I have deep appreciation for those who have invested their lives in raising up solid Christian schools, often taking major pay cuts in order to teach and administrate and serve. These people deserve the support of their churches and the encouragement of the body of Christ as a whole.

My hat is also off to those who have determined to make a difference in secular schools, swimming against the tide and putting themselves in uncomfortable situations, all with the goal of shining as lights in dark places. Would to God that there were more of these courageous people too!

But it's not easy. A college professor once called my radio show and told me that in her school, which was fairly well known in her area, she is not allowed to mention God in class, since she is not teaching religion. As hard as I found this to believe, knowing that some of her atheistic or agnostic colleagues commonly mocked God in class, she assured me that it was true. So I wonder, perhaps she needs to cross this line herself? Perhaps she needs to get Christian legal counsel and, if she's sure that her Constitutional rights are being undermined, perhaps she should intentionally violate her school's illegitimate standards? Should others do the same?

To move forward, we need to smash the idol of secular academics, a topic I addressed in my book *Revolution!*[26] I spent some of my most fulfilling years engrossed in university studies, and I have devoted even more fulfilling years to teaching in or directing Bible schools and seminaries. Thank God for literacy and the pursuit of knowledge. Yet academic pursuits, specifically secular academic pursuits, have become an idol. And this idol needs to be repudiated. Most Christian teens end up attending secular colleges in America, even though the atmosphere there is often immoral and even though the professors there are often anti-God in their philosophies. Yet it is to college—specifically, the secular university—our teens must go. Why? Because they need to get a degree! Why? Because everyone has to get a degree; or, because you can't get a good job without a degree; or, because you will not enter adult life rounded and balanced without a degree. Yet so often secular college experience doesn't prepare us for life or improve us for life or enrich us for life or expand our horizons for life. Rather, it is often something to be endured, leaving a huge financial debt in the end.

I have found it illuminating to survey college graduates (who are today believers) about their experience in secular college. Did it help them fulfill their purpose in God? Did it ultimately enrich and benefit their lives? Only a small minority say yes.[27] And yet many of these same believers will insist that *their* kids go to secular college. Why? Because everyone has to get a respected degree! God forbid that your kids enroll in a specialized vocational program that will help them do inner-city work or that the Bible college they want to attend is not listed in the nation's top schools.

How utterly worldly this mind-set is. How it smacks of bowing down to the system of this age, and how it measures itself by the standards of flesh and blood. It is especially ugly when it becomes a matter of prestige for the parents, as if sending their kids to a famous—although godless—school makes the parents look better. It is especially challenging when a particular culture *demands* that we send our kids to such schools—regardless of the financial burden entailed. This is idolatry.

Christian schools can fall into this same trap. They can bow down to the same idol. Unless they offer certain courses and meet certain guidelines, they will lose their accreditation, and if they lose their accreditation, they will lose potential students, and their degrees will not be recognized by other universities, and then that will make Christian education look bad. How so? Because the Christian college failed to live up to the standards set by the state. But why must the state (or accrediting agency) set the standards? What if that school has a unique purpose and function? What if it needs to major on things the state considers minor and minor on things the state considers major? Why must it conform? To offer degrees, of course! This too is idolatry.

Why must we prove that we are just as smart, just as educated, just as astute, just as academically excellent as the world? To whom are we proving this, and what, after all, does it prove? In the long run, will it really produce that much fruit for the gospel? Where does the Word hint at this kind of orientation?

Even godly seminaries can be snared here, spending hundreds of hours combating liberal heresies (although most of the people to whom these graduates minister will never even know these heresies exist) or making sure that graduates are of the highest intellectual caliber without also guaranteeing that they are strong in the experiential knowledge of God. Jesus is more interested in using people who know him than in using people who merely know about him.[28]

I personally long for the day when God will raise up an army of highly educated, deeply intellectual, and mentally sharp radicals: men and women like Pascal with minds on fire and souls aflame. It will be wonderful to hear them refute the cultists and confute the atheists, providing us with a revolutionary strategy to take this generation for Jesus and shake this society for the King. My own life has been shaped by my educational experiences, and I would not be able to do most of the things I now do in Jewish ministry (especially apologetics) or biblical scholarship without that training. But it is only a tool, not an idol, and I willfully—and joyfully—"go to [Jesus] outside the camp, bearing the disgrace he bore. For here we do not have an enduring city, but we are looking for the city that is to come" (Heb. 13:13–14 NIV). This is another way we live with a multigenerational mentality while recognizing that we are only passing through.

On that great day of accounting, we will stand before our God: not our professors, not our accrediting agency, not our board of regents. We must bow down to no god but him, regardless of the cost. That is how idolatry is defeated.

Along these lines, we should be encouraged by the progress made in the homeschooling revolution, where the number of kids being taught at home continues to grow[29] and the academic progress made by those kids continues to grow. Already in 2009 the *Washington Times* could report that "in reading, the average home-schooler scored at the 89th percentile; language, 84th percentile; math, 84th percentile; science, 86th percentile; and social studies, 84th percentile. In the core studies (reading, language and math), the average home-schooler scored at the 88th percentile." In contrast, "The average public school student taking these standardized tests scored at the 50th percentile in each subject area," meaning that "the average home-school test results continue to be 30-plus percentile points higher than their public school counterparts."

What explains this success, seeing that most parents are less equipped to teach school subjects than trained school teachers? In the opinion of the *Times* article,

> there are two main factors for these outstanding results: the educational environment where learning takes place, and the individualized, one-on-one instruction. Most home-school students are directly taught by their parents, who love their children enough to make the sacrifice to stay at home to make sure their child is taught in a safe and loving learning environment. Second, one-on-one instruction emphasizes the best interests of the child rather than the best interests of the group.
>
> In a sentence, home-schooling is a recipe for academic success.[30]

I'm quite aware that homeschooling is not a viable option for everyone, and it may be completely impossible in single-parent homes. But getting involved with our kids' education should be a priority for all of us, especially as we realize that education really does begin in the home and that education is far more than just taking classes. Let us educate ourselves in the things that matter most, and let us impart godly education to our children.

A faculty member at Liberty University, which now boasts a residential enrollment of 14,500 students and an online enrollment of 95,000 (!), told me that Liberty is now producing half of all military chaplains.[31] Do you think this will make a difference in the years to come?

After I spoke at a church in Indiana in 2015, a man approached me with a glowing report about what was happening in the local school district. The schools were wide open to the gospel, and local pastors were ministering to the students with extraordinary freedom and favor. He then explained to me that he was a retired school principal, and after his retirement his pastor told him that the schools there still needed him. So he became an active (and influential) member of the local school board, and he was a key reason the schools were so friendly to the churches. What if more retired teachers and administrators followed his lead?

While ministering in Korea in 2016, the pastor of the church hosting my last meeting there told me how his kids are excelling in their school's debate club. (He is an American lawyer married to a Korean woman, and he was a leading debater while a student at Liberty.) His son, now seventeen, and his daughter, now fifteen, previously divided their time between America and Korea, but they were homeschooled in both settings until recently. Now that they're in the Korean school system, which is quite rigorous, they have won national debating contests and are able to hold their own against anti-Christian instructors.

This is the potential of godly kids and godly college grads and godly retired educators, and this is the kind of vision we need to set before us for the improving of our nation. Renewing our minds and recapturing our schools is an obvious, major key.

NINE

RESTORING THUNDER TO OUR PULPITS

Is not my word like fire, declares the LORD, and
like a hammer that breaks the rock in pieces?
—JEREMIAH 23:29

ON DECEMBER 4, 1873, REVIVALIST, PASTOR, AND COLLEGE PRESI-
dent Charles G. Finney made this striking comment:

> Brethren, our preaching will bear its legitimate fruits. If immorality pre-
> vails in the land, the fault is ours in a great degree. If there is a decay of
> conscience, the pulpit is responsible for it. If the public press lacks moral
> discrimination, the pulpit is responsible for it. If the church is degenerate
> and worldly, the pulpit is responsible for it. If the world loses its interest in
> religion, the pulpit is responsible for it. If Satan rules in our halls of leg-
> islation, the pulpit is responsible for it. If our politics become so corrupt
> that the very foundations of our government are ready to fall away, the
> pulpit is responsible for it. Let us not ignore this fact, my dear brethren;
> but let us lay it to heart, and be thoroughly awake to our responsibility in
> respect to the morals of this nation.[1]

Is this true? Are the spiritual leaders of our nation largely responsible
for our moral condition? Without a doubt, in Finney's day the pulpit played
a greater role in society, and there was a greater reverence for Scripture and

respect for the church at that time. So, in that sense, his statement needs to be modified. But it should certainly not be thrown out. To the contrary, since the great majority of people in the United States of America still claim to be Christian, since our airwaves are flooded with 24–7 gospel radio and TV programs, since we have *New York Times* bestselling Christian books, and since roughly one-third of Americans attend church services on a regular basis,[2] the answer remains yes: the pulpit is largely responsible. And since Jesus said that we were the salt of the earth and the light of the world, with tens of millions of believers in our nation, we really do set the spiritual and moral climate, for better or for worse.

In the days of Jeremiah twenty-six hundred years ago, this was also God's verdict on the spiritual leaders of Judah when he laid the blame for the backslidden condition of the nation at the feet of the priests and prophets. By their bad example and their defective message, they led the chosen people into exile and judgment.[3] Similar things are happening in our day.

Let the truth be told. There is very little thunder from our pulpits, very little preaching that creates an atmosphere of holy reverence (what the Bible calls "the fear of the Lord"), very little that challenges us and confronts us and stirs us and awakens us, very little that equips us to endure hardship or to be courageous or to confront the culture or to live a sacrificial life out of love for our neighbor.

Many of our leaders preach a toothless, pep talk gospel that fits in perfectly with our convenience-store, quick-fix Christianity, promising all kinds of benefits without any requirements. What a deal! Who could refuse it? No wonder we are producing consumers rather than disciples. What else can we expect when we so studiously bypass the cross in so much of our preaching? What else can we expect when we preach God the Genie rather than God the Judge?

More than fifty years ago, in his classic article "The Old Cross and the New," A. W. Tozer wrote, "The old cross would have no truck with the world. For Adam's proud flesh it meant the end of the journey."[4] In contrast, he noted with profound insight, "the new cross does not slay the sinner, it redirects him."[5] Today we could take this one step further and say, "The new cross does not slay the sinner; it empowers him (or her)."

In today's view, Jesus came to make you into a bigger and better you.

Jesus came to help you fulfill *your* dreams and *your* destiny. Put another way, the gospel is all about you!

Our contemporary "gospel" says, "This is who I am, this is how I feel, and God is here to please me." The biblical gospel says, "This is who God is, this is how he feels, and we are here to please him." The difference between these two messages is the difference between heaven and hell.

Scan the programming on Christian TV and listen to the latest "hit" sermons, and take note of how often you hear messages about all the wonderful things God can do for you, including helping you prosper financially. Contrast that with how seldom you hear messages about the wonderful things we are called to do for the Lord. And see if you can count even five times in the last year that you heard a message challenging you to sacrificial service for Jesus (and I'm not talking about making a financial sacrifice for the TV preacher). Yet Jesus said, "If anyone would come after me, he must deny himself and take up his cross daily and follow me. For whoever wants to save his life will lose it, but whoever loses his life for my sake will save it," (Luke 9:23–24). When is the last time you were stirred to the core of your being with those words? Yet they are repeated throughout the Gospels and formed a fundamental part of the message of the Lord.[6]

"Endure hardship as a good soldier of Jesus Christ," Paul wrote to Timothy (2 Tim. 2:3 NKJV)—as opposed to, "Enjoy personal success as a good entrepreneur of Christ Jesus." And he exhorted Timothy to use the Word to "correct, rebuke and encourage—with great patience and careful instruction" (2 Tim. 4:2 NIV), warning him that "the time is coming when people will not endure sound teaching, but having itching ears they will accumulate for themselves teachers to suit their own passions, and will turn away from listening to the truth and wander off into myths" (2 Tim. 4:3–4).

We are living in such a time today, a time when the gospel of personal success, which is already dangerous, has been merged with an exaggerated message of God's love, thereby rendering the listener impervious to warning or correction or rebuke: "If it doesn't make me feel better about myself, it's not from God. If it draws attention to my sin, it's not from God. If it challenges me in any way, it's not from God. It's legalism, it's bondage, it's the law—and it's not for me."

No wonder the world is changing us rather than us changing the world.

No wonder there can be so many of us who profess to follow Jesus yet we make so little impact for him. It is because so many of us are spiritually shallow, superficial in our faith, and at surface level in our commitment. And one reason we are lacking in depth is that we are being coddled rather than challenged from the pulpits. This idea may be painful to admit, but it's true.

When is the last time you left a church service or Bible study overwhelmed with the reality of who God is or deeply gripped with the cost of discipleship or weeping under conviction at the revelation of your sin or laughing for joy at the Father's extraordinary love? When is the last time you were *moved* by what you heard—moved to fast and pray, moved to reach out to the hurting, moved to make a major life-changing decision, moved to make a break with a sinful habit, moved to take a stand, whatever the cost or consequence? How long has it been—if ever? Perhaps the problem is not entirely yours. Perhaps it is also the failure of those of us who are teachers and preachers and leaders.

Today many Christian leaders teach that it is wrong to expect born-again believers to change their conduct, calling you "religious" (as if that's a bad word) or, worse still, a "legalist" if you preach repentance to the church and to the lost. Today we can practice almost any sin, work in almost any ungodly profession, and still be accepted as followers of Jesus. How in the world did we depart so far from the transforming power of the gospel?

This is where we find ourselves today:

- A senior editor of one of the nation's leading Christian publications speaks with regret of "the long-standing evangelical myth that there should be something different about the Christian."[7]
- A glamorous spokeswoman for conservative Christian values explains that "I am a Christian, and I am a model. Models pose for pictures, including lingerie and swimwear photos."[8]
- A well-known rapper claims a conversion to Christianity and states, "I love God, Jesus Christ is my savior and I'm still out here thuggin'." He has been baptized, attends church regularly, and says, "I still love the strip club and I still smoke and drink. I'm faithful to my family, so I wanted to make an album where you could love God and be of God, but still get it poppin' in your life."[9]

- A former sex worker explains, "It may surprise many Christians to hear me say that I was a Born Again Christian the entirety of my 20 year career as a prostitute and adult entertainer. I was a Born Again Christian the entire time I was advocating for legalized brothels."[10]

I am not making this up. Yet most Christian leaders today don't dare call out anyone for their sinful, public lifestyle lest we be guilty of what is now considered the worst sin of all—the sin of judging! Yes, these days, it is considered worse to judge someone for sinning than it is to commit the sin. How did we fall so far from the lofty standards of the gospel? Who changed things?

Who changed things from the New Testament faith, where even the disciples couldn't minister without being endued by the Spirit, to today's version, where whole ministries are run with hardly any evidence of the Spirit's work? As Tozer once said, "If the Holy Spirit was withdrawn from the church today, 95 percent of what we do would go on and no one would know the difference. If the Holy Spirit had been withdrawn from the New Testament church, 95 percent of what they did would stop, and everybody would know the difference."[11] This remains true of most of the contemporary church in the West.

In the early church, Paul instructed the Corinthians to separate themselves from people who claimed to be believers but were living in outward, unrepentant sin (1 Cor. 5). Today, some of those people lead our churches and preach from our pulpits. Who changed things?

When did Jesus stop being enough? When did obedience become an option? When did keeping God's commandments out of love for him become "religious" (in the negative sense of the word)? Didn't Jesus say that if we loved him, we would keep his commandments (see John 14:15, 21)?

If we belonged to another religion that claimed to have other books that supplemented the Bible or traditions that superseded it, that would be one thing. But we don't. We believe the Scriptures alone are God's Word and that nothing that comes after the Scriptures—no tradition, no alleged revelation, no consensus—can undermine or countermand the written Word of God. So who changed things from the biblical version of the Jesus faith to the modern American version?

When did the Lord command us to fashion our preaching and our style of worship and even the way we look based on what's trending? If some church leaders choose to trust in worldly business models and carnal consulting firms, that's their choice. I say that we go with the power of the name of Jesus and the wisdom of the Word of God and the fullness of the Spirit. I say that we go with the New Testament model, applied with boldness, wisdom, and compassion to the pressing needs of the day.

It is a doomed strategy when we try to make the gospel of Jesus palatable to lost sinners, take away its offense, remove its reproach, water down its contents, and explain away its standards. In doing so, we dishonor the Lord and contribute to the damnation of the lost. It's time we wake up and repent of this worldly, faithless approach.

Let me illustrate the folly of trying to preach a palatable gospel. Suppose that a doctor made an amazing scientific breakthrough, perhaps the greatest of all time. He discovered a cure for cancer that was 100 percent successful, and it worked for all forms and all stages of cancer. Perhaps the most incredible thing of all was that just one dose of the medicine would cure the cancer for life.

The only problems were that the medicine had to be taken in pill form, each pill cost one million dollars, the pill was huge and difficult to swallow, and it left a terrible, bitter taste that lasted for seven days.

Of course, the research and development team was ecstatic over the discovery. They met with the doctor, telling him that he had to make three simple changes for his breakthrough to succeed: he needed to figure out a way to reduce the cost of each pill so it would sell for one thousand dollars per dose; he needed to reduce the size of the pill so people wouldn't choke on it; and he needed to remove the bitter taste.

After two years of hard work, the doctor called the team back, announcing that he had succeeded on all fronts. With the new formula he had developed, each pill would cost just one thousand dollars, it would be packaged in a small gel cap, and it would actually have a pleasant aftertaste. There was only one problem: the pill no longer cured cancer!

And that is exactly what we have done with the gospel. We have tried to make the narrow gate wide and tried to make the cross of Christ popular, thinking somehow we would get more people "saved." But our message no longer saves!

We have tried to make Jesus acceptable to sinners rather than making sinners acceptable to him, removing the call to submit to his lordship and live a new life in him. And we have redefined repentance, reducing it to a mere change of mind rather than a change of direction: specifically, a turning from sin and a turning to the Lord, an about-face by the grace of God and the power of the Spirit.

Belief in Jesus is now presented as a good insurance policy and packaged as a great deal at that. "Just give up your guilt and depression, and in exchange, receive success, prosperity, and eternal life!" May I ask you to show me one example of a message like that preached to the lost anywhere in the Gospels or Acts? Or do we think we know better than the apostles?

Was there a reason that Paul, when reaching out to the Roman governor Felix and speaking about "faith in Christ Jesus," also spoke to him "about righteousness, self-control and the judgment to come" (Acts 24:24–25 NIV)? Is this part of our gospel message? And was there a reason that Felix became unnerved (literally, "frightened") after hearing Paul's message? Could it be that Felix came to speak with Paul accompanied by his wife Drusilla, whom he took away from her lawful husband to have her as his personal trophy, and that's why Paul talked with him about "righteousness, self-control and the judgment to come"? Could it be that Paul indirectly confronted him about his sins?

Of course we should be people of compassion, reaching out to the lost with hearts overflowing with genuine love and care. And of course we should exercise wisdom and cultural sensitivity. But love tells the truth, and we do not win the world by becoming like the world; we win the world by becoming like Jesus—and by presenting the Jesus of the Scriptures and the gospel of the Scriptures, whether it brings offense or reproach or mockery.

Paul wrote that when Jesus returns, "He will punish those who do not know God and do not obey the gospel of our Lord Jesus" (2 Thess. 1:8 NIV). How often do we think of the gospel as something to be "obeyed"?

To quote A. W. Tozer again:

The trouble is the whole "Accept Christ" attitude is likely to be wrong. It shows Christ applying to us rather than us to Him. It makes Him stand hat-in-hand awaiting our verdict on Him, instead of our kneeling with troubled hearts awaiting His verdict on us. It may even permit us to accept Christ by an impulse of mind or emotions, painlessly, at no loss to our ego and no inconvenience to our usual way of life.[12]

Let us return to the New Testament gospel, exalting both the holiness of God and the love of God, presenting Jesus as both Lord and Savior, and preaching a message that is foolishness to those who perish but is the power of God to those who believe (1 Cor. 1:18). Let's preach the truth without compromise, empowered by the Spirit, filled with compassion, and unashamed of Jesus and the cross. As we do, God himself will back the message about his Son.

I certainly don't believe that every message should be heavy, and I fully affirm the pastoral calling to shepherd the flock—a pastor is a shepherd—and that means offering instruction, comfort, and encouragement along with all kinds of practical teaching. It is also imperative that our words are filled with kindness and tenderness and that we speak the truth in love (Eph. 4:15). But is there never a time to warn or sound the alarm? Is there never a time to raise up a spiritual army and send that army out to make an impact? Is there never a time to make the sheep uncomfortable? Given the morally confused state in which we find ourselves today, is it too much to think that our pulpits would offer clarity and guidance and sobriety? Our nation is in critical condition. How can we hold our peace?

Pastors have told me that they dare not address certain issues, because those issues are too controversial. We must act wisely, I am told by so many; but all too often, *what we call "wisdom" is simply a cloak to cover up our cowardice.* May the Lord Jesus help us to stand!

In 2014 George Barna reported the results of his latest poll, saying,

When we ask [pastors] about all the key issues of the day, [90 percent of them are] telling us, "Yes, the Bible speaks to every one of these issues." Then we ask them: "Well, are you teaching your people what the Bible says about those issues?" and the numbers drop . . . to less than 10 percent of pastors who say they will speak to it.

And what, exactly, holds them back from addressing controversial issues from the pulpit, including, "societal, moral and political issues"? According to Barna, "There are five factors that the vast majority of pastors turn to. Attendance, giving, number of programs, number of staff, and square footage."

He continued: "What I'm suggesting is [those pastors] won't probably get involved in politics because it's very controversial. Controversy keeps people from being in the seats, controversy keeps people from giving money, from attending programs."[13]

Fired up by the results of this poll, pastor and radio host Chuck Baldwin wrote:

> Please understand this: America's malaise is directly due to the deliberate disobedience of America's pastors—and the willingness of the Christians in the pews to tolerate the disobedience of their pastor. Nothing more! Nothing less! When Paul wrote his own epitaph, it read, "I have fought a good fight, I have finished my course, I have kept the faith" (2 Tim. 4:7 KJV). He didn't say, "I had a large congregation, we had big offerings, we had a lot of programs, I had a large staff, and we had large facilities."

But Baldwin wasn't done. He also gave this direct and unnerving charge:

> It is time for Christians to acknowledge that these ministers are not pastors; they are CEOs. They are not Bible teachers; they are performers. They are not shepherds; they are hirelings. It is also time for Christians to be honest with themselves: do they want a pastor who desires to be faithful to the Scriptures, or do they want a pastor who is simply trying to be "successful?"[14]

Now, I want to be the first one to say that there are many fine pastors in America. Anything but hirelings, they are overworked and underpaid while serving their communities out of love. And I recognize that churches have bills to pay and financial obligations to meet and must therefore be conscious of their budgets. If attendance goes down, giving will likely go down, and that might mean your ministry can't support a missionary over-seas or your church has to cut back on a feeding program or eliminate a children's pastor from the staff. These are certainly issues to consider.

But the sad fact is that all too many leaders *do* draw back from address-ing critically important social and moral issues for fear of losing people or losing income or losing reputation. *This is nothing other than cowardice and compromise.* Yet this very approach is put forward as a great model for church growth today.

I urge every Christian leader in America reading this book to ask them-selves some honest questions (as I ask myself as well): If your congregants are slumbering, are your words calculated to wake them up? If your con-gregants are compromised, are your words calculated to convict them? If your congregants are worldly, are your words calculated to call them to separation? I know there are many other questions to ask, including these: What if your congregants are hurting or discouraged or hopeless? Are your words calculated to heal and encourage and inspire? Those are worthy questions as well. But today we seem to put all the emphasis on the last two questions and almost no emphasis on the first three.

My dear fellow leader: Is God calling you to train a holy army of world changers, or is he calling you to build a luxurious Christian country club? Martin Luther King Jr. once said, "The church must be reminded that it is not the master or the servant of the state, but rather the conscience of the state. It must be the guide and the critic of the state, and never its tool. *If the church does not recapture its prophetic zeal, it will become an irrelevant social club without moral or spiritual authority.*"[15] Isn't that where we find ourselves today?

Yale law professor Stephen L. Carter gave us a powerful picture of what it means for the church to recapture its prophetic zeal.

> Along with many African-American theologians, I believe in the tre-mendous importance of preserving religious communities not only as centers of difference—that is, places where one grasps the meaning of the world as different from what you find in the dominant culture—but even more so as centers of resistance. These centers of resistance do not simply

proclaim "We don't believe what the rest of you believe," but say, "We are willing and ready to sacrifice, to lose something material for the sake of that difference in which we believe."

He understood that this was something the church was uniquely called to do.

Indeed, radical transformation will demand a sacrifice. But a fundamental demand for sacrifice will not arise in politics. It will have to arise from the church, which is really the only contemporary, genuine source of resistance to the existing order. Nobody else can do it. Nobody was ever persuaded to go out and risk life and limb because of reading a smart article on philosophy and public affairs. No people ever said they were going to organize a march and be beaten by the police because of something they read in *The New York Times* op-ed page. It is only religion that still has the power, at its best, to encourage sacrifice and resistance.

But, Professor Carter urged, "one should have no illusions. All too many pastors today, black and white, are so worried about filling the seats. Clergy deliver brilliant sermons that preach up to the edge of asking people to do something, and then they will pull back. Some pastors display prophetic leadership and call for sacrifice, but their numbers are small."[16]

Pastor and Oklahoma state representative Dan Fisher has called for the return of the "Black Robed Regiment," a name given by the British to American ministers who helped spark the fires of the American Revolution, preaching against the tyranny of England and even leading their congregations into battle. But he is not calling for pastors today to take up arms against the government (hardly!) nor is he seeking to foment a politically based revolution. Instead, he is calling on preachers today to follow in the footsteps of their forefathers, who knew nothing of the so-called separation of church and state. Instead, they fearlessly confronted the issues of the day, and they helped pave the way for our freedom.[17]

May that Black Robed Regiment rise again today. As a leader in the body of Christ, I say to my fellow leaders: America's well-being depends on us. It's time to let the lion roar. Let your voices be heard!

TEN

———

FROM *PLAYBOY* TO PURITY

Reversing the Sexual Revolution

*Flee from sexual immorality. Every other sin a
person commits is outside the body, but the sexually
immoral person sins against his own body.*
—1 CORINTHIANS 6:18

ON OCTOBER 12 AND 13, 2015, THE INTERNET LIT UP WITH HEADLINES:

- *Playboy* to stop publishing nude photos (*USA Today*)
- No more naked women in print *Playboy* (*Business Insider*)
- *Playboy* magazine abandons nudity (*Telegraph*, United Kingdom)
- *Playboy* magazine to stop publishing pictures
  of naked women (*The Guardian*)

After sixty-two years of featuring nudes, beginning in December
1953 with the famous Marilyn Monroe centerfold, *Playboy* was no longer
going to display pictures of naked women in its magazine. But from the
standpoint of moral values, this was actually bad news, not good news. As
one supporter of nude photos explained, "We live in a world where all the
world's porn is like three mouse clicks away, and most of it is totally free. In
a world like that, *Playboy* is redundant at best and embarrassing at worst."[1]
And remember, it was a *supporter* of nude pictures who wrote this.

Playboy was not abandoning nude pictorials because society had become more moral. It was abandoning these pictorials because society had become so immoral that *Playboy*'s relatively mild pornography was no longer a draw. Pornography of the most sordid kind was freely available everywhere, so who needed pictures of nude women in *Playboy*? Porn was now ubiquitous.

Max Benwell's article on the *Independent*'s site in England was titled, "Why You Should Be Worried About Playboy Dropping Naked Women from Its Pages," with the subtitle "This Isn't a Clear Moral Victory, but Yet Another Reminder of the Huge Power Wielded by Mainstream Pornography." Benwell noted that when *Playboy* dropped nudes from its website in August 2015, that "caused its traffic to quadruple." People were now drawn to the articles and not distracted by the relatively benign pictures.

Benwell wrote:

> The magazine becoming never-nude is heartening for anyone who cares about the media's constant objectification of women. But no one should pretend that this is a moral victory. *Playboy*, acting as any business would, dropped the nudes because there's no demand for them any more. The free market argument that supported their continued existence turned on them. But this isn't because we're all reading feminist zines on Tumblr now; *there's no demand for them because too many people are watching free online porn instead*. "You're now one click away from every sex act imaginable for free," *Playboy*'s CEO Scott Flanders has said. "And so it's just passé at this juncture." Whether this can be counted as a victory for feminist activists or not, it's yet another reminder of [how] powerful and pervasive mainstream porn has become. And if you think *Playboy* is bad, well, it doesn't even compare.[2]

When I was a worldly, drug-using, sixteen-year-old rebel, I had no access to pornography unless I knew an older person who subscribed to *Playboy*—and at that time, I didn't. I was too young to buy it, it wasn't available on TV, and if there was a porn theater somewhere, I couldn't get in even if I wanted to because of my age. As for the images found in *Playboy*, if 10 represents the worst of what's available today at the click of a mouse (or the touch of a finger on a cell phone), then *Playboy* would probably be a

1 or 2 (if that). Today there are chat rooms where women perform sex acts at your command, websites where couples (or other groups) post their sex tapes, and other sites numbering in the countless thousands featuring every imaginable (and unimaginable) perversion.

The Internet is awash with pornography, and most of it is coming from the United States, the porn capital of the world. We are literally experiencing a pornography plague, the likes of which the world has never seen, and it is affecting the most vulnerable members of our society—our daughters and sons. It's so bad now that even archliberals who steadfastly oppose censorship laws are getting concerned. As Judith Shulevitz wrote in the *New York Times*, "Left-leaning parents shy away from a cause they identify with right-wing culture warriors, but I challenge any parent to affirm that it's O.K. for her kids to become digital porn consumers at 11, the average age of a child's first encounter."[3]

Today, there are articles warning about "The Detrimental Effects of Pornography on Small Children"[4]—yes, small children—and many studies pointing to eleven as the average age that kids are first exposed to pornography. Eleven! (A guest on my radio show said that the average age of first exposure could be as low as *eight*.) This results in increased instances of sexual abuse within the family (child on child) along with misguided concepts of sex that can last a lifetime.

That early exposure to pornography can lead to sexual brokenness and deviance is confirmed by Michelle Smith, author of the book *Prodigal Pursued: Out of the Lifestyle into the Arms of Jesus: An Ex-Lesbian's Journey*.[5] She lived as an out and proud lesbian for almost twenty-five years, beginning at the age of eighteen. She traces her sexual struggles and confusion back to the age of seven, when a man first exposed her to pornography. Tragically, she is but one of millions who have been negatively affected.

Cultural commentator Bill Muehlenberg noted that "children accessing porn on the Internet and elsewhere are now acting out what they have seen. For example, child protection experts are warning that Internet porn is creating a new generation of sexual predators as young as six years of age."

Describing the situation in Australia where he lives, Muehlenberg wrote, "The Children At Risk Assessment Unit in Canberra has warned of a huge increase in kids under ten sexually abusing other kids, mainly because of browsing porn sites on the Internet. A social worker at the Unit said that many of the kids thought that pornography was the Internet's sole purpose."

To personalize this daunting information, Muehlenberg pointed to this tragic case from the United Kingdom:

A 13-year-old boy told a UK court that he raped his 8-year-old sister after viewing pornography at his friend's house. The teenager told police he "decided to try it out" on his sister because she was small and "couldn't remember stuff," reported the *Lancashire Telegraph*. The boy, who cannot be named for legal reasons, pleaded guilty on Monday in a Magistrates Court to rape, indecent assault, and inciting a minor to perform a sexual act on him. The boy has been released on bail to live with his family while his sister is receiving support from specialist officers.[6]

Sadly, as Muehlenberg observed, cases like this are becoming more and more common, which is one reason that the Republican Party platform of 2016 labeled pornography "a public health crisis" and a "public menace."[7]

But these days, it's actually hard to avoid Internet porn. A 2003 study claimed that "more than 80 percent of children using e-mail receive inappropriate spam daily," much of it sexual in content, yet that was well over a decade ago.[8] (Moments after typing these words, I checked my e-mail, and this was waiting for me in my Junk folder: "If you could only touch me . . . I'm waiting. I'm horny and have my camera going. Let's video chat . . . I can't touch you . . . But you can watch me touch myself. Best I can do until we can hook up. Watch me here!")

According to a major study conducted by the Barna Group in conjunction with the Josh McDowell Ministry,

- More than one-quarter (27 percent) of adults ages 25–30 first viewed pornography before puberty.
- Nearly half of young people actively seek out porn monthly or more often.
- Teens and young adults consider "not recycling" more immoral than viewing pornography.

- Teenage girls and young women are significantly more likely to actively seek out porn than women over age twenty-five.
- Sixty-six percent of teens and young adults have received a sexually explicit image, and 41 percent have sent one.
- More than half of Christian youth pastors have had at least one teen come to them for help in dealing with porn in the past twelve months.
- Twenty-one percent of youth pastors and 14 percent of pastors admit they currently struggle with using porn. About 12 percent of youth pastors and 5 percent of pastors say they are addicted to porn.[9]

No wonder a headline reporting on this declared, "Groundbreaking Pornography Study Yields Shocking Results: 'Our Future Is at Risk.'"[10] More disconcertingly, "Most teens (90 percent) and young adults (96 percent) also tend to have a cavalier attitude about porn, speaking about it in either accepting, encouraging or neutral ways, according to the study. This is reinforced with the finding that only one-in-20 young adults and one-in-10 teens say that their friends view looking at smut as a 'bad thing.'"[11]

As kids and young people continue to view pornography, the negative effects continue to increase. One pastor told me that he knows men *in their twenties* who need to use Viagra to have normal sexual relations. Constant exposure to pornography has made them unable to perform otherwise. Another faith leader told me he has counseled young married couples who have a totally sexless relationship. They got burned out on sex in high school and college, and they have now lost interest entirely.

Commenting on a major article in *Time* magazine posted in April 2016, Christian attorney and author David French wrote, "It turns out that some men report having trouble performing in the bedroom after living porn-saturated lives as teenagers, and some women report feeling pressure to act like porn stars during their most intimate moments. In other words, some men's minds are so damaged that they have to experience either porn or a porn-like encounter to be sexually satisfied."

He continued, "I don't know whether to laugh or cry. It's oddly funny that porn is now under fire in some quarters only because the sexual revolution is eating its own."[12] But what else should we expect? For good reason

Ben Shapiro, a leading young conservative voice, described his generation as "Porn Generation."[13]

Not only are sensitivities removed and standards lowered, but what titillated in the past doesn't titillate any longer. It must be more extreme in order to excite—more degrading, more revealing, more twisted; more sadistic, more perverted; otherwise, it just gets boring. And as hearts get harder and sensitivities are removed, what used to be forbidden becomes normalized and even romanticized. This helps explain Hollywood's well-documented promotion of incest on TV and movies.[14] Almost nothing is taboo anymore.

And what about the pressure put on women in today's overly sexualized culture? What about the pressure to look like the latest airbrushed, bikini-clad, perfectly proportioned magazine model? What about the pressure to perform in bed like a porn queen? What about the increasing number of women who themselves are indulging in pornography? What about the extraordinary sales of *Fifty Shades of Grey*? As of June 2015, this book, commonly described as "mommy porn," had sold 125 million copies worldwide and had been translated into fifty-two languages.[15]

The Bible addresses this contemporary and yet age-old problem in three words: "Flee sexual immorality!" (1 Cor. 6:18 NET). "Run from sexual sin! No other sin so clearly affects the body as this one does. For sexual immorality is a sin against your own body" (1 Cor. 6:18 NLT).[16] The Bible has rightly diagnosed the sickness, and the Bible has the cure.

Interestingly, many critics of Christian morality claim that the Word of God places too much emphasis on sexual sin and that too many preachers focus on it in their sermons. The reality is that sexual temptation has been here as long as human beings have been on the planet, and there's a reason that Paul always put sexual sin first when he listed the various sins of the flesh.[17] The Bible also tells us that King Solomon, the wisest man who ever lived and a man who penned powerful warnings about sexual sin, himself fell prey to the very sins he warned about. Sexual desires are powerful, and when improperly channeled, they can be destructive.

Let's unpack one of Solomon's warnings in the book of Proverbs. His words are all the more urgent because he failed to heed his own warnings. He is addressing men here, but his words have universal application:

My son, pay attention to my wisdom; listen carefully to my wise counsel. Then you will show discernment, and your lips will express what you've learned. For the lips of an immoral woman are as sweet as honey, and her mouth is smoother than oil. But in the end she is as bitter as poison, as dangerous as a double-edged sword. Her feet go down to death; her steps lead straight to the grave. (Prov. 5:1–5 NLT)

She looks so good. She has what you want. Look at that body. Look at those eyes. And she's smiling at you. She wants you! How can you resist? You need it. You deserve it. She's all yours.

Ah, but when you bite that apple, there's poison inside. And soon enough, you're experiencing deep regret, but it's too late to undo the damage. Your marriage has fallen apart or a sexually transmitted disease has ravaged your body or your reputation lies in tatters. All that for a few moments of carnal pleasure. In a moment of time, sin can destroy what you've worked a lifetime to achieve.

The words of Solomon shout to us today:

So now, my sons, listen to me. Never stray from what I am about to say: Stay away from her! Don't go near the door of her house! If you do, you will lose your honor and will lose to merciless people all you have achieved. Strangers will consume your wealth, and someone else will enjoy the fruit of your labor. In the end you will groan in anguish when disease consumes your body. You will say, "How I hated discipline! If only I had not ignored all the warnings! Oh, why didn't I listen to my teachers? Why didn't I pay attention to my instructors? I have come to the brink of utter ruin, and now I must face public disgrace." (Prov. 5:7–14 NLT)

Bill Clinton may have enjoyed his trysts with Monica Lewinsky, but those trysts (among others) have plagued him throughout his life. That stained dress of his young intern was nothing compared to the stained reputation of this former president of the United States. And so, when I think of the many Christian leaders who have greatly damaged or even destroyed their ministries because of sexual sin, I don't point a condemning finger at them. Rather, I grieve over the damage they have done—to themselves, to their families, to their congregations, to their larger audiences, to the reputation of the Lord—and I examine my own heart and life. If Solomon could fall, so could I. If a well-known pastor could fall, or if a devoted Christian businessman could fall, or if that sweet homeschooling mother of four could fall, so could you and so could I.

The first lesson, then, to learn from the wisdom of God's Word is that *any of us can fall and none of us are invincible*, whether it's our fleshly lusts that lead us astray or an improper friendship that betrays us. Any of us can fall, which means that all of us must be vigilant. Sexual sin is like fire, and you don't play with fire. As Solomon warned again, "Can a man scoop a flame into his lap and not have his clothes catch on fire? Can he walk on hot coals and not blister his feet? So it is with the man who sleeps with another man's wife. He who embraces her will not go unpunished" (Prov. 6:27–29 NLT).

What makes you so sure you can e-mail that girl (or guy) you dated in college without getting pulled back in? Without Facebook, you never would have found each other; but now you're only seconds away, even though you've been happily married for years. Don't play with this fire! What makes you so sure that watching those R-rated sex scenes won't lead to watching XXX-rated sex scenes? And wasn't there a time when you knew the R-rated scenes were wrong too? What makes you so sure that opening that porn e-mail in your Junk folder every so often won't turn into a full-fledged addiction? And what, exactly, do you expect to see when you click on it? Something wholesome or edifying?

This leads to the second important lesson from the Scriptures: *You must deal with sexual sin ruthlessly*. Don't cut it back; cut it out. This is how Jesus told us to deal with sexual sin:

> You have heard that it was said, "You shall not commit adultery." But I say to you that everyone who looks at a woman with lustful intent has already committed adultery with her in his heart. If your right eye causes you to sin, tear it out and throw it away. For it is better that you lose one of your members than that your whole body be thrown into hell. And if your right hand causes you to sin, cut it off and throw it away. For it is better that you lose one of your members than that your whole body go into hell. (Matt. 5:27–30)

These teachings are repeated two other times in the Gospels, suggesting that Jesus taught on this theme quite often.[18] What does this mean in practical terms? Obviously, Jesus wasn't telling us to amputate our hands or gouge out our eyes, as if our hands or eyes actually led us into sin. Instead, he was using extreme language to show us the extreme danger of sexual sin, telling us in no uncertain terms that we must deal with it decisively. To repeat: we don't cut it back, we cut it off.

If you're involved in an illicit relationship, break it off completely. This means if you're sleeping with someone you're not married to, repent before God, confess it to your spouse and your spiritual leaders, and then break off all contact, even if you have to change jobs or change churches. Or if you consistently struggle with online pornography, get accountability software, put it on every device you use, and link the software to your spouse (if you're not married, link it to someone else you don't want to betray), and let him or her monitor every single site you go to. Or if you keep messing up with porn on your cell phone, don't use a cell phone anymore until you have clearly demonstrated that you are free of it.

You may say, "That sounds radical!"

Well, the words of Jesus sound pretty radical too, don't they? Losing a hand or foot in this world is tragic. But losing your soul in the world to come is a million times more tragic, and that's the point Jesus was so graphically illustrating.

The third important scriptural lesson is this: *realize that sin is never worth it in the end*. It promises you everything and leaves you with nothing. It offers you freedom and leaves you with bondage. It guarantees you satisfaction and leaves you with insatiable desires. This is the invariable trajectory: (1) Sin never satisfies, just like that one potato chip doesn't satisfy. Instead, it creates a desire for more. (2) Because of this, sin leads to more sins, like lying to cover up the sin you just committed, or opening the door to other destructive activities and habits. (3) As a result, sin leads to worse sins. You end up doing shameful things, degrading things, things you never thought you would do (or, in some cases, things you never thought of period; they were completely outside of your world). I can assure you that when I first got high in 1969 as a fourteen-year-old kid, I would have sworn on a stack of Bibles that I would *never* shoot heroin. Not a chance!

One year later, I was shooting heroin into my veins, and it soon had me in a stranglehold.

Finally, the deadly progression leads here: sin enslaves. That desire or that act or that lust now has you completely bound. You used to be so free, living your life without needing that drug or drink or cigarette or food or sexual fix. Now your hands shake and you break into a cold sweat if you can't temporarily satisfy that urge, which has become physical, mental, emotional, and spiritual. Wouldn't it be wonderful to be free again? Sin is not worth it!

Have you met a drug addict who is thrilled to be addicted or an alcoholic who is so happy he or she is totally bound? There is nothing like being free, and no sin that exists—including sexual sin—is worth sacrificing your freedom for.

Can I ask you some honest questions? If you are a follower of Jesus and you have watched pornography, were you pleased with yourself afterward? Did you say, "Boy, I'm so glad I did that!"? Or did you say, "I can't believe I watched that trash!"? If you ever cheated on your spouse, did you say to yourself in the days that followed, "I am so glad we had sex! That was one of the best decisions of my life!"? Or did you weep with regret and shame, pleading for the chance to make things right again in your marriage? The one thing constant about sin is this: it is never worth it in the end.[19]

And here's one more lesson from the Bible about sexual sin: *If you want to be free, run away from what is wrong and run straight toward what is right, and don't try to do it alone.* This was Paul's counsel to Timothy: "Flee youthful passions and pursue righteousness, faith, love, and peace, along with those who call on the Lord from a pure heart" (2 Tim. 2:22). This verse means that you don't intentionally put yourself in tempting situations and try to tough it out, like a guy going to a strip club but trying to watch his eyes. No, you get out of that strip club (flee!), and you stay out. But that's not all you do. "Instead, pursue righteous living, faithfulness, love, and peace. Enjoy the companionship of those who call on the Lord with pure hearts" (2 Tim. 2:22 NLT).

To repeat, run from what is wrong and run toward what is right. If you fill your mind with God's Word on a daily basis, you'll lose your appetite for those controlling sins, and you'll understand what the psalmist meant when he said, "I have stored up your word in my heart, that I might not sin against you" (Ps. 119:11). It's amazing to see how our desires change when we feast on the Scriptures day and night, reading the Word as much as we can, memorizing verses (or, keeping verses in front of us as much as possible), speaking those verses out loud and meditating on them as we fall asleep. Love for God and love for his ways will dominate your thinking, leaving little room for sexual fantasies and sinful acts. This is part of what Paul meant when he wrote, "Do not be conformed to this world, but be transformed by the renewal of your mind" (Rom. 12:2).

But don't try to do all this alone (although renewing your mind is something that only you can do for yourself). Find other believers who share your heart, either in your own congregation or at work or in your neighborhood or even online, and encourage one another and build each other up. Paul said to the Corinthians, "Do not be deceived: 'Bad company ruins good morals'" (1 Cor. 15:33). But it is also true that good company builds and reinforces good morals, which is why the scripture teaches, "Whoever walks with the wise becomes wise" (Prov. 13:20). So, whenever possible, spend time with other believers who challenge you to go deeper in God. And these days, with a wealth of online resources at your fingertips (provided that it's safe for you to use the Internet!), you can be challenged and edified by the hour.

The Bible makes clear that sex is something wonderful that God created for procreation and for enjoyment, but only in the context of marriage. Interestingly, it is within marriage that couples find the most lasting contentment—meaning that, on average, those who engage in one-night stands or go from partner to partner are far less sexually satisfied than those who are happily married.[20] They may have more "excitement," but they will have far less fulfillment and satisfaction than those who enjoy sex with one lifelong, faithful partner. And is that extra excitement worth the STDs that often come along with promiscuity but are unknown to faithfully married couples?

Earlier in this book, I emphasized that God's ways are ways of life. I should also emphasize that *God's ways work*, which means that spurning God's ways does *not* work. That's why, on average, couples who live together before wedlock have less stable marriages than those who don't live together before wedlock.[21] And that's why a new study has found that "women with between zero and one sexual partner are the least likely to divorce later on, with women who had 10 or more partners emerging as the most likely to see their marriages end, according to the Institute for Family Studies."

As reported on TheBlaze.com,

"Earlier research found that having multiple sex partners prior to marriage could lead to less happy marriages, and often increased the odds of divorce," Professor Nicholas Wolfinger wrote in a blog post that announced the analysis. "But sexual attitudes and behaviors continue to change in America, and some of the strongest predictors of divorce in years gone by no longer matter as much as they once did."

Allow me to quote a few more paragraphs from this article. The statistics are quite alarming:

Wolfinger, professor of family and consumer studies and sociology at the University of Utah, noted that 43 percent of women had only one sexual partner before marriage in the 1970s, but said that this figure later plummeted.

"Even in the 1980s, slightly over half of women had a maximum of one sex partner before walking down the aisle," he wrote. "Things looked very different at the start of the new millennium. By the 2010s, only 5 percent of new brides were virgins."

Wolfinger continued, "At the other end of the distribution, the number of future wives who had ten or more sex partners increased from 2 percent in the 1970s to 14 percent in the 2000s, and then to 18 percent in the 2010s."

In the end, after analyzing the data, the professor concluded that those with fewer partners are less likely to see their marriages end in divorce. Thus, marrying as a virgin left women in a better situation when it came to their chances for future divorce.[22]

Yes, God's ways work!

I'd be curious to see what the data says about men who marry as virgins, but presumably the conclusions would be the same. As for young people reading this chapter who are discouraged by this news, saying, "I already slept with a few partners and I'm not yet married," that is not the end of your story. If you'll truly ask the Lord for forgiveness and, using some of the principles laid out in this chapter, abstain from having sex until you're married, God's blessing can overtake you and your spouse for life. You can be richly blessed!

Right now, the bad news is that sexual sin is destroying our culture. The good news is that there's nothing stopping tens of millions of us who know the Lord from living godly lives, and by adhering to his life-giving standards, we can have wonderful marriages and experience sexual fulfillment.

So, how about a brand-new sexual revolution—a revolution of purity? Are you in? This is how America can rise again.

ELEVEN

FROM EXCESS TO SELF-CONTROL

The fruit of the Spirit is . . . self-control.
—GALATIANS 5:22–23

AMERICANS ARE GETTING FATTER AND FATTER. OUR GIRTH IS growing at an alarming rate, and our waistlines are expanding to danger-ous levels. Obesity has become a major health crisis in our land. Just look around and see how many seriously overweight people there are. Perhaps you don't have to look any further than your own mirror.[1]

Throughout much of human history, and to this day in many parts of the world, people have had to fight and scratch just to survive. Today we live in a culture of opulence and decadence that presents a whole new set of challenges. We are not meeting them well, not realizing the dangers that come with luxury. As Juvenal wrote nineteen hundred years ago, "Luxury, more savage than arms, has oppressed Rome, and avenges a conquered world" (*Satire VI*). *There are real challenges in having too much.*

A 2015 article announced, "The average American woman is now the same weight as the average 1960s man," offering these three bullet points:

- Modern American women are an average 166.2 pounds, while the typical man in the 1960s was 166.3 pounds.
- The weight gain has been blamed on Americans overeating unhealthy foods and scaling back on exercise.
- During the same period, men put on an average of 30 pounds.[2]

But this is not simply a question of our appearance. The fatter we get, the unhealthier we get. A major study by the RAND Corporation confirmed what many other studies have found, namely, that "obesity is linked to very high rates of chronic illnesses—higher than living in poverty, and much higher than smoking or drinking."[3] That's why a leading medical doctor wrote that we Americans are "Digging Our Graves with Forks and Knives."[4] As the RAND study concluded, "Not only does obesity have more negative health consequences than smoking, drinking, or poverty, it also affects more people. Approximately 23 percent of Americans are obese. An additional 36 percent are overweight. By contrast, only 6 percent are heavy drinkers, 19 percent are daily smokers, and 14 percent live in poverty."[5]

In 2012, articles were written about the soaring costs associated with our growing waistlines. As reported by Reuters, "U.S. hospitals are ripping out wall-mounted toilets and replacing them with floor models to better support obese patients. The Federal Transit Administration wants buses to be tested for the impact of heavier riders on steering and braking. Cars are burning nearly a billion gallons of gasoline more a year than if passengers weighed what they did in 1960."[6]

> Because obesity raises the risk of a host of medical conditions, from heart disease to chronic pain, the obese are absent from work more often than people of healthy weight. The most obese men take 5.9 more sick days a year; the most obese women, 9.4 days more. Obesity-related absenteeism costs employers as much as $6.4 billion a year, health economists led by Eric Finkelstein of Duke University calculated.[7]

The very real costs are staggering. So why are we getting fatter and fatter? Before we answer that question, let's switch topics from eating to spending. Why are we getting more and more in debt?

I don't want to depress you with these figures, but our debt is growing just like our waistlines are growing. As reported in 2010,

> Back in the late 1940s and early 1950s, the average American consumer had less than two thousand dollars in total personal debt, but that amount has increased steadily during the past fifty years.

This year, according to a recent report on the financial website The Motley Fool, "The average American household has total debt of more than $90,000, which includes households that live debt free. The average household with debt owes more than $130,000."[8]

Returning to our food issues, note these alarming statistics from the CDC:

- Childhood obesity has more than doubled in children and quadrupled in adolescents in the past thirty years.
- The percentage of children aged 6–11 years in the United States who were obese increased from 7 percent in 1980 to nearly 18 percent in 2012. Similarly, the percentage of adolescents aged 12–19 years who were obese increased from 5 percent to nearly 21 percent over the same period.
- In 2012, more than one-third of children and adolescents were overweight or obese.[9]

So, it's not just that we're getting fatter as a society, but our kids are getting fatter at younger and younger ages. Accordingly, the American Heart Association's website reminds us that "with good reason, childhood obesity is now the No. 1 health concern among parents in the United States, topping drug abuse and smoking." The website also quotes former Surgeon General Richard Carmona, who warned that, "because of the increasing rates of obesity, unhealthy eating habits and physical inactivity, we may see the first generation that will be less healthy and have a shorter life expectancy than their parents."[10]

How do we reverse these dangerous trends?

Once again, God's Word has the answers. We must recapture the biblical themes of stewardship and self-control: our bodies and our finances belong to the Lord, and we must take care of both as responsible stewards.

According to Paul, some people have their stomachs as their god (so, food is an idol in their lives) while others have made money into their god (he explicitly said that covetousness is idolatry).[11] So we must beware the idolatry of a wrong attachment to food and money.

Here, then, are biblical principles that will help us get physically and financially fit. We'll start with the issue of unhealthy eating, but first, a word of encouragement. On August 24, 2014, I weighed 275 pounds, and despite being almost 6' 3" and working out (so I did have some muscle too), I was obese. My big problem, though, was not really gluttony per se, since I exercised a certain amount of discipline every day. My big problem was unhealthy eating—being addicted to chocolate (or at least to sugar) for most of my life (I ate Oreos for breakfast as a boy), and eating pizza and pasta on a weekly (or daily) basis, along with plenty of snacks like pretzels or jelly beans. And my favorite ice cream desserts were hard-core, like Ben and Jerry's New York Super Fudge Chocolate (I'd eat the whole pint in two sittings during the same night when I splurged) or a large Chocolate Extreme Blizzard from Dairy Queen (sometimes I would skip a meal to "justify" having this decadent treat).

By God's grace and with Nancy's help, I made a total lifestyle change, eating foods I had never eaten before and getting rid of most of the foods I had eaten my entire life. Simply stated, I changed my whole relationship to food. Within eight months, I had lost 95 pounds (and I've kept it off since). My health is more vibrant than I can remember in decades, showing radical, positive changes in my blood pressure, cholesterol levels, and more. And at age 62 as of this writing, I can out-exercise most men one-third my age.

If I could make these radical changes (Nancy made them in her life, too) in my food intake, so can you. It's simply a matter of applying the wise principles of the Word to your eating habits, leaning on him for grace and help, through which you too can go from indulgence to self-control.[12]

Principle 1: Our bodies belong to the Lord.

When the Lord saved us from our sins, he purchased us in full—spirit, soul, and body. We now belong to him in the entirety of our beings. In light of that, Paul wrote to the Corinthians: "Do you not know that your body is a temple of the Holy Spirit within you, whom you have from God? You are not your own, for you were bought with a price. So glorify God in your body" (1 Cor. 6:19–20).

The context refers to abstaining from sexual immorality (see chapter 10 for more on that), but it's clear that this text can refer to healthy eating as well. So let's rephrase this in the form of a series of questions: Are you glorifying God in your body if you are destroying it willfully? Are you glorifying God in your body if you are shouting to the whole world, "I'm out of control when it comes to my appetite!"? Are you glorifying God in your body if you are unable to run your race effectively because of sickness and tiredness brought on by unhealthy eating? How does any of this glorify the Lord?

Principle 2: Your stomach is not your god.

Look at how strongly Paul spoke against certain false teachers in his day: "For many, of whom I have often told you and now tell you even with tears, walk as enemies of the cross of Christ. Their end is destruction, their god is their belly, and they glory in their shame, with minds set on earthly things" (Phil. 3:18–19). Read those words again, slowly and carefully. These people are bound by fleshly sins and controlled by carnal desires—*and their god is their belly.*

Jesus taught that "no one can serve two masters, for either he will hate the one and love the other, or he will be devoted to the one and despise the other. You cannot serve God and money" (Matt. 6:24). We'll come back to this verse in a moment when we talk about money, but once more, the same principle applies: if your stomach is your god, then your heart is divided, and as a child of God, you should not be a slave to carnal appetites.

Principle 3: Gluttony is a sin.

Notice the different contexts in which gluttony is referenced. Then ask yourself if you want to fit into any of these categories:

- "This our son is stubborn and rebellious; he will not obey our voice; he is a glutton and a drunkard" (Deut. 21:20).
- "Be not among drunkards or among gluttonous eaters of meat, for the drunkard and the glutton will come to poverty, and slumber will clothe them with rags" (Prov. 23:20–21).
- "The one who keeps the law is a son with understanding, but a companion of gluttons shames his father" (Prov. 28:7).

- "One of the Cretans, a prophet of their own, said,
  'Cretans are always liars, evil beasts, lazy gluttons.' This
  testimony is true. Therefore rebuke them sharply, that
  they may be sound in the faith" (Titus 1:12–13).

Gluttony is associated with stubbornness, rebellion, drunkenness, lying, evil, and laziness that results in shame, poverty, and judgment. Gluttony should not characterize you and me!

Principle 4: Practice self-control.

Jesus preached that we, his followers, need to deny ourselves (see Luke 9:23); the world (along with what is preached from many a pulpit) tells us to indulge ourselves. Whose advice will we follow? Proverbs offers us this practical counsel: "When you sit down to dine with a ruler, think carefully about who is before you. If you have a big appetite, put a knife to your throat! Don't be greedy for his delicacies, for they are deceptive food" (Prov. 23:1–3 cjb).

Today most Americans can eat like kings (meaning in the most indulgent, decadent ways imaginable), from appetizers to main courses to desserts to snacks. We can gorge ourselves to our stomachs' content (and more), and we hardly realize what we're doing.

We need to put into practice this word from Proverbs on a daily basis by saying no to unhealthy foods (the king's dainties!) putting a knife to our throats, figuratively speaking, and by exercising discipline. Paul told us that we, just like Olympic athletes, should exercise self-control in all things, seeing that the crown we're competing for is far more valuable and enduring (see 1 Cor. 9:24–27). But notice carefully his language: "Everyone who competes in the games goes into strict training. *They do it* to get a crown that will not last, *but we do it* to get a crown that will last forever" (1 Cor. 9:25 niv, emphasis added). We are called to self-discipline as disciples, and that includes exercising moderation in our diets. As Proverbs exhorts, "If you have found honey, eat only enough for you, lest you have your fill of it and vomit it" (Prov. 25:16). Proverbs also states, "A man without self-control is like a city broken into and left without walls" (Prov. 25:28). Surely you do not want your life to look like this.

Principle 5: We will reap what we sow.[13]

We'll return to this principle as well when it comes to our money, reminding us that the same principles that bring life and health and well-being in one area of life are the same principles that bring life and health and well-being in other areas of life. When it comes to food, as a general rule, we can be sure that if we sow to health—meaning eating healthy foods, walking in self-control, and exercising—we will reap health. But if we sow to indulgence—meaning eating whatever we like in whatever amounts we desire and being couch potatoes—we will reap destruction, in the form of sickness, tiredness, shame, depression, and even premature death. God's ways are ways of life.

Just like get-rich-quick schemes don't work (as we will see shortly), so also fad diets don't work.[14] The right way is often the hard way, but it's always the blessed way.

Now, let's turn to financial issues and see what the Word has to say. Many books have been written on biblical principles of finance, since the Bible contains hundreds of verses relevant to money. We'll just touch on a few here now.

Principle 1: There's no substitute for good, hard work.

Just like *glutton* is a bad word in the Bible, so also is *sluggard* (meaning "lazy person"). *Sluggard* occurs more frequently.[15] Look at how foolish a lazy person is: "The sluggard says, 'There is a lion in the road! There is a lion in the streets!'" In other words, he makes lame excuses for his inactivity. "As a door turns on its hinges, so does a sluggard on his bed." What a graphic picture! "The sluggard buries his hand in the dish; it wears him out to bring it back to his mouth." Talk about lazy! Yet the sluggard thinks he's so wise: "The sluggard is wiser in his own eyes than seven men who can answer sensibly" (Prov. 26:13–16). What a pathetic figure.

And the consequences of laziness are nothing to laugh about: "How long will you lie there, O sluggard? When will you arise from your sleep? A little sleep, a little slumber, a little folding of the hands to rest, and poverty will come upon you like a robber, and want like an armed man" (Prov. 6:9–11).

God's Word calls us to serious, hard work, counseling the lazy person to learn from some tiny, industrious creatures made by the Lord: "Go to the ant, O sluggard; consider her ways, and be wise. Without having any chief, officer, or ruler, she prepares her bread in summer and gathers her food in harvest" (Prov. 6:6–8). We must take responsibility for our finances, we must work hard, and we must plan ahead. So simple! As we'll see in the next chapter, Paul instructed his followers that if they weren't willing to work, they shouldn't be allowed to eat.

So, if you're healthy and able-bodied, get out of that bed, get out of your room, and get to work. And if you can't find work, then do something productive with your time, volunteering to help others. Whatever you do, don't look to others to give you a handout (we'll have much more to say about that in the next chapter), take full responsibility for your life, and learn some good lessons from the ant.

Principle 2: Get-rich-quick schemes are doomed to fail.

Have you ever tracked what happened to winners of the lottery? Most of them end up in far worse shape after winning than before they became multimillionaires: some have destroyed marriages, some have destroyed personal lives, and many have destroyed finances.[16] It's the same with people who lose lots of weight on reality TV shows.[17] Most of them end up heavier in the end. In short, quick-fix solutions do not work for the long haul, be they get-rich-quick schemes or fad diets.

Principle 3: You can't serve God and money.

When Jesus spoke these words (Matt. 6:24), the word he used for money was *mammon*, which comes from the Greek *mammōnas*, which in turn comes from the Aramaic word *mammōnā*. What, exactly, does it mean? One lexicon explains that it occurs "usually in a derogatory sense" with reference to "*property, wealth, earthly goods*" (as in Luke 16:9), while here, in Matthew 6:24, it is a personification of "*Mammon*, the Syrian god of riches," hence, money as some kind of deity.[18] Yes, people often make a god out of money, and Jesus said you can't serve that god and the one true God at the same time.

In practical terms, just as *food is the fuel* for healthy living, *money is the tool* for productive living. And so, rather than pursuing wealth, we work hard to meet our needs and the needs of those we're responsible for with the goal of making extra money to give away to meet the needs of others. (If you can learn to give money away with joy, you're certainly free from the god of money.)

Many people think that the more we have, the more we are. Not so. As Jesus said, "Take care, and be on your guard against all covetousness, for one's life does not consist in the abundance of his possessions" (Luke 12:15). As rendered in the *New Living Translation* (NLT): "Beware! Guard against every kind of greed. Life is not measured by how much you own."

We often hear that money is the root of all evil, but as you probably know, that's a misquotation of Paul. What he spoke against was not money, which in and of itself is totally neutral, but rather the love of money, issuing this strong warning: "Those who desire to be rich fall into temptation, into a snare, into many senseless and harmful desires that plunge people into ruin and destruction. For the love of money is a root of all kinds of evils. It is through this craving that some have wandered away from the faith and pierced themselves with many pangs" (1 Tim. 6:9–10). A man of God, like Timothy, to whom he was writing, should have a different set of priorities: "But as for you, O man of God, flee these things. Pursue righteousness, godliness, faith, love, steadfastness, gentleness" (v. 11).

I have good friends who are successful businesspeople, and they are highly motivated to succeed and make lots of money. But they do not love money, and they are not trying to get rich. Instead they want to succeed so they will have more funds to invest in the gospel and in helping the poor and the needy, and their greatest goal is to win other businesspeople to the Lord.

God may have genuinely called you to be wealthy and to earn millions of dollars, but that is a calling fraught with many dangers. To succeed in that calling, you will have to destroy the idol of mammon and die to the love of money. Then you can be free to pursue your high calling.

Principle 4: Debt is dangerous and draining.

Also in 1 Timothy 6, Paul counseled believers to be content with what they had, writing, "But godliness with contentment is great gain, for we brought nothing into the world, and we cannot take anything out of the world. But if we have food and clothing, with these we will be content" (vv. 6–8). Many of us find this difficult to do, especially with the constant bombardment of advertising that most of us are subject to day and night: You need this! You really want this! You cannot live without this! So, we fall into debt rather than live within our means, thereby becoming slaves to a monthly bill that often consumes us. Is it really worth it? Is it really wise?

I don't believe the primary debt issue is having an affordable mortgage on our homes (which is often much better than paying rent) or making affordable payments on a car (although many financial advisors say that we can afford only what we can buy with cash). The issue is falling into debt because we're not willing to live within our means, and the Word warns us about this too: "Owe no one anything, except to love each other, for the one who loves another has fulfilled the law" (Rom. 13:8). And, "The rich rules over the poor, and the borrower is the slave of the lender" (Prov. 22:7).

There's a reason that some of the best books on finances are written by Christian leaders (such as Dave Ramsey and Larry Burkett). And if every American (including our government) lived by these biblically based financial principles, we would have no national debt (can you imagine that?), we would have no national poverty, and we would have billions of dollars to invest in needy causes around the world.

Principle 5: Store up treasure in heaven.

One of the greatest ways to get free from the love of money and to embrace money as a practical tool for productive living is to store up treasure in heaven, since our hearts will follow our treasure (see Matt. 6:19–21). But how exactly do we do that?

Think of it as putting money in the bank or investing in a retirement fund. You put aside money today to be used tomorrow. We do the same thing when it comes to the world to come: we invest our earthly finances in heavenly treasures, meaning that we use our money to help those who cannot repay us and to advance the work of the gospel.

Proverbs teaches, "Whoever is generous to the poor lends to the LORD, and he will repay him for his deed" (19:17). We might get that divine repayment in this world, or we might get it in the world to come, but our ultimate focus should be on the eternal repayment. As Jesus taught:

When you give a dinner or a banquet, do not invite your friends or your brothers or your relatives or rich neighbors, lest they also invite you in return and you be repaid. But when you give a feast, invite the poor, the crippled, the lame, the blind, and you will be blessed, because they cannot repay you. For you will be repaid at the resurrection of the just. (Luke 14:12–14)

What a radical concept, what a freeing concept, and what a blessed concept. As Jesus also taught, "It is more blessed to give than to receive" (Acts 20:35b).

And when you invest in world missions and reaching the lost with the gospel, you actually make eternal friends in the process. In the words of Jesus again, "And I tell you, make friends for yourselves by how you use worldly wealth, so that when it runs out you will be welcomed into the eternal homes" (Luke 16:9 NET).[19] This too is a radical concept, one that frees us from the love of money and instead transforms money into something that will last forever.

I once read a joke about a wealthy believer who made a deal with the Lord that when he died, he would be allowed to bring one large package with him into heaven. Moments after his death, he found himself in front of the proverbial pearly gates, dragging a massive sack behind him. He was immediately told by the gatekeeper that he could not enter heaven with any of his possessions, but when the gatekeeper checked the records, to his surprise he saw that an exception had been made for this man.

"I just need to see what's in your sack," the gatekeeper said.

The rich man then opened his sack carefully, only to reveal an absolutely massive and weighty gold bar worth hundreds of millions of dollars.

The gatekeeper said, "Okay, you can come through, but why in the world did you bring concrete?"

Yes, in the New Jerusalem the streets are made of gold. (Actually, the whole city is made of gold! See Rev. 21:18, 21.) How this changes our perspective on things.

As followers of Jesus, we are in this world but not of it (John 17:11–16), and though we go to school and get jobs and raise families and play sports and listen to music and go on vacations like everyone else, we have a very different perspective on what matters most, and we live in the light of eternity. So, if we *eat to live* rather than live to eat, we also *live to give*, to quote a famous phrase from missionary Wayne Meyers. And in so doing, we receive our Father's blessings both in this world and in the world to come.

Here too we reap what we sow. As Paul explained so beautifully:

> The point is this: whoever sows sparingly will also reap sparingly, and whoever sows bountifully will also reap bountifully. Each one must give as he has decided in his heart, not reluctantly or under compulsion, for God loves a cheerful giver. And God is able to make all grace abound to you, so that having all sufficiency in all things at all times, you may abound in every good work. As it is written, "He has distributed freely, he has given to the poor; his righteousness endures forever." He who supplies seed to the sower and bread for food will supply and multiply your seed for sowing and increase the harvest of your righteousness. You will be enriched in every way to be generous in every way, which through us will produce thanksgiving to God." (2 Cor. 9:6–11)

Principle 6: Recognize the deceitfulness of wealth.

Jesus said in one of his parables that "the cares of the world and the deceitfulness of riches and the desires for other things" are like thorns that "choke the word"—pictured as a plant—thereby making it unfruitful (Mark 4:19). In what ways are riches deceitful? First, having lots of money and possessions can give us a false sense of security, as if nothing can touch us. This is clearly false, and what we have can be taken from us in a moment of time. Second, wealth can give us a false sense of identity, as if the more we own, the more important we are. This too is false, since what is highly esteemed among people is often detestable in God's sight (see Luke 16:15 and note that this writing was spoken in the context of money; see v. 14). And the richest people in the world are sometimes the most miserable, experiencing more divorces, more depression, and more problems with their kids. That's one reason I never envy the "rich and famous" of the world.

Let's go back to Proverbs 23, where we were told to put a knife to our throats if we were gluttons sitting at the king's table. The text continues, "Do not toil to acquire wealth; be discerning enough to desist. When your eyes light on it, it is gone, for suddenly it sprouts wings, flying like an eagle toward heaven" (Prov. 23:4–5). In this light, Paul gave this wise counsel to Timothy, telling him to exhort the rich to be generous with a view toward the world to come:

> As for the rich in this present age, charge them not to be haughty, nor to set their hopes on the uncertainty of riches, but on God, who richly provides us with everything to enjoy. They are to do good, to be rich in good works, to be generous and ready to share, thus storing up treasure for themselves as a good foundation for the future, so that they may take hold of that which is truly life. (1 Tim. 6:17–19)

Being rich is fine. There are many rich, godly Christians. But an attitude of generosity is the way to avoid the sorrows that wealth often brings as well as the way to store up true riches.

Scripture teaches many other financial principles (including the importance of putting your money to work, which can be deduced from a parable taught in Matt. 25:14–30), but since so many excellent books and online resources are available, I'll stop here. Suffice it to say that once more, to the extent that we live in harmony with the Scriptures we can see our nation changed for the best, breaking with the culture of indulgence and laying the foundation for a culture of self-control and frugality. That is the culture that is blessed!

TWELVE

———

PUTTING AN END TO THE BLAME GAME AND SAYING GOODBYE TO THE ENTITLEMENT MENTALITY

If anyone is not willing to work, neither should he eat.
—2 THESSALONIANS 3:10 NET

THERE IS NOTHING NEW UNDER THE SUN! THE TEACHER IN THE book of Ecclesiastes penned those words many centuries ago, and they ring true today. He wrote, "What has been is what will be, and what has been done is what will be done, and there is nothing new under the sun. Is there a thing of which it is said, 'See, this is new'? It has been already in the ages before us" (Eccl. 1:9–10). Nations will rise and fall. Maps will be rewritten. New discoveries will be made. Technology will change. But human nature remains the same. There is nothing new under the sun!

The problems and challenges we face today, although packaged differently than in past centuries, are the same problems and challenges experienced by previous generations. We have the same fears, desires, lusts, loves, hopes, and dreams, whether we live in the twenty-first century A.D. or the twenty-first century B.C. This is another reason God's Word is so amazingly relevant: Our Maker knows us better than we know ourselves, and the sins and shortcomings and weaknesses of our forefathers—going all the way back to the garden of Eden—are our sins and shortcomings and weaknesses today. In many ways, we are just like Adam and Eve.

Let's go back, then, to the beginning, to an earthly paradise called the garden of Eden. We know the story all too well. Eve was deceived by the serpent, and she ate of the tree of the knowledge of good and evil, giving the fruit to her husband, Adam, who also ate of it. This is what is known as the fall of man.

Immediately, Adam and Eve were conscious of their nakedness. Before that they had the innocence of little children and were unaware they were unclothed. Now they had to cover up. For the first time they also experienced guilt and fear. They hid from the presence of the Lord, whose commandments they had violated. *They also learned how to make excuses and pass the buck.* The narrative in Genesis 3 is remarkable:

> Then the LORD God called to the man, "Where are you?"
>
> He replied, "I heard you walking in the garden, so I hid. I was afraid because I was naked."
>
> "Who told you that you were naked?" the LORD God asked. "Have you eaten from the tree whose fruit I commanded you not to eat?"
>
> The man replied, "It was the woman you gave me who gave me the fruit, and I ate it."
>
> Then the LORD God asked the woman, "What have you done?"
>
> "The serpent deceived me," she replied. "That's why I ate it." (vv. 9–13 NLT)

This sounds just like you and me: "Lord, it's not my fault! Someone else is to blame!"

When God confronted Adam, the man in essence replied, "It's not my fault! It was that woman that you gave me. She's guilty. And for the record, I never asked you for a companion. That was all your idea. You're the one who put her in the garden with me, so in reality, *you're the one responsible for what I did.*"

When God confronted Eve, she replied, "It's not my fault! The snake tricked me! And just for the record, although I'm not actually saying it out loud, *you* were the one who put that deceiver in the garden with me. Otherwise, I would never have thought of disobeying you. Not in a million years. So, if there's anyone to blame, it's *you* for putting that arch deceiver right in my own backyard."

How did God respond? First he pronounced a curse on the snake, then on the woman, then on the man (Gen. 3:14–19). Everyone is responsible before the Lord, and excuses evaporate in his presence. The blame game doesn't work before an all-seeing God. To paraphrase the old joke, you can't kill your parents and then plead for leniency from the court because you're an orphan. Not in God's court!

The Lord calls us to take responsibility for our actions, refusing to entertain our facile excuses. This is something you find throughout the Gospels, where Jesus, who was so full of compassion and long-suffering and kindness and tenderness, showed no tolerance for excuses. He cut through them like a knife cuts through butter. He exposed them for what they were: empty words used to cover up a lack of willingness. That's why, when Jesus was on the earth, he didn't entrust himself to people, "because he knew all people and needed no one to bear witness about man, for he himself knew what was in man" (John 2:24–25).[1] He also knew that there was nothing new under the sun when it came to the human race.

When, in response to Jesus' command to "follow me," a man said, "Lord, let me first go and bury my father," Jesus replied, "Leave the dead to bury their own dead. But as for you, go and proclaim the kingdom of God" (Luke 9:59–60).

What? Jesus didn't have the sensitivity to let this man bury his own father, something which was a sacred responsibility in Judaism? I thought Jesus was all about honoring one's father and mother!

The fact is that Jesus *was* sensitive, and he *was* committed to honoring one's parents (see especially Mark 7:1–13). But he saw through this man's excuse, recognizing that the man was procrastinating—there are different theories on the potential background to this story—and that's why he responded so strongly. "Let the dead bury their own dead! You've got better things to do as one of my followers."

The account continues: "Yet another said, 'I will follow you, Lord, but let me first say farewell to those at my home.' Jesus said to him, 'No one who puts his hand to the plow and looks back is fit for the kingdom of God'" (Luke 9:61–62).

Jesus might seem harsh and uncaring. He's hardly like the Jesus we hear preached from our pulpits these days. The contemporary Jesus would never hurt anyone's feelings like this. But that, of course, is one of the big differences between the real Jesus—the Jesus of the Scriptures who is the same yesterday, today, and forever (Heb. 13:8)—and the modern, fairy-tale version of Jesus.

Luke shows us how the Lord did not tolerate excuses, seeing right through this man's seemingly fair request (after all, he might not return for days or weeks or months, so of course he should go home and say goodbye to his family). In the eyes of the Lord, this was nothing less than double-mindedness, and a double-minded man—someone with dual affections and dual devotions, someone with divided loyalties and divided interests—could never be a true disciple of Jesus. In reality, a person can serve only one master, and Jesus required his followers to choose.

It is absolutely true that we are saved by grace, not by works, and that eternal life is a gift. In a million years we could not earn the mercy or forgiveness of God. The Father loves us because of his goodness, and it was while we were still ungodly sinners, still rebels, still guilty, that Jesus died for us.[2] All of us can shout out, "Amazing grace, how sweet the sound, that saved a wretch like me!" This is something that Paul emphasized again and again in his writings as he gloried in the grace of God.

But Paul also made clear that with grace came responsibility, writing, "I therefore, a prisoner for the Lord, urge you to *walk in a manner worthy* of the calling to which you have been called" (Eph. 4:1, emphasis added). And, "Therefore I exhort you, brothers and sisters, by the mercies of God, to *present your bodies as a sacrifice*—alive, holy, and pleasing to God—which is your reasonable service. Do not be conformed to this present world, but be transformed by the renewing of your mind, so that you may test and approve what is the will of God—what is good and well-pleasing and perfect" (Rom. 12:1–2 NET, emphasis added).

We who are saved have a sacred responsibility, and it requires the complete surrender of the entirety of our beings to the Lord. After all, he paid for all of our sins, not half of our sins, right? And we expect him to save us in full, not in part, correct? Then how much of us does he own? All of us! And what does he expect from us? Everything!

To quote Paul again,

For you were bought with a price. So glorify God in your body. . . . For you have died, and your life is hidden with Christ in God. When Christ who is your life appears, then you also will appear with him in glory. Put to death therefore what is earthly in you: sexual immorality, impurity, passion, evil desire, and covetousness, which is idolatry. . . . For the love of Christ controls us, because we have concluded this: that one has died for all, therefore all have died; and he died for all, that those who live might no longer live for themselves but for him who for their sake died and was raised. (1 Cor. 6:20; Col. 3:3–5; 2 Cor. 5:14–15)

Paul also had no place for empty excuses, telling the believers in Rome that "each of us will give an account of himself to God" and explaining to the believers in Corinth that "we must all appear before the judgment seat of Christ, so that each one may receive what is due for what he has done in the body, whether good or evil" (Rom. 14:12; 2 Cor. 5:10).

These are sobering words. As children of God, we will give account to our Father one day, not to determine if we are saved or lost but to determine our future reward.

This is something to think about: *one day you will stand before Almighty God and give account for your life.* Have you heard this preached lately? Fellow leaders and pastors, have you preached on this yourselves?

Take a few minutes and read some of the parables of Jesus that illustrate how we will give account to the Lord. You'll find them in passages like Matthew 25. Our God will hold us responsible for our actions (and for our failures to act), as well as search out our motives. Will he say to us on that day, "Well done, my good and faithful servant. . . . Let's celebrate together!" (Matt. 25:21 NLT)? Or will he first burn up our excuses with the fire of his all-seeing eyes (see 1 Cor. 3:10–15)?

It is true that he is for us, not against us; that he desires to bless, not curse; that there is no condemnation for those who are in Messiah Jesus; that Christ himself is our advocate, which means he is pleading our cause. All this is gloriously and wonderfully true, and so we submit to the Lord out of love rather than cower before him in servile fear. But we also have a healthy reverence for him, and because we are receiving an inheritance in his eternal and unshakable kingdom, we should "offer to God acceptable worship, with reverence and awe, for our God is a consuming fire" (Heb. 12:28–29).

This also means that we take responsibility for our sins, which is something else we don't hear about too often these days. As Christian apologist Jeremiah Johnson observed, instead of repentance we hear "a lot of talk about brokenness and negativity, as if Christ humbled Himself to the point of death to cure depression and fix bad attitudes. The modern church has largely done away with the biblical language of sin and salvation, replacing it with gooey postmodern verbiage that appeals to a generation raised on psychobabble and self-help seminars."[3]

Johnson then quoted Pastor John MacArthur:

That kind of thinking has all but driven words like *sin, repentance, contrition, atonement, restitution,* and *redemption* out of public discourse. If no one is supposed to feel guilty, how could anyone be a sinner? Modern culture has the answer: people are *victims.* Victims are not responsible for what they do; they are casualties of what happens to them. So every human failing must be described in terms of how the perpetrator has been victimized. We are all supposed to be "sensitive" and "compassionate" enough to see that the very behaviors we used to label "sin" are actually evidence of victimization.

Victimization has gained so much influence that as far as society is concerned, there is practically no such thing as sin anymore. Anyone can escape responsibility for his or her wrongdoing simply by claiming the status of a victim. It has radically changed the way our society looks at human behavior.[4]

We're not sinners anymore; we're morally challenged. We don't break God's commandments; we have a disease.[5] We're not wicked; we're weak. And above all, we're not guilty, since guilt implies responsibility and God knows we are not responsible. Someone else is to blame!

The bottom line is this: If you want to grow spiritually, if you want to become mature, if you want to fulfill your God-given destiny, then adopt a no-excuses policy for your life. You alone are responsible for your success or failure, and the quicker you learn to embrace this way of thinking, the quicker you will make progress—real, discernible progress. No one will be able to stop you from living a productive, meaningful life, and every stumbling block will become a stepping-stone. His grace will empower you as you give yourself to him.

It's true that people often hurt us and that circumstances are often against us, and many times we do suffer because of other people's sins and negligence and misdeeds. But making excuses will make things worse, not better, while shifting the blame will not provide you with a single constructive solution. And as the popular saying goes, if it doesn't kill you, it makes you stronger—meaning that the more things are stacked against you, the more you can overcome. Look at these challenges as opportunities rather than obstacles, and soon you'll be unstoppable.

But there's one more step to take if you really want to swim against the tide of today's society, and so I encourage you to embrace this attitude as well: *nobody owes me anything, and I am not "entitled" to a wonderful life.* Unfortunately, many Americans hold the exact opposite of this belief, and this crippling entitlement mentality dominates much of our nation today. It is the mind-set that says, "Society owes me a better life."

Conservapedia.com defines the *entitlement mentality* as "a state of mind in which an individual comes to believe that privileges are instead rights, and that they are to be expected as a matter of course."[6] In the words of Aletheia Luna, "A sense of entitlement is established and upheld by the belief that *we* are the center of the universe, and if the universe doesn't meet *our* needs and desires, all hell will break loose."[7] According to Conservapedia. com, the entitlement mentality is characterized by:

- A lack of appreciation for the sacrifices of others. . . .
- Lack of personal responsibility. . . .
- An inability to accept that actions carry consequences. . . .
- Increased dependency on Nanny state big government intervention, and an expectation that the government will intervene to solve personal problems. Upon losing a job, for instance, someone with an entitlement mentality is likely to turn to the government for unemployment handouts rather than immediately seeking another job.
- Ignorance of the Bill of Rights. Those with an entitlement mentality

frequently imagine so-called rights that are in no way guaranteed—for instance, the "right to employment," or the "right to not be offended" or the "right to healthcare." Moreover, they misinterpret the Declaration of Independence's affirmation of their right to *pursue* happiness as a Constitutional *guarantee* of happiness.

- Support for wholesale expansion of Welfare state social programs as a cure-all for perceived "injustice."[8]

Now, if we go back to the garden, back to Adam and Eve, we can see that the entitlement mentality is the flip side of the blame-shifting mentality. Blame-shifting says, "I'm not responsible for my failure; someone else is," while entitlement says, "I'm not responsible for improving my situation; someone else is." Either way, someone else is to blame for my current situation, and if I don't find myself where I want to be today, it's someone else's fault.

This dangerous attitude is crippling a whole generation, but once again, this attitude is nothing new. It is just greatly on the rise in our day. As expressed by Kate S. Rourke, "Children in the most recent generation of adults born between 1982 and 1995, known as 'Generation Y,' were raised to believe that it is their right to have everything given to them more than any other previous generation."[9] This mind-set has been here before; it has just become much worse.

Two thousand years ago Paul had to deal with believers in Thessalonica who had become dependent and irresponsible, so he wrote to them, reminding them of the way he and his team conducted themselves when they were together: "For you yourselves know how you ought to imitate us, because we were not idle when we were with you, nor did we eat anyone's bread without paying for it, but with toil and labor we worked night and day, that we might not be a burden to any of you. It was not because we do not have that right, but to give you in ourselves an example to imitate" (2 Thess. 3:7–9).

Even though Paul was an apostle and had every right to be supported by his congregations, he didn't take this support, wanting to set an example of hard work and independence. But Paul not only reminded the Thessalonians of his own example. He also reminded them of what he taught when he was with them. "For even when we were with you, we would give you this command: *If anyone is not willing to work, let him not eat*" (v. 10, emphasis added). I would say that sums things up!

If you're not willing to work, then don't eat. The choice is entirely yours. (Obviously, there was work to be found in Thessalonica.) Paul then concluded, "For we hear that some among you walk in idleness, not busy at work, but busybodies. Now such persons we command and encourage in the Lord Jesus Christ to do their work quietly and to earn their own living" (v. 11–12). Did I say already that no one is entitled to a free lunch?

Once again, God's Word has a major word of correction and redirection for America. The entitlement mentality is destroying our culture and hurting a whole generation. The Bible's directive to take full responsibility for our lives and quit making excuses is just what we need.

Paul also had some practical words for the believers in Ephesus, writing, "Let the thief no longer steal, but rather let him labor, doing honest work with his own hands, so that he may have something to share with anyone in need" (Eph. 4:28). The thief not only had to stop stealing, which is the ultimate expression of entitlement, since it says, "I want what you worked so hard for, so I will simply take it;" the thief also had to learn to do useful, honest work. And since the thief was now a follower of Jesus, he wasn't only working to make a living. He was working to have extra money to help those in need. This is the complete crucifixion of the entitlement mentality. *Others are not responsible for me; I'm responsible for others.*

I believe that the entitlement mentality has one of the greatest strongholds on our society today. It undercuts initiative, encourages apathy, and discourages visionary sacrifice. Worst of all, it is so deeply embedded that we're not even conscious of it, making it harder to resist and overcome. But resist it and overcome it we must. Otherwise, we'll be stuck on a merry-go-round of blame-shifting and victimhood, getting angry, pointing our fingers, making accusations, and going nowhere.

To repeat: It's high time we embrace the mentality of "No excuses! I'm responsible for myself." This is the first step to progress and success.

Jesus gives us three practical principles in Luke 16:

1. "One who is faithful in a very little is also faithful in much, and one who is dishonest in a very little is also dishonest in much"

(v. 10). You will not be trusted with much until you prove yourself trustworthy with very little. In my early days of radio broadcasting when I was on a few smaller stations, I said to the Lord, "If you will give me a million listeners a day, I'll make this the best radio show possible." No sooner did I say the words than I knew what his answer would be: "Make this the best show possible, and I'll give you a million listeners."

2. If you're not faithful with money (what Jesus calls "the unrighteous wealth"), you won't be faithful with true riches (v. 11). Many of us want to be spiritual heroes, but our earthly lives are a wreck due to our own irresponsibility, particularly when it comes to handling money. Of course, God doesn't expect all of us to be financial wizards, but he does require us to be good financial stewards, and that means paying our bills on time, being generous, and being wise. (For some biblical guidelines on finances, see chapter 11.) Don't expect the Lord to give you a massive, world-changing ministry if you fail to pay your electric bill because of bad spending habits.

3. "And if you have not been faithful in that which is another's, who will give you that which is your own?" (v. 12). The principle again is simple: If you are irresponsible with things that don't belong to you, caring for them as if they were your own, then you'll never be entrusted with things that are your own. If you don't take care of your parents' car when they loan it to you, you're not ready for a car of your own. If you won't serve faithfully in someone else's company (or church), you're not ready for a company (or church) of your own.

In sum, the bigger the stakes, the more our good habits (and bad habits) will be magnified. So, faithful with little, faithful with much; faithful with earthly riches, faithful with spiritual riches; faithful with that which belongs to someone else, faithful with that which belongs to you.

None of this is rocket science, but once again, that's what is so wonderful about God's Word. It is as practical as it is profound and as pragmatic as it is penetrating. The Word of God is wise, and we do well to live by the wisdom of the Word. And the Word of God destroys the entitlement mentality, giving us something far better in its place. Just think of what would happen if every American said, "Nobody owes me anything, and I am responsible for my own actions. If I want my life (or my family's life) to change, with God's help, it can change."

You might say, "Every American? Now that's a tall order."

I agree! So how about starting with you and me? I'm all in. Are you?

Dr. John Townsend wrote,

> There is a solution to entitlement, which I call the *Hard Way*. The Hard Way is the entitlement cure. It is a path of behaviors and attitudes that undo the negative effects of entitlement, whether in ourselves or in others.

This was his definition of the Hard Way: "The habit of doing what is best, rather than what is comfortable, to achieve a worthwhile outcome."[10]

It is the hard way that pays long-term dividends, the hard way that produces long-term fruit, the hard way that yields long-term gratification. So quit passing the buck and shirking responsibility; don't blame others for where you find yourself today; and determine, with God's help, to be a giver not a taker, a producer not a drainer, one who lifts others up rather than drags them down. To quote Paul once again, "Do everything without complaining and arguing, so that no one can criticize you. Live clean, innocent lives as children of God, shining like bright lights in a world full of crooked and perverse people" (Phil. 2:14–15 NLT).

That's our calling, that's who we are, and that's who our nation needs us to be. So, let's wake up from our slumber. It's literally time to rise and shine.

THIRTEEN

The Universe Does Not Revolve Around Me

Let each of you look not only to his own
interests, but also to the interests of others.
—PHILIPPIANS 2:4

SOMETHING ELSE IS GOING ON WITH OUR ENTITLEMENT MENTALITY, something more foundational that has even affected messages preached from our pulpits. It's the notion that the universe revolves around me. In this view I am not here to serve God, he is here to serve me; I am not here to serve society, society is here to serve me. In short, it's all about *me*. The world revolves around *my* needs and *my* desires and *my* wants and *my* sensitivities, and anything that doesn't make *me* happy or make *me* feel good, or anything that makes *me* uncomfortable or challenges *me* is wrong, wrong, wrong.

With this me-centered mind-set I evaluate everything by how it affects me, and if I find your words or actions offensive or insulting or derogatory or attacking or demeaning, then you have committed a grave, cardinal sin. You are guilty of a microaggression.

What exactly is a *microaggression*? According to an article on Buzzfeed. com by Heben Nigatu:

The term "microaggression" was used by Columbia professor Derald Sue to refer to "brief and commonplace daily verbal, behavioral, or environmental indignities, whether intentional or unintentional, that communicate hostile, derogatory, or negative racial slights and insults toward people of color." Sue borrowed the term from psychiatrist Dr. Chester Pierce who coined the term in the '70s.[1]

The definition has now been expanded to include almost anything that could potentially offend any other "marginalized" group, leading to absurd situations like this:

Guidelines issued on the [University of North Carolina's] Employee Forum aim to help staff avoid microaggressions in their interactions by cautioning against offensive phrases such as "Christmas vacation," "husband/boyfriend" and "golf outing."

Seriously? Talking about a Christmas vacation or inviting someone to play a round of golf could be perceived as a microaggression? Precisely so. And that's just the beginning.

Under the "Religion" tab, the guidebook says organizing vacations around Christian holidays further "centers the Christian faith and minimizes non-Christian spiritual rituals and observances."

With regard to "gender" microaggressions, the guidelines discourage comments such as "I love your shoes!" to female colleagues or otherwise complimenting the appearance of women.

To compliment a woman on her appearance, the guidance warns, is essentially to say, "I notice how you look and dress more than I value your intellectual contributions. How you look is really important."

The guide also discourages staff from inviting others to play a "round of golf," which assumes "employees have the financial resources/exposure to a fairly expensive and inaccessible sport."

On the matter of race, telling someone that you "don't see color" is equivalent to "minimizing/denying a person of color's racial/ethnic experiences," the guide says.

Microaggressions against "sexual orientation" include using the terms "husband" or "boyfriend" when addressing a female colleague, or "wife" or "girlfriend" when addressing a male colleague, instead of the asexual "partner" or "spouse."[2]

The university quickly removed the guidelines after an outcry from campus conservatives,[3] but these guidelines represent a prevalent contemporary mentality: my feelings set the tone, my feelings are what matter, and my feelings evaluate what is true. (Today, people even speak of "my truth," as if truth were defined as whatever I perceive it to be.)

And what if my sensitivities offend your sensitivities? What if *my* reaction to *your* words strikes *you* as a microaggression? What if *you* are offended because *I* was offended by *your* use of the term *Merry Christmas*? You can see what a ridiculous situation this creates, but that's what happens when the universe revolves around me (or you!).

In her book, *Generation Me*, psychology professor Jean M. Twenge noted that the generation born in the 1950s was called "the Me Generation." But, she wrote, "Compared to today's young people, they were posers," and she illustrated her point by describing a woman named Linda, who was born in the fifties, and whose "youngest child, Jessica, was born years after Whitney Houston's No. 1 hit song 'Greatest Love of All' declared that loving yourself was the greatest love." What is life like for Jessica?

Jessica's elementary school teachers believed that they should help Jessica feel good about herself. Jessica scribbled in a coloring book called We Are All Special, got a sticker on her worksheet just for filling it out, and did a sixth-grade project called "All About Me." When she wondered how to act on her first date, her mother told her, "Just be yourself." Eventually, Jessica got her lower lip pierced and got a large tattoo on her lower back because, she said, she wanted to express herself. She dreams of being a model or a singer, takes numerous "selfies" a day, and recently reached her personal goal of acquiring 5,000 followers on Instagram. She does not expect to marry until she is in her late 20s, and neither she nor her older sisters have any children yet. "You have to love yourself before you can love someone else," she says. This generation is unapologetically focused on the individual, a true Generation Me.[4]

How did we become so self-centered and thin-skinned? A friend of mine in the business world told me that it's common now for college and university grads to have trouble on their jobs, but not because they lack intelligence or the necessary academic training. Instead, it's because they can't take correction, having been shielded from it during much of their upbringing and education. "You may be my boss, but you're making me feel bad, which makes you a bad person, since I'm a good person and therefore a good employee." I may be exaggerating the sentiments, but not by much.

So I ask again, how did we get so self-centered? What's at the root of Generation Me? Obviously, human beings have always been self-centered (that's the nature of sin), but there seem to be several reasons that this generation is more self-centered than previous generations. Needless to say, members of this younger generation do have many excellent qualities, but their tendency to extreme self-centeredness is not one of them.[5] What, then, has contributed to this attitude?

One factor is the rise of personal technology, from the PC to the cell phone, through which we have become more individualistic. Life used to be lived more communally, by necessity as much as by choice, but now we spend more time alone in our rooms or, even if in public, alone with our gadgets. Have you ever seen an entire family having dinner together at a restaurant but none of them are talking and all of them are on their phones, either texting or surfing the Internet or playing games or answering e-mails or even chatting online? Isn't this a vivid illustration of Generation Me? Twenty years ago, you wouldn't have seen everyone in the family sitting at a restaurant reading their own books.

Added to this issue is the nature of social media, which gives pride of place to self-expression. This ability can be terrific, potentially giving everyone a voice. But it can also be destructive, since the main focus is on what *I* have to say. As a long-time youth minister said to me, "Kids today are especially good at stating who they are and describing what they're doing." Let me talk to you about *me*! They're also good at taking selfies. Come to think of it, most of us are becoming good at taking selfies. Here's the latest picture of *me*!

This can easily lead to all kinds of obsessive behavior. As Patrick Nelson reported on Networld.com:

We're obsessed with our phones, a new study has found. The heaviest smartphone users click, tap or swipe on their phone 5,427 times a day, according to researcher Dscout.

That's the top 10 percent of phone users, so one would expect it to be excessive. However, the rest of us still touch the addictive things 2,617 times a day on average. No small number.[6]

Really—2,617 times a day? Do I do that? Do you?[7]

But it's not just an addictive behavior in the sense that we get used to doing it all the time. There's also something going on in the brain, as with other addictions. As explained by the behavioral scientist Susan Weinschenk:

> Do you ever feel like you are addicted to email or twitter or texting? Do you find it impossible to ignore your email if you see that there are messages in your inbox? Do you think that if you could ignore your incoming email or messages you might actually be able to get something done at work? You are right!
>
> The culprit is dopamine—dopamine was "discovered" in 1958 by Arvid Carlsson and Nils-Ake Hillarp at the National Heart Institute of Sweden. Dopamine is created in various parts of the brain and is critical in all sorts of brain functions, including thinking, moving, sleeping, mood, attention, motivation, seeking and reward.

How exactly does this apply to e-mailing and texting and posting on social media?

> With the internet, twitter, and texting you now have almost instant gratification of your desire to seek. Want to talk to someone right away? Send a text and they respond in a few seconds. Want to look up some information? Just type your request into google. Want to see what your colleagues are up to? Go to LinkedIn. It's easy to get in a dopamine induced loop. Dopamine starts you seeking, then you get rewarded for the seeking which makes you seek more. It becomes harder and harder to stop looking at email, stop texting, or stop checking your cell phone to see if you have a message or a new text.[8]

I can absolutely relate to this, and a few times I've almost found myself panicking when my e-mail wasn't working, as if my world (or the whole world!) would collapse if I couldn't send or receive these messages. It is downright difficult to disconnect and disengage. And as a writer, constantly posting articles online (or posting memes on social media), I understand the concept of instant gratification. *Within seconds* of posting something, I begin to see the first Likes and Shares and, if it's a good post or article, *within minutes* the responses and comments are flooding my cell phone or computer by the thousands or tens of thousands. Instant gratification indeed.

When I was a kid, you would write a letter to someone and wait days for it to arrive, after which you'd wait several more days (at least) for the response to get back to you. And in prior generations, before mail would travel on trucks or trains or planes, cross-country communication would take weeks and overseas communication months. Not anymore! Everything is virtually instant, and we can easily become consumed with this wired world that pulls us away from normal emotional development. We could say that this is the largest social experiment in history.

Another factor in our self-absorption is the exponential increase in the availability of entertainment. There were no video games when I grew up, no twenty-four-hour sports networks, no movie channels, no cable TV, no Internet. Kids back then would be more prone to play with friends or have a constructive hobby or read a book or do something outside. But with so much entertainment available today, we are now "amusing ourselves to death," to borrow the title of the modern classic by Neil Postman.[9] This has led to the dumbing down of society (we need sound bites, not long discourses) and also makes us more superficial in our attitudes. It has also produced another kind of addiction—narcissistic addiction—which, by nature, revolves around self.

But I don't say this to condemn. People living in America today, especially younger people, have a new set of challenges unknown to previous generations. They have more potential distractions, and they have been immersed in TV and movies and (more recently) Internet from their earliest cognitive stages. Many of us have also been raised with the "you are special and therefore entitled" mentality, and when you put all these factors together, you have a recipe for self-centeredness.

Earlier in this chapter, I mentioned Jean Twenge's book *Generation Me*. Together with the social psychologist W. Keith Campbell, Twenge authored *The Narcissism Epidemic: Living in the Age of Entitlement*.[10] The authors speak of "the relentless rise of narcissism in our culture," also referencing a popular song that declared, "I believe that the world should revolve around me!"[11] Chapter titles in their book include "Parenting: Raising Royalty"; "Superspreaders!"; "The Celebrity and Media Transmission of Narcissism"; "Look at Me on MySpace [yes, this is a few years old!]: Web 2.0 and the Quest for Attention"; and "I Deserve the Best at 18% APR: Easy Credit and the Repeal of the Reality Principle."

Interestingly enough, Postman's *Amusing Ourselves to Death* was written back in 1985, which feels like centuries ago in terms of social change. Yet even then he was sounding an alarm about the dangers of our media-soaked society. In a special introduction written in honor of the book's twentieth anniversary, Andrew Postman, Neil's son, referenced a professor who would require her students to go on a twenty-four-hour media fast, meaning abstaining from all electronic media, from TV to cell phones to the Internet. And if they broke the media fast for any reason, they had to start over. Once they were done, they had to write a paper detailing their experiences, which varied from "The Worst Day of My Life" to "The Best Experience I Ever Had." One student wrote, "I thought I was going to die."

Invariably, Postman reported, the students "take time to do things they haven't done in years. They actually walk down the street to visit their friend. They have extended conversations. One wrote, 'I thought to do things I hadn't thought to do *ever*.' The experience changes them," often in a lasting way.[12] A fast like this forces people to deal with their addictions (or, perhaps, reveals those addictions to them), it breaks the cycle of immediate gratification, and it challenges them to do something else—something productive, something enriching, even something outside of themselves.

Now if you're a traditional Jew, you do this media fast once a week, abstaining from all use of electronics (among other things) for the twenty-four hours of the Sabbath. And this brings us back to God's Word again. Not only does the Word have much to say about the cycle of life—with the Sabbath being a day for rest, renewal, and re-creation—but the Scriptures also call us out of self-centeredness, challenging us to live by divine principles that are as counterintuitive as they are trustworthy. The Bible has the cure for Generation Me.

Why do I say these divine principles are counterintuitive? Jesus taught that the way up is down and the way down is up. He taught that you keep things by giving them away and you lose things by keeping them. He taught that the way to receive is to give and that the way to be effective publicly is to be faithful privately.[13] In short, he said that if you save your life, you'll lose it; if you lose your life for him, you'll save it.[14] What in the world does all this mean?

Jesus calls us to bless those who curse us and to do good to those who hate us and use us.[15] How can this be? Jesus even said this: "Truly, truly, I say to you, unless a grain of wheat falls into the earth and dies, it remains alone; but if it dies, it bears much fruit. Whoever loves his life loses it, and whoever hates his life in this world will keep it for eternal life" (John 12:24–25).

What? Jesus wants us to *hate* our lives? Does that mean we should cut ourselves and whip ourselves or even kill ourselves? Does that mean that we should have a terrible self-image and beat ourselves up psychologically? Not at all. It means that we renounce the claims to our own lives because we realize we belong to the Lord. And when we understand that we do not belong to ourselves and that the purpose of our lives is to glorify him, we suddenly find freedom. We discover the meaning and purpose of our lives. We are liberated!

But when we try to hold on, when we make everything about ourselves, we lose our very souls. In short, it is only by surrendering the control of our lives to God and focusing on his purposes that we discover our real purpose and destiny. Put another way, *it is only by dying to self that we learn to live, and it is only when we live to God—and for God—that we experience the fullness of life.* After all, he's the one who designed us.

Before digging into some of these liberating scriptural truths, let me give you a practical illustration. We refer to a generous person as openhanded and a stingy person as tightfisted, but have you ever thought through the imagery? Let's say you have a hundred-dollar bill in your hand, and you are determined to hold on to it. You really need that money. A friend comes to you asking if there's any way you could help her out. Could you loan her one hundred dollars? No way! Your fist is tightly clenched, and that's the end of the story.

Yes, it's true that you kept your money, but there's a big problem. You can't receive anything, either. Your hand is tightly closed.

Now put yourself in the shoes of the openhanded person. That friend asks for a hundred-dollar loan, and you open your hand and say, "I happen to have one hundred dollars right here. Don't worry about paying me back. It's yours." Well, you no longer have that hundred-dollar bill, but your hand is open, which means you can receive hundreds of hundred-dollar bills.

This example illustrates a biblical principle: you receive by giving; you gain by relinquishing. As stated in Proverbs, "One gives freely, yet grows all the richer; another withholds what he should give, and only suffers want" (Prov. 11:24). It takes a step of faith and it requires the crucifixion of *me*, but it is so liberating and rewarding. Instead of being stuck to the ground—meaning grounded by your own limitations and the four walls of your world—you can fly. The possibilities are endless.

Do you remember learning how to ride a bike? When you first start out, you're holding on so tight, trying to keep that bike going straight, but you keep falling over, maybe into your dad's arms as he runs alongside you. But then something happens and you get the hang of it, and instead of the tightness, there's lightness. The next thing you know, you're riding with joyful abandon half a block away from Dad, who's now smiling and cheering you on. That's what it feels like spiritually when you lose your life and then find it—except it's infinitely more wonderful, intense, and rewarding.

It's the same thing with our lives: When you focus on you, when you put you first, when life revolves around you, you stagnate, becoming ingrown and stifled in your vision. When you look out—out to God and out to others, putting others first and having your life revolve around the Lord—you find your wings and learn to fly. So why stay cooped up in that smelly little nest when you can soar like an eagle?

That's the great question for Generation Me, and that's the great question for each of us: Are you tenaciously holding on to your life, fighting for *your* will and making *your* demands and insisting on *your* desires? Or have you let go and surrendered everything to Jesus, saying, "Lord, *Your* will and *Your* demands and *Your* desires"? How incredibly freeing this is! How vision-expanding this is! Only at this point of surrender do we discover the design and purpose for our lives. Only then do we really begin to live.

So, the key to breaking free from the Generation Me mentality is not to berate yourself and say, "You are so selfish! You are so self-absorbed! You should feel terrible about yourself, and you should start putting others first." The key is to realize that the me-centered mentality is self-defeating, self-destructive, and self-limiting, and it is only by dying to self that you will discover your divinely given destiny and purpose. It comes by surrendering to the will of God and giving yourself to serve others.

Something else happens when you die to self and live to God. You become free from the fear of man and free from the praise of man. By becoming God's slave, you are free from slavery to others, and so *you gain your freedom by becoming a slave.* (I told you this was counterintuitive.) As a colleague of mine once said, "I am not moved by criticism because I am not moved by praise."[16] He only cares for God's approval. He hit the bull's-eye!

The Christian leader George Müller (1805–1898) was a man of tremendous faith who cared for thousands of orphans for decades, providing them with food and shelter and education. Before he knew the Lord, he lived a decadent and unruly life, but Jesus got hold of him and transformed him. Then, years later as a believer, something dramatic happened to Müller. As he described it, "There was a day when I died, utterly died to my opinions, preferences, tastes, and will—died to the world, its approval or censure— died to the approval or blame even of my brethren and friends, and since then I have studied only to show myself approved unto God."[17] The day Müller died was the day he found freedom.

Now let's go back to the words of Jesus again and see if they're making more sense: "Truly, truly, I say to you, unless a grain of wheat falls into the earth and dies, it remains alone; but if it dies, it bears much fruit. Whoever loves his life loses it, and whoever hates his life in this world will keep it for eternal life" (John 12:24–25). How terribly small my world is when it revolves around Michael Brown. How extraordinarily large it is when it revolves around the Creator of the universe.

One of my closest friends is an incredibly generous man, always paying for everyone at his table in the restaurant, always putting others first, always looking for opportunities to serve. Many years ago we were at a meeting with other leaders, sitting together and munching on some snacks. My friend went to another room to get us something to drink, returning with a glass in each hand. But when he walked back to where we had been sitting, he saw that another friend had joined us. So he gave one glass to him and one glass to me, as if that had been his plan the whole time. I thought to myself, *What a giving guy!*

His house is constantly filled with guests, and he and his family are always preparing meals. The kids often give up their own bedrooms to accommodate the many visitors. That's how he and his family have lived for years.

About ten years ago, he launched a ministry to help poor believers in Israel, but he had no real funding. Suddenly, without solicitation, money began to pour into his ministry, and he has since given away hundreds of thousands of dollars. He lives to give and to help others, and the money keeps pouring into his hands because he keeps giving it away. And as he focuses on others, all his needs are met.[18]

Think again of the principle of being tightfisted versus openhanded; then apply that principle to every area of your life, and consider the grace that comes to you as you live to please others rather than yourself. As Paul exhorted his readers, "We who are strong have an obligation to bear with the failings of the weak, and not to please ourselves. Let each of us please his neighbor for his good, to build him up" (Rom. 15:1–2).

There is a verse that says, "Cast your bread upon the waters, for you will find it after many days" (Eccl. 11:1). Or, in another translation, "Send your grain overseas, for after many days you will get a return" (NET). If you keep it—whatever that "it" might be—you'll never experience the full return. If you send it away, it will come back. In the words of Jesus, "Give, and it will be given to you. A good measure, pressed down, shaken together and running over, will be poured into your lap. For with the measure you use, it will be measured to you" (Luke 6:38 NIV).

Do you want to receive? Then give—but don't give with the purpose of getting a return. Give with the purpose of giving, understanding that "it is more blessed to give than receive" (Acts 20:35; these are also the words of Jesus). When you learn to live like that, you tap into God's infinite supply, and you become a channel of blessing and refreshing. In the process you will find your own life enriched in many ways (and my focus is not on money here).

This is the Jesus way, and it is diametrically opposed to the Generation Me type of thinking: "Judge not," our Lord said, "and you will not be judged; condemn not, and you will not be condemned; forgive, and you will be forgiven" (Luke 6:37). To repeat the Lord's words again, "For with the measure you use, it will be measured to you."

That generous friend of mine whom I just mentioned spent more than two decades pastoring. And when someone in the church would complain and say to him, "The people here aren't friendly. Nobody asks me out to eat," he would reply, "Then you ask someone out!" In other words, if you want friends, be a friend; if you want community, build community; if no one cares about you, then reach out to others who are lonely.

When I was in graduate school I would take the train into New York City for classes, and in the last few years of my doctoral work, I had quite a long commute from where I lived on Long Island. On one particular day, I was really tired and wanted to catch a short nap, after which I would finish preparing for class. Sitting next to me was a pleasant older woman who seemed very open to the gospel, but I didn't want to talk because I needed my sleep. If I missed my power nap, my mind wouldn't be sharp and I wouldn't be able to finish my class preparation.

But I knew this woman had to come first, and so I pursued the conversation with her and we had a great talk about the Lord, because of which I missed my designated nap time. Yet when she got off the train at her stop, I realized immediately that something felt different: I was invigorated, my mind was unusually sharp, and there was joy in my spirit. And I got all my work done on time too. I've seen this happen countless times in all kinds of situations where I put others first or sacrificed something for the Lord's work. The tiny amount I lost was nothing in comparison to the great amount that I gained.

In the context of giving our money to help the poor, Paul wrote, "Remember this: Whoever sows sparingly will also reap sparingly, and whoever sows generously will also reap generously" (2 Cor. 9:6 NIV). But this principle also applies in every area of life: When we generously sow the seeds of our talents, our treasures, and our time, living an openhanded, self-denying life, we reap an abundant harvest. We reap the fullness of life. Is this making sense to you now?

Proverbs says, "Whoever brings blessing will be enriched, and one who waters will himself be watered" (11:25). I can see you nodding your head as you read. The light is going on, and life outside the confines of the nest is becoming more and more appealing. It's time to learn to fly!

Let me leave you with one more piece of biblical wisdom, another building block in the renewing of America. It is the importance of being thankful, which ties in directly with both the entitlement mentality discussed in chapter 12 and the Generation Me mentality, which is obviously closely related. According to Dennis Prager, selfishness is also related to the economic philosophy of socialism, a philosophy that was embraced by many young people who were enamored by the promises of Democratic presidential candidate Bernie Sanders.

In his PragerU video "Socialism Makes People Selfish," he explained, "After all, why would a person be grateful for receiving an entitlement? Who's going to be grateful for getting what they're entitled to?" Instead, Prager noted, people begin to think that these "entitlements" are actually "rights," and there's little reason for someone to be thankful for receiving what they believe is rightfully theirs.[19] When you pay for an item in the store, do you thank the store manager for allowing you to take it home with you?

So an excellent way to combat this ungrateful mind-set is to develop a lifestyle of thanksgiving, something we are encouraged to do throughout the Scriptures. Here are just a few examples:

- Praise the LORD! Oh give thanks to the LORD, for he is good, for his steadfast love endures forever! (Ps. 106:1)
- Give thanks to the LORD, for he is good, for his steadfast love endures forever. (Ps. 136:1)
- Giving thanks always and for everything to God the Father in the name of our Lord Jesus Christ. (Eph. 5:20)
- Give thanks in all circumstances; for this is the will of God in Christ Jesus for you. (1 Thess. 5:18)

Even when we pray, asking God for help, the Scriptures remind us to be thankful: "Do not be anxious about anything, but in every situation, by prayer and petition, *with thanksgiving*, present your requests to God" (Phil. 4:6 NIV, emphasis added).

There is tremendous power in having an "attitude of gratitude."[20] It works against a grumbling, complaining, fault-finding, me-centered mindset, and it helps us overcome the entitlement mentality. And as we thank God for who he is, we turn our focus away from our problems and self-interests and look instead to his incredible goodness, which lifts us up into a beautiful, heavenly realm. To say it once again, having a grateful attitude is so liberating!

And as we express appreciation to the Lord and to others, even for the little things, we realize that the universe does not revolve around ourselves, that the very breath we breathe is a gift from God, that the forgiveness of our sins is a gift from God, that every good thing we have is a gift from God. Our attention, then, is not set on ourselves but on him—our Lord, our Savior, our Redeemer, our Deliverer, our King.

The universe quite literally revolves around him. In Paul's words, "he is before all things, and in him all things hold together" (Col. 1:17). And when we make him—not ourselves—the center of our universe, everything gets properly aligned. This is an alignment adjustment America desperately needs, and once again, it starts with each one of us.

FOURTEEN

The Church's Great
Opportunity

The darkness is passing away and the
true light is already shining.
—1 JOHN 2:8

WITH AMERICA IN SUCH A WRETCHED CONDITION TODAY, IT'S EASY
to get discouraged, especially when so much of the church is complacent
and compromised. Could it be that we have passed the point of no return?
Could it be that our beloved country is beyond hope? Could it be that the
only thing we have to look forward to is divine judgment?

Christian leaders have been sounding the alarm for decades, urgently
calling on American believers to wake up, passionately calling for revival
and reformation and revolution—or else. In 1978 Louis Drummond wrote
The Awakening That Must Come, in 1981 Francis Schaeffer penned *A
Christian Manifesto*, in 1982 John Whitehead wrote *The Second American
Revolution*, and in 1985 David Wilkerson published *Set the Trumpet to Thy
Mouth*, just to give a representative sampling.[1] And things are a whole lot
worse today than they were thirty years ago. Is it too late for America?

What does God say? What is the verdict of the Lord? Has he written us
off forever—or at least, for a generation or more? There is certainly reason
for grave concern. America *is* ripe for judgment, and we know that God's
judgments are right and just and fair. Have we spurned the Lord's patience
and mercy for too long?

That is certainly possible, and we do well to have a sense of urgency in our prayers and our efforts. But there is another side to the story, one that sees the darkness as an opportunity for the light to shine. We see this illustrated in a fascinating account in John 9, where Jesus and his disciples encounter a man who had been blind from birth. When the disciples saw the man, they asked, "Rabbi, who sinned, this man or his parents, that he was born blind?" (John 9:2).

From the perspective of these Jewish followers of Jesus, this was a perfectly logical question, since sin and sickness were often intertwined in the Hebrew Scriptures and since some of their traditions suggested that a baby could sin in its mother's womb, causing the child to be born with handicaps or sickness.[2] So, these disciples wondered, which was it? Did the parents sin or did the man himself sin?

Jesus answered, "It was not that this man sinned, or his parents, but that the works of God might be displayed in him." What an incredible perspective! It is true that this man had suffered his entire lifetime, but Jesus saw his hardship as a divine opportunity. He added, "We must work the works of him who sent me while it is day; night is coming, when no one can work. As long as I am in the world, I am the light of the world" (John 9:3–5).

What's interesting is that Jesus never said that his Father made the man blind. Instead, without giving an explicit answer, he made clear that the man's blindness was not the result of personal sin and that his condition should be seen as an opportunity for God to be glorified. Yes, this happened "that the works of God might be displayed in him."

This is the perspective of light, which views every negative and destructive and hopeless situation as an opportunity through which the Lord can be glorified, regardless of the cause of that situation. In contrast, the perspective of darkness only sees the problem (he's blind), only points accusing fingers ("Who sinned to cause this?"), only imagines things going from bad to worse (What possible good could come out of being blind?). As someone once said, "The optimist sees opportunity in every calamity. A pessimist, calamity in every opportunity."[3]

We see this same contrast in perspectives in John 11, where Jesus learned that Lazarus, his dear friend, was sick and in need of healing. How did the Lord respond? "This illness does not lead to death," he said. "It is for the glory of God, so that the Son of God may be glorified through it" (John 11:4). There it is again! The serious illness Lazarus was suffering from was simply an opportunity for the Son of God to be glorified. Jesus actually waited until Lazarus died before going to raise him from the dead. The Lord was determined to get maximum glory out of Lazarus's sickness.

What do the disciples say when Jesus announces that it's time to visit Lazarus, which would mean going to back to Judea? "'Rabbi,' the disciples say to him, 'just now the Judean leaders were trying to stone You! And You're going back there again?'" (John 11:8 TLV). To paraphrase, "Yeshua, this is not a good move. It's dangerous in that neck of the woods! You'd be crazy to go back there."

Jesus answered, "Are there not twelve hours in the day? If anyone walks in the day, he does not stumble, because he sees the light of this world. But if anyone walks in the night, he stumbles, because the light is not in him" (John 11:9–10). What an amazing outlook!

The disciples suffered from limited vision because they were walking in darkness, seeing only fear and death. Jesus viewed things through the perspective of light, which says: This difficult situation is actually a divine setup. This is an opportunity to display God's power. This is a platform for the glory of God through which many will come to faith (see John 11:40).

This does not mean that blindness or sickness or premature death is necessarily a gift from God. Jesus never once said that.[4] He never said, "God is being glorified through this man being born blind and remaining blind the rest of his life, or through Lazarus getting sick and dying and never being healed or raised from the dead."[5] Rather, blindness and sickness and death are platforms through which God could be glorified, regardless of the origin of those conditions. And so Jesus was showing us that whatever comes our way, however painful it may be and whatever its ultimate cause may be, it can be a potential opportunity for God to be glorified. Sickness is an opportunity for healing; death is an opportunity for resurrection; destruction is an opportunity for restoration. This is the perspective of the light. What, then, would Jesus say about America's condition today? What is the perspective of the light?

Light certainly does expose sin and corruption (Eph. 5:7–14), calling for repentance and for acts of justice and morality (Rev. 3:19). And with more light, there is greater judgment (John 9:39–41; Luke 12:42–48). But light always seeks to be redemptive and restorative, and light can see a mighty apostle behind a murderous persecutor of believers (think Saul of Tarsus), and light can see a courageous leader behind a fisherman who denies the Lord (think Peter). And this doesn't just apply to the apostles. Light can also look down on a rebellious, proud, sixteen-year-old, heroin-shooting, LSD-using, Jewish hippie rock drummer who steals money from his own father and lies to cover it up; and light can then use that person to debate rabbis at Oxford University and agnostics at Ohio State University and deliver scholarly papers at Harvard University and do outreach lectures at Yale University and the Hebrew University. The more unworthy the vessel, the more glory goes to the Lord.

Light sees hope where darkness sees despair. Light sees life where darkness sees death. Light sees potential where darkness sees pitfalls. What is the perspective of light when it comes to America?

While ministering in Korea in the summer of 2016, I saw an old friend from Germany, Walter Heidenreich, who was speaking at the same conference as me. I said to him, with pain in my voice, "So, what's happening in your country? What's going on with the Muslim refugees?"

I had been reading all the bad reports about Germany, hearing how some Muslim migrants were assaulting German women and causing lots of disruption, and I wanted to show him my sympathy. But when I asked him, "So, what about Germany?" his eyes got wide, and he said, with a great big smile, "God is moving in Germany! Thousands of Muslims are coming to faith! It's harvest time in Germany! We could never get into Syria to reach these people, so God has sent them to us. What an opportunity we have!"

As Walter emphasized when I interviewed him on my radio show, we should operate from the perspective of faith, not fear.[6] That sounds just like Jesus! As long as he was in the world, he was the light of the world. Once he left the world, this became our sacred responsibility. We are now called to be God's light in this dark and dying place, and it is we who are to shine like torches, we who are to turn stumbling blocks into stepping-stones, we who are to redeem hopeless situations for the glory of God.[7] By his grace, we can!

The story is told about an American shoe company that decided to expand overseas, sending their best salesman to start a new branch in

Africa. Before he arrived, the company spent years in strategic planning, targeting this particular region as ideal for their global expansion and shipping thousands of boxes of shoes to their huge new warehouse. But within hours of his arrival, the salesman called the company headquarters in a panic. "Get me out of here!" he exclaimed. "No one here wears shoes!"

They flew him home immediately, temporarily halting their plans, and then met as leaders to reevaluate their strategy. After lengthy discussion, they decided that their plan was sound and sent their second-best salesman.

Once again, within hours of the second salesman's arrival, he called headquarters with an urgent message. But this time his tone was very different. "We need thousands more boxes of shoes!" he exclaimed. "Nobody here has any shoes!" That is the mentality we must embrace here in the United States of America today in the midst of massive societal decline. *Everyone needs what we have to offer.*

Without a doubt, our nation is desperately sick, on the edge of spiraling into moral and cultural chaos. And without a doubt, much of the church is backslidden, having been seduced into apathy, lethargy, and carnality by a compromised, watered-down "gospel" and by the endless temptations of the age. In many ways, these are dark days for our country spiritually and morally, and we must not minimize the urgency of the hour. But rather than throw our hands up in despair, we should recognize that this is the perfect opportunity for the church of Jesus to rise up in the truth and power of the Spirit, bringing the message of life and transformation to our sick country. This is the church's great opportunity. This is our time to stand.

On May 6, 2016, Harvard Law professor Mark Tushnet declared, "*The culture wars are over; they lost, we won*," before recommending that the victors (meaning his side, the so-called progressive side) take "a hard line" against "the losers in the culture wars," by which he meant conservative Christians, whom he implicitly compared to slave traders and Nazis.[8]

In response I wrote, "Perhaps, sir, your view of history is shortsighted? . . . Perhaps there will be a healthy pushback against some of these purported advances?"[9] Perhaps this learned professor underestimated the vibrancy of the New Testament faith?

As documented frequently, Christianity is on the rise, not decline, worldwide. And there's no reason that it could not be revived here in

America. The *Washington Post* noted in 2015, "Over the past 100 years, Christians grew from less than 10 percent of Africa's population to its nearly 500 million today. One out of four Christians in the world presently is an Africa[n], and the Pew Research Center estimates that will grow to 40 percent by 2030."

The article also stated, "Asia is also experiencing growth as world Christianity's center has moved not only South, but also East. In the last century, Christianity grew at twice the rate of population in that continent. Asia's Christian population of 350 million is projected to grow to 460 million by 2025."[10]

As for religious faith in America, notable times of spiritual decline have occurred throughout our history—as far back as the seventeen hundreds—and all were followed by seasons of awakening and revival. Professor Tushnet didn't have to look any further than Yale University for quite a few relevant examples, as recently as the beginning of the twentieth century. Yale has had numerous seasons of awakening throughout its history.[11]

It is reported that in the early eighteen hundreds, Supreme Court Chief Justice John Marshall wrote to Bishop Madison of Virginia, "The church is too far gone ever to be redeemed."[12] His observations were quickly swept away by the Second Great Awakening and seem shockingly ill-advised in retrospect. So much for the esteemed justice's foresight.

One century earlier, Rev. Samuel Blair, who became chaplain of the Congress of Pennsylvania, stated, "Religion lay as it were dying, and ready to expire its last breath of life in this part of the visible church."[13] This was shortly before the First Great Awakening, led by the great philosopher Jonathan Edwards, that radically affected the society. "Religion" had hardly expired and breathed its last breath.

Perhaps Professor Tushnet's words will be swept away by another great awakening? As I asked him in my article, "Are you 100 percent sure that this will not happen again? If not, you can hardly pronounce the culture wars over."[14] G. K. Chesterton wrote, "At least five times, the Faith has to all appearances gone to the dogs. In each of these five cases, it was the dog that died."[15] Indeed!

John Zmirak, a conservative Catholic columnist who holds a PhD in English from Louisiana State University, told me that when he was a student at Yale, his professors uniformly praised communism, making clear that communism, not capitalism, was the key to the world's future success. They were quite confident that this socialist system was here to stay and that its sphere of influence was growing by the decade. Who would have imagined how dramatically and quickly it would collapse around the globe? And, Zmirak asked, who would have believed that the principal players who would help topple communism would be a former Hollywood actor (Reagan); a female prime minister in England, the daughter of a lay preacher and grocer (Thatcher); a shipyard worker who became the head of a Polish trade union (Walesa); and a Polish pope (John Paul II)?[16]

What does God have planned for America? What unlikely players is he preparing to use? Who can tell how swiftly and dramatically the tide could turn in our land? And if we as his people truly humble ourselves, confessing our sins, recognizing our need, and giving ourselves unconditionally to the Lord, what surprises will he have in store for our nation? Could it be that our greatest awakening is ahead of us rather than behind us?

Things look so bad today that many believers wonder if God can really save our sick nation. But if he truly is God (and he is!), the answer is simple: all things are possible to him (or her) who believes (see Mark 9:23–24). The question is: Do we really believe? If we really do believe God and his Word, then we will be willing to take holy, Jesus-glorifying, countercultural action based on our faith, regardless of cost or consequence. Forward in faith without flinching!

On April 8, 1966, *Time* magazine featured a stark front cover (for the first time, without a picture of any kind) simply asking the question in bold text, "Is God Dead?" Five years later, on June 21, 1971, the *Time* cover story featured a picture of a hippie-like Jesus with the caption, "The Jesus Revolution." Who saw this coming?

Even more interesting, pollsters in the early 1960s predicted that the young generation would be a joy to work with, a generation that really honored authority.[17] Not quite! These pollsters had no clue that a massive counterculture revolution was about to rise, a nation-shaking revolution led almost entirely by young people. And these same pollsters never could have imagined that in the midst of this rebellious movement a sweeping religious revival known as the Jesus Revolution would arise as well. Perhaps another great awakening is right around the corner for us—an awakening as near as it is undetected.

We dare not minimize the urgency of the hour in our land. America stands at a critical juncture, and it is possible that in just a few years our religious liberties will be gone, our children will face overwhelming obstacles, and the sun will have set for good (or at least for a generation) over what was once "the land of the free and the home of the brave." We have no guarantee that this will not happen.

But there is still time for change: the door of opportunity remains open, and this could be our greatest hour. America can be transformed! Our nation can be redeemed! Our sin-sick land can be healed! But we must get desperate if we want to see change come, and we must continue to cry out to God and reach out to people until we see America rocked with the glory of God.

Leonard Ravenhill was a saintly man of prayer who died in 1994. He wrote these words several decades ago:

> When a nation calls its prime men to battle, homes are broken, weeping sweethearts say their good-byes, businesses are closed, college careers are wrecked, factories are refitted for wartime production, rationing and discomforts are accepted—all for war. Can we do less for the greatest fight that this world has ever known outside of the cross—this end-time siege on sanity, morality, and spirituality?[18]

Ravenhill also wrote, "The true man of God is heartsick, grieved at the worldliness of the Church, grieved at the toleration of sin in the Church, grieved at the prayerlessness in the Church. He is disturbed that the corporate prayer of the Church no longer pulls down the strongholds of the devil." What would he say today, when America has plunged to almost unimaginable depths and the church has become even less vigilant? How urgently should we be living, and how passionately should we be praying?

If we are to see change come to our nation, we must focus on three essential actions.

1. We must give ourselves to focused, fervent, passionate, persistent prayer for revival in the church and for awakening in society.

   In the words of A. T. Pierson:

   > From the day of Pentecost, there has been not one great spiritual awakening in any land which has not begun in a union of prayer, though only among two or three; no such outward, upward movement has continued after such prayer meetings have declined; and it is in exact proportion to the maintenance of such joint and believing supplication and intercession that the word of the Lord in any land or locality has had free course and been glorified.[19]

   This is our great (really, greatest) secret weapon, something every one of us can do, something that exchanges our limited abilities for the limitless power of God. History is filled with the incredible stories of what God has done in answer to faith-filled, persevering prayer. Sadly, many churches have no corporate prayer gatherings, and very little private prayer goes on in the homes of the believers. But the good news is that, to my knowledge, America now has more prayer networks and prayer movements and houses of prayer than at any time in recent history. Many groups are engaging in prayer and worship twenty-four hours a day, seven days a week (some have gone on like this for years now), and there have been gatherings of up to several hundred thousand coming together for a day of prayer and fasting, right here in the United States of America. Will God ignore these prayers?

   Evan Roberts, leader of the Welsh Revival from 1904 to 1905, said this: "My mission is first to the churches. When the churches are aroused to their duty, men of the world will be swept into the Kingdom. A whole church on its knees is irresistible."[20] That remains true to this day.

2. We must give ourselves to the Great Commission here in the United States of America, winning the lost and making disciples.

   Yes, we must get back to the basics, back to carrying a burden for those who do not know the Lord, back to seeing them as lost and in need of a Savior, back to the joy of sharing our faith, back to looking for opportunities to be witnesses for our Lord. There are no greater ministries than the ministry of prayer and the ministry of evangelism, and these are ministries that every one of us can engage in.

For those of us who once lived worldly, sinful lives before coming to faith, our first weeks and months in the Lord were often the richest in terms of evangelism, since we were still in contact with old friends who saw the undeniable change in our lives, and we were so free in telling them about Jesus. That's why many of them came to believe as well. But as the years go on, we end up much more focused on our church communities and much more silent about our faith in the public square, so that decades can go by without us leading a single person to the Lord. Is it any wonder, then, that so much stagnation exists in so many of our churches? New souls are the lifeblood of the body of Christ, and without them, we become ingrown and stale.

And all the while, Jehovah's Witnesses knock on doors day in and day out, sharing their defective faith, and Mormon young people give two years of their lives to the mission field, showing more devotion to Joseph Smith than many of us do to Jesus. And Islam and atheism and a host of others are shouting out their messages while we who have the words of eternal life have grown quiet. This cannot continue.

Evangelist Reinhard Bonnke, who has seen tens of millions of Africans come to faith, once said, "If you want to catch fish, don't throw your net into the bathtub." Exactly. We must *reach out* to the lost, wherever they are. And all of us must have some lost people we know—family, friends, coworkers, neighbors. Why not pray that in the next twelve months, the Lord will allow you to win at least one nonbeliever to the Lord, helping to disciple them and teaching them to go and do the same? If all of us did this, as absolutely tiny as it seems, repeating it every year, the face of America would be radically changed within a decade. And what if we could win numerous souls to the Lord each year? What then?

Oswald J. Smith famously said, "The church that does not evangelize will fossilize."[21] Conversely, the church that *does* evangelize is revitalized, and those we disciple in turn go and make disciples. This is God's ultimate way to change the world, the heart essence of the Jesus revolution: changed people go out and change their generation.

All of us are called to be witnesses in one way or another, and we can support those on the front lines of evangelism with our prayers and with our finances while we look for opportunities to share the good news with those we get to meet. And just think: When you are able to lead someone to Jesus, they literally pass from death to life and their eternal destiny is changed. Forever you will share the joy with them. What price can be put on that?

3. We must live out our faith without excuse, without compromise, and without hypocrisy.

One reason that many Americans have turned against the faith in recent years is the hypocrisy they see in the church. They see sex scandals among Catholic priests and evangelical superstars; they see us live just like the world while we get outraged over the immoral ways of the world. Of course they are leaving the church. Why should that surprise us?

But once again, there is a positive side to this: these people expect followers of Jesus to be different, and when we are different—not perfect, but different—they will listen to us. It's true that there are critics who mock the Bible, the faith, and the Christians, no matter how we live or what we say. But many in the world (including those who were once in the church) expect Christians to live godly lives, expect Christians to help the poor and needy, expect Christians to have solid marriages and families, expect Christian leaders to be people of integrity.

Let us, then, get our own houses in order (which is really the subject of this entire book) by walking in integrity, walking in purity, walking in mercy, walking in truth, walking in justice, walking in faith. Let us recover a spirit of authority with humility and a spirit of boldness with compassion. We have just what America so desperately needs, and as simple as it sounds, *the greatest need in America is for the church to be the church.*

So let us cast off a defeated, pessimistic, cowardly attitude. There is no place for it, and there is no reason for it. Jesus rose from the dead and ascended to heaven, and all authority in heaven and earth has been given to him (Matt. 28:18). We take up that authority when we use his name, and in his name the Iron Curtain and the Bamboo Curtain have been penetrated and torn in two, while the veil of Islam has been pulled back through the message of the gospel. Is there any power in America that can withstand his name? Jesus has already broken the back of Satan, and it is up to us now to walk in that reality, recognizing that we have authority over his power and that, in Jesus, we are more than conquerors.[22]

It is true that in many ways America is post-Christian, yet my concern is not so much with a post-Christian society as with an unchristian church. Let us rise up into the fullness of Jesus, into the reality of the Spirit, into the power of the Word, and let us make a positive, life-giving, truly transformative impact on every area of society.

Will God say no to this? Will he turn a deaf ear to the cries of his people? Will he thwart our efforts to win the lost? Will he oppose our efforts to turn to him with all our hearts and our souls? Will he not richly bless us as we kneel before him with tears of repentance, as we stand up and proclaim Jesus to the lost, as we seek to live lives that please him and glorify him? Will he not go before us and stand with us and do the impossible for us—and for the sake of this nation and for the sake of his name?

Let us cast all fear aside, let us look beyond our difficult and sometimes depressing surroundings, and let us say with one voice, "Here we are! Send us! Use us! America must be saved." What will our Father say in response? I believe he will say to each one of us, "Yes, I am sending *you.*"

Will you go?

NOTES

Chapter 1: How Good Were the Good Old Days?

1. See, conveniently, "List of *Dennis the Menace* (1959 TV series) Episodes," Wikipedia, accessed January 18, 2017, https://en.wikipedia.org/wiki /List_of_Dennis_the_Menace_(1959_TV_series)_episodes.

2. Eliot A. Cohen, "The Age of Trump," *The American Interest*, February 26, 2016, http://www.the-american-interest.com/2016/02/26/the-age-of-trump/.

3. Irwin Unger and Debi Unger, eds., *The Times Were a Changin': The Sixties Reader* (New York: Three Rivers Press, 1998), 2.

4. "Parents Guide for *Midnight Cowboy*," Internet Movie Database, accessed January 18, 2017, http://www.imdb.com/title/tt0064665/parentalguide.

5. Unger and Unger, *The Times Were a Changin'*, 7.

6. Rev. Jesse Lee Peterson, *The Antidote: Healing America from the Poison of Hate, Blame, and Victimhood* (Washington, DC: WND Books, 2015), 138–39.

7. David G. Myers, "Wanting More in an Age of Plenty," *Christianity Today*, April 24, 2000, 95. Adapted from his book *The American Paradox: Spiritual Hunger in an Age of Plenty* (New Haven, CT: Yale University Press, 2000).

8. Bella DePaulo, "7 Stunning Ways Life Was Different in the 1960s," *Psychology Today*, September 6, 2014, https://www.psychologytoday.com /blog/living-single/201409/7-stunning-ways-life-was-different-in-the-1960s (emphasis in the original).

9. "Adolescent Suicide," MedBroadcast, accessed January 26, 2017, http://www .medbroadcast.com/Condition/GetCondition/Adolescent-Suicide.

10. Cheryl Wetzstein, "Census: More First-Time Mothers Give Birth out of Wedlock," *Washington Times*, July 8, 2014, http://www.washingtontimes .com/news/2014/jul/8/census-more-first-time-mothers-give-birth-out-wedl /?page=all.

11. Cotton Mather, *Magnalia Christi: The Great Works of Christ in America* (1853; repr., Carlisle, PA: Banner of Truth, 1979), 25.

12. Matthew Spalding, *We Still Hold These Truths: Rediscovering Our Principles, Reclaiming Our Future* (Wilmington, DE: ISI Books, 2010), 15.

13. For more on this subject, see chapter 2.

Chapter 2: The Bible in American History

1. See, conveniently, "The Old Deluder Act (1647)," *Constitution Society*, accessed January 18, 2017, http://www.constitution.org/primarysources /deluder.html. The English is updated from the original spelling and punctuation. The Act continued with further instructions for larger communities.

2. Cited in Stephen McDowell, *The Bible: America's Source of Law and Liberty* (Charlottesville, VA: Providence Foundation, 2016), Kindle locations 638–40.

3. Karen L. Willoughby, "Long Island Student Fights for School Club, Religious Expression," *Christian Examiner*, November 21, 2014, http://www .christianexaminer.com/article/long-island-student-fights-for-school-club -religious-expression/47653.htm.

4. Todd Starnes, "Teacher Tells Student He Can't Read the Bible in Classroom," Fox News, May 5, 2014, http://www.foxnews.com/opinion/2014/05/05 /teacher-tells-student-cant-read-bible-in-my-classroom.html.

5. "Bible Makes List of Books Most Challenged at Libraries, Public Schools," Fox News, April 12, 2016, http://www.foxnews.com/us/2016/04/12/bible -makes-list-books-most-challenged-at-libraries-public-schools.html.

6. Susan Edelman, "Parent Furor at Bawdy Sex Ed," *New York Post*, October 23, 2011, http://nypost.com/2011/10/23/parent-furor-at-bawdy-sex-ed/.

7. Ibid.

8. "California Governor Signs Bill Requiring Schools to Teach Gay History," CNN, July 15, 2011, http://www.cnn.com/2011/US/07/14/california.lgbt .education/.

9. For discussion, see David L. Barr and Nicholas Piediscalzi, eds., *The Bible in American Education: From Source Book to Textbook* (Chico, CA: Scholars Press, 1982).

10. See ibid. for further background.

11. I cited the account from "An Outline History of Religion in American Schools," Free Republic, updated January 2009, http://www.freerepublic.com/focus/religion/2201818/posts, almost verbatim.

12. *The New England Primer* (Boston, 1777), Kindle edition.

13. "An Outline History of Religion."

14. Noah Webster, *The Original Blue Back Speller* (New York, 1824; repr., San Antonio: Vision Forum, 2002), 43.

15. Ibid., 16.

16. Greg Pfundstein, "Sex Ed Mandates and Children's Innocence," *Public Discourse*, August 17, 2011, http://www.thepublicdiscourse.com/2011/08/3699/.

17. Webster, *Blue Back Speller*, 81.

18. "An Outline History of Religion."

19. See John H. Westerhoff III, "The Struggle for a Common Culture: Biblical Images in Nineteenth-Century Schoolbooks," in David L. Barr and Nicholas Piediscalzi, eds., *The Bible in American Education: From Source Book to Textbook* (Atlanta: SBL Press, 1982), 26–40.

20. "Kansas Teachers' Union—1892," accessed January 18, 2017, http://www.theroadtoemmaus.org/RdLb/21PbAr/Ed/KS%20TchrUn.htm.

21. "An Outline History of Religion."

22. "Laws and Statutes for Students of Harvard College," from *Collections of the Massachusetts Historical Society*, vol. 1 (1792), 242–48, http://boldhearts.com/massachusetts.htm. Under Rev. John Leverett, president of Harvard from 1708 to 1724, standards temporarily declined and there were complaints of "profane swearing," "riotous Actions," and "bringing Cards into the College." Can you imagine such actions creating a stir on our campuses today, especially "bringing Cards into the College"?

23. "The Seal of Princeton University," in Alexander Leitch, *A Princeton Companion* (Princeton: Princeton University Press, 1978), http://etcweb.princeton.edu/CampusWWW/Companion/princeton_university_seal.html.

24. "The Founding of Princeton," in Leitch, *A Princeton Companion*, http://etcweb.princeton.edu/CampusWWW/Companion/founding_princeton.html.

25. "A Brief History of Columbia," Columbia University, accessed January 18, 2017, http://www.columbia.edu/about_columbia/history.html.

26. *A History of Columbia University, 1754–1904: Published in Commemoration of the One Hundred and Fiftieth Anniversary of the Founding of King's College (1904)* (Ithaca, NY: Cornell University Library, 2010), 443–44.

27. Robert Allan Hill, "POV: BU Continues to Reflect Its Methodist Origins," *BU Today*, November 4, 2013, https://www.bu.edu/today/2013/pov-bu -continues-to-reflect-its-methodist-origins/.

28. "A Guide to the Usage of the Seal and Arms of the University of Pennsylvania," Penn University Archives and Records Center, accessed January 18, 2017, http://www.archives.upenn.edu/histy/features/vis_obj /heraldry/guide.html.

29. Laura Gibbs, "Leges sine moribus vanae," *Bestiaria Latina* (blog), April 16, 2007, http://audiolatinproverbs.blogspot.com/2007/04/leges-sine-moribus -vanae.html.

30. See "Presidential Inauguration: Pageantry and Colors," Rutgers University, April 13, 2003, http://ruweb.rutgers.edu/inauguration/media-color.html.

31. "Charter of a College to Be Erected in New Jersey, by the Name of Queen's-College," National Library of Australia Catalogue, accessed November 11, 2016, http://catalogue.nla.gov.au/Record/3377105.

32. My appreciation to Truls Liland, a FIRE School of Ministry graduate, for locating this quote for me and pointing out that it came from Dwight's Baccalaureate Discourse of 1814.

33. Mortimer Adler, ed., *The Annals of America* (Chicago: Encyclopedia Britannica, 1968), 1:464; for the quote online and for additional information about early American education, see Dave Miller, "The Purpose of Education," Apologetics Press, 2007, accessed January 18, 2017, http://www .apologeticspress.com/articles/3392.

34. I owe this information about compulsory chapel attendance to the late John McCandlish Phillips, a *New York Times*, Pulitzer Prize–winning journalist who was heavily involved in Ivy League campus ministry for the last decades of his life.

35. According to Kevin Seamus Hasson in *Believers, Thinkers, and Founders: How We Came to Be One Nation Under God* (New York: Image, 2016), the God referred to by the founders in our nation's key documents was "the God of the Philosophers," and thus not primarily the God of Christianity. With respect to the author's long-term interest in this subject, I believe he minimizes the degree of overlap between these concepts in the minds of some of the founders.

36. *The Constitution of the United States of America and Selected Writings of the Founding Fathers* (New York: Barnes & Noble, 2012), 21.

37. See Bill Muehlenberg, "On the Witchcraft Trials," January 19, 2015, https:// billmuehlenberg.com/2015/01/19/on-the-witchcraft-trials/.

38. Joshua Charles, *Liberty's Secrets: The Lost Wisdom of America's Founders* (Washington, DC: WND Books, 2015), [[page number]].

39. Harry Alonzo Cushing, ed., *The Writings of Samuel Adams*, vol. 4 (New York: G. P. Putman's Sons, 1908), 124.

40. This is the first definition offered on Dictionary.com for *theocracy*; the second definition is "a system of government by priests claiming a divine commission." We'll discuss this subject in more depth in the next chapter.

Chapter 3: The Bible, Not a Theocracy, Is the Answer

1. Wayne Besen, "We Are Now All Members of Billy Graham's Church . . . Whether We Like It or Not," *Truth Wins Out*, May 3, 2012, https://www.truthwinsout.org/blog/2012/05/24826/.

2. John McCandlish Phillips, "When Columnists Cry 'Jihad,'" *Washington Post*, May 4, 2005, http://www.washingtonpost.com/wp-dyn/content/article/2005/05/03/AR2005050301277.html.

3. Markos Moulitsas, *American Taliban: How War, Sex, Sin, and Power Bind Jihadists and the Radical Right* (Sausalito, CA: PoliPointPress, 2010), introduction.

4. Matt Vespa, "Matthews Likens Paul Ryan's Pro-Life Views to Sharia Law," *NewsBusters*, October 17, 2012, http://newsbusters.org/blogs/matt-vespa/2012/10/17/matthews-likens-paul-ryans-pro-life-views-sharia-law. He was referring to Ryan's "personhood" argument, which would grant Fourteenth Amendment rights to the baby in the womb.

5. Michael Brown, "When Committed Christians Are Compared to ISIS," *Townhall*, September 13, 2015, http://townhall.com/columnists/michaelbrown/2015/09/13/when-committed-christians-are-compared-to-isis-n2051359/page/full.

6. Michael Foust, "Talk Show Host Montel Williams Compares Gay Marriage Opponents to ISIS, Taliban," *Christian Examiner*, June 29, 2015, http://www.christianexaminer.com/article/talk-show-host-montel-williams-compares-opponents-of-gay-marriage-to-isis-taliban/49174.htm.

7. Jenny Stanton, "An Eye for an Eye: Iran Sentences 27-Year-Old to Have Eyes Gouged Out After Damaging Sight of Another Man in Street Brawl," *Daily Mail*, August 6, 2015, http://www.dailymail.co.uk/news/article-3186052/An-eye-eye-Iran-sentences-27-year-old-eyes-GOUGED-damaging-sight-man-street-brawl.html#ixzz44hKzPFyS.

8. Excerpted from John Pollock, *George Whitefield and the Great Awakening* (Oxford, England: Lion Publishing, 1972), 164–66.

9. George Whitefield, *George Whitefield's Journals* (Carlisle, PA: Banner of Truth, 1965), 479.

10. McDowell, *The Bible*, Kindle locations 447–96.

11. For a related study, see James A. Monroe, *Hellfire Nation: The Politics of Sin in American History* (New Haven: Yale University Press, 2004).

12. Alexis de Tocqueville, *Democracy in America, and Two Essays on America*, trans. Gerald E. Bevan (New York: Penguin Books, 2003), 345; to locate this quote in any edition, see Alexis de Tocqueville, *Democracy in America*, vol. 1, pt. 2, ch. 9, "The Main Causes which Tend to Maintain a Democratic Republic in the United States."

13. Tocqueville, *Democracy in America*, 543–44; for the universal citation, see Tocqueville, *Democracy in America* (vol. 2, pt. 1, ch. 13, "How Literature Appears in Democratic Times").

14. The complete quote is: "I sought for the key to the greatness and genius of America in her harbors . . . ; in her fertile fields and boundless forests; in her rich mines and vast world commerce; in her public school system and institutions of learning. I sought for it in her democratic Congress and in her matchless Constitution.

   "Not until I went into the churches of America and heard her pulpits flame with righteousness did I understand the secret of her genius and power. America is great because America is good, and if America ever ceases to be good, America will cease to be great." The quote (in one form or another) was circulating as early as 1886 (Tocqueville died in 1859). See, e.g., http://www.barrypopik.com/index.php/new_york_city/entry/america_is_great_because_she_is_good/.

15. Tocqueville, *Democracy in America*, 343; for the universal citation, see Tocqueville, *Democracy in America*, vol. 1, pt. 2, ch. 9, "The Main Causes which Tend to Maintain a Democratic Republic in the United States."

16. "Washington's Farewell Address" (speech, September 19, 1796), Heritage Foundation, accessed January 18, 2017, http://www.heritage.org/initiatives/first-principles/primary-sources/washingtons-farewell-address.

17. Carson Holloway, "Tocqueville on Christianity and American Democracy," Heritage Foundation, March 7, 2016, http://www.heritage.org/research/reports/2016/03/tocqueville-on-christianity-and-american-democracy#_ftn1.

18. Os Guinness, *Renaissance: The Power of the Gospel However Dark the Times* (Downers Grove, IL: InterVarsity Press, 2014), 60.

Chapter 4: The Bible Is Still Relevant in America

1. As noted earlier in chapters 2 and 3.

2. Dennis Prager, *The Ten Commandments: Still the Best Moral Code* (Washington, DC: Regnery, 2015), 5–6.

3. See, conveniently, "Dr. Benjamin Rush," http://www.faithofourfathers.net/rush.html. The quote is from Benjamin Rush's open letter, "To the Citizens of Philadelphia: A Plan for Free Schools," dated March 28, 1787.

4. Spalding, *We Still Hold These Truths*, 22.

5. McDowell, *The Bible*, Kindle locations 768–73, citing Donald Lutz, "The Relative Influence of European Writers on Late 18th Century American Political Thought," *American Political Science Review*, 28 (1984), 189–97. For a criticism on the use of the Lutz article, see Ed Brayton, "Bill Federer Lies About Lutz Study," *Dispatches from the Culture Wars*, September 19, 2016, http://www.patheos.com/blogs/dispatches/2016/09/19/bill-federer-lies-about-lutz-study/.

6. Paul Wallace, "Too Simple to Be Wrong: Atheism's Bronze-Age Goat Herder Conceit," *Huffington Post*, March 11, 2013, http://www.huffingtonpost.com/paul-wallace/atheisms-bronze-age-goat-herder-conceit_b_2398220.html.

7. Michael L. Brown's Facebook page, post by Jason Hughes, April 11, 2016, https://www.facebook.com/DrMichaelBrown.

8. "Evil Bible Home Page," Evil Bible: Fighting Against Immorality in Religion, accessed January 20, 2017, http://www.evilbible.com/.

9. Richard Dawkins, *The God Delusion* (New York: Houghton Mifflin, 2006), 51.

10. Gabriel Sivan, *The Bible and Civilization* (New York: Quadrangle/New York Times Books, 1974), 3, 6.

11. Herbert Friedenwald, "Adams, John," *The Jewish Encyclopedia*, accessed January 20, 2017, http://www.jewishencyclopedia.com/articles/767-adams-john.

12. Cited in Travis Gettys, "Tennessee Lawmakers Named the Bible as State Book—and Some Christians Are Furious," RawStory, April 6, 2016, https://www.rawstory.com/2016/04/tennessee-lawmakers-named-the-bible-as-state-book-and-some-christians-are-furious/.

13. Of course many American Christians were pro-slavery, but the driving force of the abolitionists was solidly Christian, and it was that force that won the day.

14. Peter J. Paris, "The Bible and Black Churches," in Ernest R. Sandeen, ed., *The Bible and Social Reform* (Philadelphia/Chico, CA: Fortress/Scholars Press, 1982), 140. Paris also discussed the pastoral strand, the reform strand, and the nationalist strand, all part of "the black Christian tradition." See

ibid., 133–54. He explained that "the Bible is utilized whenever it is helpful in verifying and justifying the aims of the various strands of the black Christian tradition" (ibid., 152). To a certain extent, however, Paris overly subjugated the Bible to race relations in black churches, as if the Bible were only a tool to accomplish a social goal.

15. Sivan, *The Bible and Civilization*, 107.

16. Gordon Wood, ed., *John Adams: Revolutionary Writings 1755–1775* (New York: The Library of America, 2011), 7.

17. Guinness, *Renaissance*, 21.

18. Rodney Stark, *The Rise of Christianity: How the Obscure, Marginal Jesus Movement Became the Dominant Religious Force in the Western World in a Few Centuries* (Princeton, NJ: Princeton University Press, 1996), 95.

19. Ibid., 103.

20. Ibid., 104.

21. Ibid., 97.

22. Ibid., 98–99.

23. Ibid., 104.

24. Ibid., 104, 110.

25. From his *Short History of the English People* (1874), cited in Sivan, *The Bible and Civilization*, 55 (emphasis mine).

26. C. Ben Mitchell, "The Christian Origins of Hospitals," *BibleMesh*, February 6, 2012, http://biblemesh.com/blog/the-christian-origins-of-hospitals/.

27. H. E. Sigerist, *Civilization and Disease* (Chicago: University of Chicago Press, 1943), 69. In the words of D. J. Seel, "Early in my manhood I said I could not be a physician unless I were first a disciple of Jesus Christ. . . . *Jesus healed.* It follows that the gospel of Jesus cannot be complete without that compassionate ministry. Jesus demonstrated that our God is compassionate, that He is moved by human suffering. And therefore Christ's disciples must seek to be instruments of healing, in one or more of the various avenues available for medical ministry. Christian medicine must be above all else an exhibit, a demonstration, of the character of God." Seel, *Proceedings of the Consultation on the Study Program of Healing Ministry, October 30–November 1, 1980* (Seoul, Korea: Asian Center for Theological Studies and Mission/Korea Christian Medico-Evangelical Association, n.d.), 3, 5.

28. Mitchell, "The Christian Origins of Hospitals," citing Albert R. Jonsen, *A Short History of Medical Ethics* (2000; repr., Oxford: Oxford University Press, 2008).

29. Mitchell, "The Christian Origins of Hospitals," citing Charles E. Rosenberg,

The Care of Strangers, The Rise of America's Hospital System (Baltimore: Johns Hopkins University Press, 1995).

30. Rodney Stark, *The Triumph of Faith: Why the World Is More Religious Than Ever* (Wilmington, DE: Intercollegiate Studies Institute, 2015), 47.

31. Ibid., 50.

32. "0.0% of Icelanders 25 Years or Younger Believe God Created the World, New Poll Reveals," *Iceland Magazine*, January 14, 2016, http://icelandmag .visir.is/article/00-icelanders-25-years-or-younger-believe-god-created-world -new-poll-reveals.

33. Stark, *Triumph of Faith*, 6.

34. Ibid., 50.

35. For details on this quote, see, "When Man Ceases to Worship God," *The American Chesterton Society*, accessed January 20, 2017, http://www .chesterton.org/ceases-to-worship/. For further confirmation of this phenomenon, note that the same magazine that reported on the rapidly rising tide of atheism in Iceland also carried this article: "Why Has the Ancient Sumerian Religion Zuism Become the Fastest Growing Religion in Iceland?," *Iceland Magazine*, December 3, 2015, http://icelandmag.visir.is /article/why-has-ancient-sumerian-religion-zuism-become-fastest-growing -religion-iceland.

36. Adolf Hitler, *Hitler's Table Talk: 1941–1944*, ed. H. R. Trevor-Roper (New York: Enigma Books, 2007), 48.

Chapter 5: Created in the Image of God

1. Matthew Cullinan Hoffman, "Famous Pro-Abortion Feminist Calls Unborn Child a 'Tumor,'" *LifeSite News*, November 23, 2010, https://www.lifesitenews .com/news/famous-pro-abortion-feminist-calls-unborn-child-a-tumor.

2. Alan Rappenport, "Hillary Clinton Roundly Criticized for Referring to the Unborn as a 'Person,'" *New York Times*, April 4, 2016, http://www.nytimes .com/politics/first-draft/2016/04/04/hillary-clinton-roundly-criticized-for -referring-to-the-unborn-as-a-person/.

3. Bradford Richardson, "Marsha Blackburn Says Hillary Clinton's 'Unborn Person' Comment 'Shocks the Conscience,'" *Washington Times*, April 5, 2016, http://www.washingtontimes.com/news/2016/apr/5/marsha-blackburn -says-hillary-clintons-unborn-pers/.

4. Ibid.

5. See Shout Your Abortion at http://shoutyourabortion.com/.

6. Vishal Mangalwadi, *The Book That Made Your World: How the Bible Created the Soul of Western Civilization* (Nashville: Thomas Nelson, 2011), 60.

7. Ibid., 63.

8. This is the Google definition; as Hindus, this couple would not technically subscribe to naturalism, but their decisions regarding their daughter were clearly based on naturalistic thinking.

9. In particular, the controversy over the age of the Earth, a subject that need not detain us here. For a leading old Earth site, see Reasons to Believe at http://www.reasons.org/; for a leading young Earth site, see Creation Ministries International at http://creation.com/.

10. Two of the Hebrew words are simply direct-object markers, and so there are really five actual words in the sentence. Some interpreters, dating back more than a millennium in the Jewish tradition, understand Genesis 1:1 slightly differently, joining this verse in a dependent clause with the next two verses, hence, "When God began to create heaven and earth—the earth being unformed and void, with darkness over the surface of the deep and a wind from God sweeping over the water—God said, 'Let there be light'; and there was light" (Gen. 1:1–3, NJV).

11. See, conveniently, "Cosmological Theories Through History," The Physics of the Universe, accessed January 21, 2017, http://www.physicsoftheuniverse .com/cosmological.html.

12. See J. B. Pritchard, ed., *The Ancient Near Eastern Texts Relating to the Old Testament*, 3rd ed. with supplement (Princeton: Princeton University Press, 1969), 63.

13. Ibid.

14. When speaking of God triumphing over hostile forces in Genesis 1, I'm referring to his causing light to shine out of darkness; the waters (which represent chaos powers in the ancient world) shut up within boundaries; the beasts of the sea, land, and sky are mere creations.

15. Gerald Schroeder, "The Age of the Universe," accessed January 21, 2017, http://www.geraldschroeder.com/AgeUniverse.aspx.

16. "'And God Said, Let There Be Light': The Big Bang, Creation, and Acoustics," *Creation Revolution*, November 11, 2010, http://creationrevolution.com/%E2 %80%9Cand-god-said-let-there-be-light%E2%80%9D-the-big-bang-creation -and-acoustics/.

17. Mangalwadi, *The Book That Made Your World*, 56.

18. Ibid., 47.

19. Originally expressed in Latin as *Cogito ergo sum*.

20. For more on this concept, see chapter 13 of this book.

21. From the publisher's blurb to Frank Turek, *Stealing from God: Why Atheists Need God to Make Their Case* (Nashville: NavPress, 2014).

22. C. S. Lewis, *Mere Christianity* (New York: MacMillan Publishing Company, 1952) 38–39.

23. Mangalwadi, *The Book That Made Your World*, 70.

24. Ibid., 71.

25. Ibid.

26. Lewis, *Mere Christianity*, 154.

27. According to Pope Francis, the contemporary war on gender is a war on the image of God: "We are living a moment of annihilation of man as image of God," he said. Associated Press, "Pope Francis Denounces Transgender People as 'Annihilation of Man,'" LGBTQ Nation, August 3, 2016, http://www.lgbtqnation.com/2016/08/pope-francis-denounces-transgender-people-annihilation-man/.

Chapter 6: From *The Walking Dead* to a Culture of Life

1. "Children, Violence, and the Media: A Report for Parents and Policy Makers," Senate Committee on the Judiciary, September 14, 1999, quoted in "Television and Children: Literature Cited," University of Michigan: Michigan Medicine, accessed January 21, 2017, http://www.med.umich.edu/yourchild/topics/tvc.htm#ref15.

2. "Media Violence Content," Parents Television Council, accessed January 21, 2017, http://w2.parentstv.org/main/Research/Studies/CableViolence/cv_f.aspx. Note that the October 2016 opening episode of *The Walking Dead* was so gory that, according to Paul Schrodt, "Parents Want to Change TV Ratings After That 'Brutally Explicit' 'Walking Dead' Episode," *Business Insider*, October 26, 2016, http://www.businessinsider.com/parents-tv-ratings-violent-walking-dead-episode-2016–10.

3. James Delingpole, "Torture and Murder with the Addictive Glamour of Hollywood: James Delingpole Gives His Verdict on Latest *Grand Theft Auto* Game," *Daily Mail*, September 17, 2013, http://www.dailymail.co.uk/news/article-2424124/Grand-Theft-Auto-V-James-Delingpole-gives-verdict-latest-game.html.

4. Ibid.

5. Monica Davey and Mitch Smith, "Murder Rates Rising Sharply in Many U.S.

Cities," *New York Times*, August 31, 2015, http://www.nytimes.com/2015
/09/01/us/murder-rates-rising-sharply-in-many-us-cities.html.

6. See, e.g., Matt Vasilogambros, "Rising Suicide Rates," *The Atlantic*, April 22,
2016, http://www.theatlantic.com/health/archive/2016/04/rising-suicide-rates
/479475/.

7. Dave Andrusko, "Remembering When Mother Teresa Left Hillary Clinton
in Stunned Silence on Abortion," Live Action News, August 5, 2016, http://
liveactionnews.org/remembering-when-mother-teresa-left-hillary-clinton
-in-stunned-silence-on-abortion/.

8. Camille Paglia, "Camille Paglia: Feminists Have Abortion Wrong, Trump
and Hillary Miscues Highlight a Frozen National Debate," April 7, 2016,
http://www.salon.com/2016/04/07/camille_paglia_feminists_have_abortion
_wrong_trump_and_hillary_miscues_highlight_a_frozen_national_debate/.

9. Mother Teresa, "Whatsoever You Do" (speech, National Prayer Breakfast,
Washington, DC, February 3, 1994), http://www.priestsforlife.org/brochures
/mtspeech.html.

10. Life Defender Team, "Mother Teresa's 10 Most Compassionate Pro-Life
Quotes," American Life League Life Defenders, September 1, 2016, http://
lifedefender.org/2016/09/mother-teresas-10-most-compassionate-pro-life
-quotes/. Quote is used without attribution.

11. See John 1:4; 3:15–16; 4:13–14; 5:21; 6:54, 68; 8:12; 10:10; 14:6; 17:3.

12. Note that the Hebrew word translated here as "corrupt" in other contexts can
mean "destroy." The concepts are thus intertwined.

13. In Hebrew, the literal translation of *bloodshed* is "blood."

14. See Norma McCovey and Gary Thomas, *Won by Love* (Manhattan Beach,
CA: Jan Dennis Books, 1997).

15. For a perfect description of what I mean by being an achiever, see Clifton
StrengthsFinders "Achiever," *Business Journal*, accessed January 21, 2017,
http://www.gallup.com/businessjournal/622/achiever.aspx.

16. One more thing we can do to be pro-life is to celebrate marriage and
family—meaning, to see children as a precious gift from God. We'll talk
about this more in the next chapter.

Chapter 7: Having a Multigenerational Mentality

1. Scholars debate the chronology of Hezekiah's reign, but the data presented
here is based on the most straightforward reading of the relevant texts.

2. No other sons of Hezekiah are mentioned in Scripture. Since his eldest son

would presumably have been his heir, and since Manasseh, his son, began to reign at the age of twelve, this would mean that he was born three years after Hezekiah's healing, since the king lived fifteen more years.

3. The Hebrew word for son is *ben*, the Aramaic word is *bar*, and the Arabic is *ibn*. Readers will immediately think of Peter's name, Simon bar Jonah, meaning "Simon, son of Jonah." The Hebrew name of the famous Jewish scholar Maimonides is Moshe Ben Maimon ("Moses son of Maimon"), while Arabic names with *ibn* in the middle also mean "son of," as in the full Arabic name of Osama ibn Laden, which is Usama bin Mohammed bin Awad bin Laden (*bin* has been substituted for *ibn* in English). So, this practice remains common to this day.

4. Because the Bible records that Absalom did have sons (2 Sam. 14:27), scholars assume that they all died before he did.

5. Traditional Jewish interpretation interprets this promise to refer to "the thousandth generation"; most Christian translations render it as "the thousands," speaking of people rather than generations.

6. I agree that what ultimately matters is where we spend eternity. I also agree that a good case can be made for cataclysmic events occurring at the end of this age. But I strongly reject the defeatist, escapist mentality.

7. "Samsung Predicts the World 100 Years from Now," *Future Timeline*, February 24, 2016, http://www.futuretimeline.net/blog/2016/02/24.htm#.V6FYJrgrI2w.

8. Maggie Aderin-Pocock et al., "SmartThings Future Living Report," Samsung, accessed January 21, 2017, http://www.samsung.com/uk/pdf /smartthings/future-living-report.pdf?CID=AFL-hq-mul-0813–11000279.

9. Ibid., 3.

10. Ibid.

11. Dargan Thompson, "11 Essential Bonhoeffer Quotes," *Relevant Magazine*, April 8, 2016, http://www.relevantmagazine.com/culture/books/12-essential -bonhoeffer-quotes.

12. Joshua Charles, "Thinking Only One Election at a Time Is Killing the Conservative Movement," *The Stream*, August 13, 2016, https://stream.org /thinking-only-one-election-at-a-time-is-killing-the-conservative-movement/.

13. For a biting commentary to this effect, see Fred Clark, "Happy Birthday, Hal Lindsey—Still Defying Prophecy After All These Years," *Patheos* (blog), November 23, 2014, http://www.patheos.com/blogs/slacktivist/2014/11/23 /happy-birthday-hal-lindsey-still-defying-prophecy-after-all-these-years/.

14. See, for example, 2 Cor. 5:1–4; 1 Pet. 2:11.

15. Michael L. Brown, *Outlasting the Gay Revolution: Where Homosexual Activism Is Really Going and How to Turn the Tide* (Washington, DC: WND Books, 2015).

16. Carle E. Zimmerman, *Family and Civilization*, ed. James Kurth (Wilmington, DE: ISI Books, 2008). As noted in Carlson's introduction, in the years following World War II, with the rise of the baby boomer generation, it appeared that the tide was turning in a positive way, contrary to Zimmerman's theses; but not long after, his predictions proved true.

17. In popular form, see Mark Steyn, *America Alone: The End of the World as We Know It* (Washington, DC: Regnery, 2006).

18. As cited by Carlson in Zimmerman, *Family and Civilization*, xiii (bracketed clarifications are omitted).

19. Of course, as mentioned earlier, adoption is another excellent way to celebrate children, and there is a growing adoption movement in contemporary evangelical circles. Christian attorney David French has responded to critics of that movement in his article, "Is the Left Launching an Attack on Evangelical Adoption?" *National Review*, April 25, 2013, http://www.nationalreview.com/corner/346643/left-launching-attack-evangelical-adoption-david-french.

20. By *spouse* I mean, of course, a spouse of the opposite sex, as intended by God. For my response to "gay Christian" arguments against this, see Michael L. Brown, *Can You Be Gay and Christian? Responding with Love and Truth to Questions About Homosexuality* (Lake Mary, FL: Frontline, 2014).

21. Dan Silverman, "The Jewish View of Marriage," Aish.com, accessed January 21, 2017, http://www.aish.com/f/m/98914744.html.

22. At the same time, male irresponsibility is at an all-time high in our land, so we have a generation of biological reproducers who do not serve as fathers. This has created a perfect storm.

23. Jake Fillis, "23 Quotes from Feminists That Will Make You Rethink Feminism," *Thought Catalog*, May 17, 2014, http://thoughtcatalog.com/jake-fillis/2014/05/23-quotes-from-feminists-that-will-make-you-rethink-feminism/.

24. Ibid.

25. Ibid.

26. Carl Wittman, "A Gay Manifesto (1970)," Gay Homeland Foundation, accessed January 21, 2017, http://library.gayhomeland.org/0006/EN/A_Gay_Manifesto.htm.

27. Jack Nichols, *The Gay Agenda: Talking Back to the Fundamentalists* (New York: Prometheus Books, 1996), 78.

28. See, for example, Mark Oppenheimer, "Married, with Infidelities: Dan Savage on the Virtue of Infidelity," *New York Times*, June 30, 2011, http://www.nytimes.com/2011/07/03/magazine/infidelity-will-keep-us-together

.html; Kelly Boggs, "Sexual Anarchy: America's Demise?," *Crosswalk*, July 27, 2009, http://www.crosswalk.com/family/marriage/sexual-anarchy -americas-demise-11606599.html; Spencer McNaughton, "Sleeping with Other People: How Gay Men Are Making Open Relationships Work," *The Guardian*, July 22, 2016, https://www.theguardian.com/lifeandstyle/2016 /jul/22/gay-dating-open-relationships-work-study.

29. See, for example, Catherine Briggs, "Porn Use Can Lead to Divorce: Study," *LifeSite News*, June 9, 2014, https://www.lifesitenews.com/news/porn-use-can -lead-to-divorce-study.

30. "The Future of American Jewry: Will Your Grandchild Be Jewish? (Revisited)," Simple to Remember: Judaism Online, accessed January 21, 2017, http://www.simpletoremember.com/vitals/will-your-grandchild-be -jewish-chart-graph.htm (this chart reflects data from 2005). This graphic updates an earlier version: Matitia Chetrit, "Giving Your Child a Better Chance in School—The Ten Advantages of a Jewish Education," accessed January 21, 2017, http://www.oocities.org/~jwnet/jwscl8i.htm.

31. Around the world today Islam is also growing rapidly, but it is not primarily through conversion. Instead, it is through having large families, and within those families loyalty to Islam is stressed.

32. "The Future of American Jewry."

33. See, e.g., Craig S. Keener, *And Marries Another: Divorce and Remarriage in the Teaching of the New Testament* (Grand Rapids, MI: Baker Academic, 1991); David Instone-Brewer, *Divorce and Remarriage in the Church: Biblical Solutions for Pastoral Realities* (Downers Grove, IL: InterVarsity Academic, 2009).

34. While there are some difficulties in the Hebrew text, it seems clear that the text declares that God hates divorce.

35. "Divorce Continues to Take a Psychological Toll on Kids," *The Guardian*, July 31, 2016, https://www.theguardian.com/lifeandstyle/2016/jul/31/divorce -psychological-toll-on-kids-children.

36. As popularized by Dr. Gary Chapman's many teachings on the "five love languages."

37. Prager, *The Ten Commandments*, 36.

Chapter 8: Reclaiming Our Schools and Learning How to Think Again

1. Roger Kimball, *Tenured Radicals: How Politics Has Corrupted Our Higher Education*, rev. ed. (Chicago: Ivan R. Dee, 1998), x.

2. Cited in ibid., xiv.

3. Ibid., 217. For other important studies from the 1990s and earlier, see Thomas Sowell, *Inside American Education: The Decline, the Deception, the Dogmas* (New York: Free Press, 1993); see also the watershed study of Alan Bloom, *The Closing of the American Mind* (New York: Simon and Schuster, 1987).

4. See, e.g., "World University Rankings 2015–2016," Times Higher Education, accessed January 21, 2017, https://www.timeshighereducation.com/world-university-rankings/2016/world-ranking#!/page/0/length/25/sort_by/rank_label/sort_order/asc/cols/rank_only.

5. James Marshall Crotty, "7 Signs That U.S. Education Decline Is Jeopardizing Its National Security," *Forbes*, March 26, 2012, http://www.forbes.com/sites/jamesmarshallcrotty/2012/03/26/7-signs-that-americas-educational-decline-is-jeopardizing-its-national-security/#521d6a805999.

6. Martha C. White, "The Real Reason New College Grads Can't Get Hired," *Time*, November 10, 2013, http://business.time.com/2013/11/10/the-real-reason-new-college-grads-cant-get-hired/.

7. Rachel Pells, "University Students Are Struggling to Read Entire Books," *Independent*, April 15, 2016, http://www.independent.co.uk/news/education/university-students-are-struggling-to-read-entire-books-a6986361.html.

8. In making this comment, I am not, of course, denying the reality of medical conditions like ADHD.

9. Samuel D. James, "America's Lost Boys," *First Things*, August 2, 2016, https://www.firstthings.com/blogs/firstthoughts/2016/08/americas-lost-boys.

10. For the phenomenon of microaggressions, see chapter 13 of this book.

11. Bloom, *The Closing of the American Mind*, n. 225.

12. Greg Lukianoff and Jonathan Haidt, "The Coddling of the American Mind," *The Atlantic*, September 2015, http://www.theatlantic.com/magazine/archive/2015/09/the-coddling-of-the-american-mind/399356/.

13. Eric Owens, "Fancypants College in Cleveland Offers Safe Space for Students Traumatized by Republican Convention," *Daily Caller*, July 20, 2016, http://dailycaller.com/2016/07/20/fancypants-college-in-cleveland-offers-safe-space-for-students-traumatized-by-republican-convention/#ixzz4FTT7qIAe.

14. Karin Agness, "Dear Universities: There Should Be No Safe Spaces from Intellectual Thought," *Time*, May 11, 2015, http://time.com/3848947/dear-universities-there-should-be-no-safe-spaces-from-intellectual-thought/. See also Dr. Everett Piper, "This Is Not a Day Care. It's a University!" Oklahoma Wesleyan University, accessed January 21, 2017, http://www.okwu.edu/blog/2015/11/this-is-not-a-day-care-its-a-university/. (Note that Piper is the president of Oklahoma Wesleyan University.); David Schaper, "University

of Chicago Tells Freshmen It Does Not Support 'Trigger Warnings,'" NPR, August 26, 2016, http://www.npr.org/2016/08/26/491531869/university-of -chicago-tells-freshmen-it-does-not-support-trigger-warnings. (Note that the university faced considerable pushback for its decision.)

15. See a list of representative studies here: Google search, "Democrat Republican Law Professors Percentage," accessed January 21, 2017, https://www.google.com/search?q=democrat%20republican%20law%20 professors%20percentage&rct=j.

16. "Liberals to Outnumber Conservative Graduation Speakers 4-to-1," *Campus Reform*, May 5, 2016, https://www.campusreform.org/?ID=7554; for a summary of left-leaning abuses, see "Leftist Abuses and Bias on Campus," *Campus Reform*, accessed January 21, 2017, https://www.campusreform.org /img/writings/Left_Bias_and_Abuse.pdf; for an assessment by a university professor, see George Yancey, *Compromising Scholarship: Religious and Political Bias in American Higher Education* (Baylor, TX: Baylor University Press, 2010).

17. Amarnath Amarasingam, "Are American College Professors Religious?" *Huffington Post*, October 6, 2010, http://www.huffingtonpost.com/ amarnath-amarasingam/how-religious-are-america_b_749630.html.

18. Criminology professor Mike Adams has documented the extreme, anti-conservative political correctness that exists in many universities, and the accounts he relates in his syndicated columns are so wild that you don't know whether to laugh or cry. See "Mike Adams Articles," Townhall, accessed January 21, 2017, http://townhall.com/columnists/mikeadams/. From the perspective of a student, Ben Shapiro wrote *Brainwashed: How Universities Indoctrinate America's Youth* (Nashville: WND Books, 2004). Not surprisingly, Shapiro dedicated the book to his parents, who, he said, "taught me the difference between right and wrong and gave me the strength to confront falsehood." That prepared him well for the secular university. See also Dinesh D'Souza, *Illiberal Education: The Politics of Race and Sex on Campus* (New York: Free Press, 1991); David Horowitz, *Reforming Our Universities* (Washington, DC: Regnery, 2010).

19. Bill Korach, "New Web Show 'Queer Kids Stuff' Targets Preschool," The Report Card, July 11, 2016, http://education-curriculum-reform-government -schools.org/w/2016/07/new-web-show-queer-kids-stuff-targets-pre-school/.

20. See further Michael L. Brown, *A Queer Thing Happened to America: And What a Long, Strange Trip It's Been* (Concord, NC: EqualTime Books, 2011), 85–119.

21. Spalding, *We Still Hold These Truths*, 15.

22. Kraig Beyerlein, "Educational Elites and the Movement to Secularize Public Education: The Case of the National Education Association," in Christian Smith, ed., *The Secular Revolution: Power, Interests, and Conflict in the Secularization of American Public Life* (Berkeley, CA: University of California Press, 2003), 160, 194. The entire volume is relevant to the present topic.

23. Linda Harvey, "NEA Teachers Union 2014 More Extreme Than Ever," *Mission: America*, July 28, 2014, http://missionamerica.com/article/nea-teachers-union -2014-more-extreme-than-ever/.

24. For relevant links, see Michael Brown, "When a Child Asks, 'What If I Identify as a Dinosaur?,'" *Charisma News*, July 15, 2016, http://www .charismanews.com/opinion/in-the-line-of-fire/58623-when-a-child -asks-what-if-i-identify-as-a-dinosaur.

25. John Taylor Gatto, *Weapons of Mass Instruction: A Schoolteacher's Journey Through the Dark World of Compulsory Schooling* (Gabriola Island, BC: New Society Publishers, 2010), xv.

26. I have adapted material here from Michael L. Brown, *Revolution! The Call to Holy War* (Ventura, CA: Renew, 2000), 139–43.

27. This stands in stark contrast with the responses given by graduates of Christian colleges, the vast majority of whom say that their college experience did, in fact, help them move toward fulfilling God's purposes for their lives.

28. For another, related critique, compare David F. Wells, "The D-Min-ization of the Ministry," in Os Guinness and John Seel, *No God But God* (Chicago: Moody, 1992), 175–88 (compare more fully David F. Wells, *No Place for Truth* [Grand Rapids: Eerdmans, 1992]). For an even sharper critique, compare Eta Linnemann, *Historical Criticism of the Bible: Methodology or Ideology?* trans. Robert W. Yarbrough (Grand Rapids: Baker, 1990). No doubt there is an important place in Christian college and seminary curriculum for apologetics, if only for the sake of the students, who may have been bombarded with unbiblical concepts and perspectives for years. Still, there is often the subtle, underlying feeling that as Christian professors and academicians, we must prove our intellectual integrity over and over again, spending more time refuting error than learning truth.

29. Terrence P. Jeffrey, "1,773,000: Homeschooled Children Up 61.8% in 10 Years," CNS News, May 19, 2015, http://www.cnsnews.com/news/article /terence-p-jeffrey/1773000-homeschooled-children-618–10-years.

30. "Home-schooling: Outstanding Results on National Tests," *Washington Times*, August 30, 2009, http://www.washingtontimes.com/news/2009 /aug/30/home-schooling-outstanding-results-national-tests/.

31. "Liberty University Quick Facts," Liberty University, accessed January 21, 2017, http://www.liberty.edu/aboutliberty/?PID=6925.

Chapter 9: Restoring Thunder to Our Pulpits

1. Charles G. Finney, "The Decay of Conscience," *Independent*, December 4, 1873, quoted in *The Gospel Truth*, http://www.gospeltruth.net/1868 _75Independent/731204_conscience.htm.

2. Kelly Shattuck, "7 Startling Facts: An Up Close Look at Church Attendance in America," Church Leaders, December 29, 2015, http://www.churchleaders .com/pastors/pastor-articles/139575–7-startling-facts-an-up-close-look-at -church-attendance-in-america.html. I'm aware that there are different estimates about church attendance in America, but the figures cited here represent solid research and polling.

3. See especially Jer. 23:9–15.

4. Tozer's article has been posted frequently online; see, e.g., http://www .ldolphin.org/oldcross.html.

5. A. W. Tozer, "The Old Cross and the New," in *Man, the Dwelling Place of God: What It Means to Have Christ Living in You* (Camp Hill, PA: Wingspread Publishers, 2008), 22.

6. See Matt. 10:37–39; 16:24–25; Mark 8:34–35; 14:26–33; Luke 17:32–33; John 12:24–25.

7. See Michael L. Brown, "Appalling Grace: A Response to Mark Galli's 'The Scandal of the Public Evangelical,'" *The Voice of Revolution*, July 4, 2009, http://www.voiceofrevolution.com/2009/07/04/apalling-grace-a-response-to -mark-gallis-the-scandal-of-the-public-evangelical/.

8. These are the words of the former Miss California, Carrie Prejean; see http:// www.wava.com/11603023/.

9. These are the words of the rapper The Game; S. Samuel, "Game Says Lord Have Mercy: 'Christ Is My Savior & I'm Still Out Here Thuggin'," SOHH. com, October 31, 2012, http://www.sohh.com/game-says-lord-have-mercy -christ-is-my-savior-im-still-out-here-thuggin/.

10. Michael Brown, "A Born-Again Christian Prostitute?," *Charisma News*, April 5, 2013, http://www.charismanews.com/opinion/38964-a-born-again -christian-prostitute.

11. Frequently posted online and cited in books, always attributed to Tozer, but without original attribution.

12. A. W. Tozer, *The Best of A. W. Tozer* (Grand Rapids, MI: Baker, 1978), 101; originally from his book *The Incredible Christian*.

13. Quoted in Heather Clark, "Study Reveals Most American Pastors Silent on Current Issues Despite Biblical Beliefs," *Christian News Network*, August 12, 2014, http://christiannews.net/2014/08/12/study-reveals-most-american-pastors -silent-on-current-issues-despite-biblical-beliefs/.

14. Ibid.

15. Martin Luther King Jr., "A Knock at Midnight" (sermon, June 11, 1967), http:// kingencyclopedia.stanford.edu/encyclopedia/documentsentry/doc_a_knock _at_midnight.1.html (emphasis mine). This text was originally published in Martin Luther King Jr., *Strength to Love* (New York: Harper & Row, 1963).

16. Stephen L. Carter, "The Freedom to Resist," *Christianity Today*, June 12, 2000, http://www.christianitytoday.com/ct/2000/june12/5.58.html.

17. For Fisher's resources, which include his one-man play (dressed in American Revolutionary garb), see http://www.theresonancemovement.com/.

Chapter 10: From Playboy to Purity

1. Jack Moore, "Why Playboy's Decision to No Longer Feature Nude Photos Is Smart (and, Really, Long Overdue)," *GQ*, October 13, 2015, http://www .gq.com/story/playboy-no-more-nude-photos. Ironically, early in 2017, Playboy returned to featuring nudes. See "Playboy Returns to Nudity in New Issue," Fox News, February 13, 2017, http://www.foxnews.com /entertainment/2017/02/13/playboy-returns-to-nudity-in-new-issue.html.

2. Max Benwell, "Why You Should Be Worried About Playboy Dropping Naked Women from Its Pages," *The Independent*, October 13, 2015, http://www .independent.co.uk/voices/why-you-should-be-worried-about-playboy -dropping-naked-women-from-its-pages-a6692756.html, emphasis mine.

3. Judith Shulevitz, "It's O.K., Liberal Parents, You Can Freak Out About Porn," *New York Times*, July 17, 2016; http://www.nytimes.com/2016/07/17/opinion /sunday/its-ok-liberal-parents-you-can-freak-out-about-porn.html.

4. Russ Warner, "The Detrimental Effects of Pornography on Small Children," *Net Nanny*, May 1, 2013, https://www.netnanny.com/blog/the-detrimental -effects-of-pornography-on-small-children/.

5. Michelle X. Smith, *Prodigal Pursued: Out of the Lifestyle into the Arms of Jesus: An Ex-Lesbian's Journey* (Prodigal Pursued Ministries, 2016).

6. Bill Muehlenberg, "Children and Pornography," *Culture Watch*, February 7, 2016, https://billmuehlenberg.com/2016/02/07/children-and-pornography/.

7. Among many online reports, see Liz Goodwin, "Porn Is a 'Public Health Crisis' and a Menace, GOP Committee Says in Platform Draft," *Yahoo! News*, July 11, 2016, https://www.yahoo.com/news/rnc-platform-draft-porn-000000329.html.

8. "Symantec Survey Reveals More Than 80 Percent of Children Using Email Receive Inappropriate Spam Daily," *Symantec*, June 9, 2003, https://www.symantec.com/en/hk/about/newsroom/press-releases/2003/symantec_0609_03.

9. Advertisement for *The Porn Phenomenon*, *Barna*, accessed November 21, 2016, https://barna-resources.myshopify.com/products/porn-phenomenon.

10. Billy Hallowell, "Groundbreaking Pornography Study Yields Shocking Results: 'Our Future Is at Risk,'" *The Blaze*, January 20, 2016, http://www.theblaze.com/stories/2016/01/20/groundbreaking-pornography-study-yields-shocking-results-our-future-is-at-risk/.

11. Ibid.

12. David French, "America's *Real* Porn Problem," April 7, 2016, *National Review*, http://www.nationalreview.com/article/433805/pornography-destroys-american-morals-and-culture.

13. Ben Shapiro, *Porn Generation: How Social Liberalism Is Corrupting Our Future* (Washington, DC: Regnery, 2013).

14. See Michael Brown, "Here Comes Incest, Just as Predicted," *Charisma News*, September 14, 2012, http://www.charismanews.com/opinion/34146-here-come-incest-just; Brown, "Next Stop on Slippery Slope: Incest," *World Net Daily*, July 23, 2014, http://www.wnd.com/2014/07/next-stop-on-slippery-slope-incest/.

15. See "Fifty Shades of Grey," *Wikipedia*, accessed November 21, 2016, https://en.wikipedia.org/wiki/Fifty_Shades_of_Grey.

16. According to the Lutheran scholar R. C. H. Lenski, "Paul again states undeniable facts in comparing sinful acts in general with that of fornication in particular. Also this is only a necessary preliminary statement that paves the way for the following. It really states the major premise of a syllogism: Fornication, as does no other sin, violates the body. The minor premise will follow: The Christian's body is the Spirit's sanctuary. And then the conclusion of this syllogism is plain: Fornication, as does no other sin, desecrates the very sanctuary of God." *The Interpretation of St. Paul's First and Second Epistle to the Corinthians* (Minneapolis: Augsburg, 1963), 267–68.

17. See, e.g., 1 Cor. 6:9–10; Gal. 5:19–21; Col. 3:5.

18. See Matt. 5:27–30; 18:7–9, 18; Mark 9:43, 45, 47–48.

19. For the principle of the *acharit* (pronounced "a-kha-reet" in Hebrew), which refers to the final consequences, the end results, the end, see Michael L. Brown, *Go and Sin No More: A Call to Holiness* (Ventura, CA: Regal, 1999), 75–89. For a short article related to this subject, see Michael L. Brown, "Cigarette Smoking Kills the Third Marlboro Man," AskDrBrown, January 31, 2014, https://askdrbrown.org/library/cigarette-smoking-kills -third-marlboro-man.

20. I have heard this anecdotally for years from those who once lived promiscuously but are now in committed marital relations. For studies that support this with detailed data, see http://marri.us/research/sexuality/.

21. See Glenn T. Stanton, *The Ring Makes All the Difference: The Hidden Consequences of Cohabitation and the Strong Benefits of Marriage* (Chicago: Moody Press, 2011). For other problems with cohabitation, see Laurie DeRose, "Increasing Cohabitation and Family Instability for Children," *Family Studies*, July 12, 2016, http://family-studies.org/increasing -cohabitation-and-family-instability-for-children/.

22. Billy Hallowell, "Study Reveals Key Detail About Women Who Are Virgins When They Get Married," *The Blaze*, June 7, 2016, http://www.theblaze.com /stories/2016/06/07/study-reveals-key-detail-about-women-who-are-virgins -before-they-get-married/.

Chapter 11: From Excess to Self-Control

1. For those struggling with overeating, obesity, or health problems related to unhealthy eating, see Michael L. Brown and Nancy Brown, *Breaking the Stronghold of Food: How We Conquered Food Addictions and Discovered a Whole New Way of Living* (Lake Mary, FL: Siloam, 2017).

2. "The Average American Woman Is Now the Same Weight as the Average 1960s Man," *Daily Mail*, June 15, 2015, http://www.dailymail.co.uk/news /article-3124838/The-average-American-woman-weight-average-1960s-man .html#ixzz4EdT8NbaI.

3. Roland Sturm and Kenneth B. Wells, "The Health Risks of Obesity: Worse Than Smoking, Drinking or Poverty," RAND Corporation, accessed January 23, 2017, http://www.rand.org/pubs/research_briefs/RB4549.html.

4. Joel Fuhrman, MD, *Eat to Live: The Amazing Nutrient-Rich Program for Fast and Sustained Weight Loss,* revised edition (New York: Little, Brown, and Company, 2011).

5. Sturm and Wells, "The Health Risks of Obesity."

6. Sharon Begley, "As America's Waistline Expands, Costs Soar," *Reuters*, April 30, 2012, http://www.reuters.com/article/us-obesity-idUSBRE83T0C820120430.

7. Ibid.

8. Matthew Frankel, "The Average American Household Owes $90,336—How Do You Compare?," The Motley Fool, May 8, 2016, http://www.fool.com /retirement/general/2016/05/08/the-average-american-household-owes -90336-how-do-y.aspx.

9. "Childhood Obesity Facts," Centers for Disease Control and Prevention, accessed January 20, 2017, https://www.cdc.gov/healthyschools/obesity/facts.htm.

10. "Overweight in Children," American Heart Association, http://www .heart.org/HEARTORG/HealthyLiving/HealthyKids/ChildhoodObesity /Overweight-in-Children_UCM_304054_Article.jsp#.V4l83LgrLb0; for some other perspectives, see Laura Gray, "Will Today's Children Die Earlier Than Their Parents?," *BBC News*, July 8, 2014, http://www.bbc.com/news /magazine-28191865.

11. See Col. 3:5.

12. I tell my story in full, as does my wife, Nancy, in *Breaking the Stronghold of Food*.

13. See especially Gal. 6:7–8.

14. See, e.g., "Why Are Yo-Yo Diets So Bad? Dr. Joel Furhman," YouTube video, 5:26, recorded at the Health, Happiness Expo, Las Vegas, Nevada, June 12, 2015, posted by HappyCow Vegan Guide, July 15, 2015, https://www.youtube .com/watch?v=KUBlI3MzzLM.

15. In Proverbs, see 6:6, 9; 10:26; 13:4; 15:19; 19:24; 20:4; 21:25; 22:13; 24:30; 26:13–16; see also 19:15.

16. See, e.g., Michael B. Kelley and Pamela Engel, "21 Lottery Winners Who Blew It All," *Business Insider*, February 11, 2015, http://www.businessinsider .com/lottery-winners-who-lost-everything-2015-2.

17. See, e.g., Madelyn Fernstorm, "'The Biggest Loser' Contestants Gain Again: Why Weight Keeps Coming Back," *Today*, May 30, 2016, http://www.today .com/health/biggest-loser-contestants-gain-again-why-weight-keeps-coming -back-t90261.

18. Timothy Friberg, Barbara Friberg, and Neva F. Miller, *Analytical Greek Lexicon* (Victoria, BC: Trafford Publishing, 2005), ad loc., their emphasis.

19. The meaning of this difficult verse is disputed, but the *New English Translation* (NET), cited here, presents a widely accepted understanding of the text.

Chapter 12: Putting an End to the Blame Game and Saying Goodbye to the Entitlement Mentality

1. The Greek for John 2:24b is literally "because he knew all," normally taken to mean "he knew all people."

2. See, e.g., Eph. 2:1–10; Rom. 5:1–12.

3. Jeremiah Johnson, "Whatever Happened to Sin?" *Grace to You*, June 1, 2015, https://www.gty.org/blog/B150601/whatever-happened-to-sin.

4. Ibid., citing John MacArthur, *The Vanishing Conscience* (Nashville: Thomas Nelson, 1994), 21.

5. "Alcoholism: Sin or Sickness?" The Bridge of Overcomers Outreach, accessed January 25, 2017, http://overcomersoutreach.org/blog/new-pamphlets-2 /alcohol-sin-or-sickness/; Gary D. Robinson, "Whatever Happened to Sin?," *Breakpoint*, May 20, 2008, http://www.breakpoint.org/features-columns /articles/entry/12/9249.

6. "Entitlement Mentality," Conservapedia, accessed January 25, 2017, http:// www.conservapedia.com/Entitlement_mentality.

7. Aletheia Luna, "16 Signs You Have a Sense of Entitlement Complex," *Loner Wolf*, accessed January 25, 2017, http://lonerwolf.com/sense-of-entitlement/.

8. "Entitlement Mentality."

9. Kate S. Rourke, "You Owe Me: Examining a Generation of Entitlement," *Inquiries Journal* 3, no. 1 (2011), 1, http://www.inquiriesjournal.com/articles /362/you-owe-me-examining-a-generation-of-entitlement.

10. Dr. John Townsend, *The Entitlement Cure: Finding Success in Doing Hard Things the Right Way* (Grand Rapids, MI: Zondervan, 2015), 26.

Chapter 13: The Universe Does Not Revolve around Me

1. Heben Nigatu, "21 Racial Microaggressions You Hear on a Daily Basis, " Buzzfeed, December 9, 2013, https://www.buzzfeed.com/hnigatu/racial -microaggressions-you-hear-on-a-daily-basis?utm_term=.rheD1rqMJ#. ktPPXrVgp.

2. Bradford Richardson, "'Christmas Vacation,' 'Round of Golf' Are Microaggressions at UNC," *Washington Times*, June 26, 2016, http://www .washingtontimes.com/news/2016/jun/26/university-of-north-carolina-saying -christmas-vaca/.

3. Andrew Egger, "A Dustup at UNC over Christmas Vacation and Other Microaggressions," *The Daily Signal*, June 30, 2016, http://dailysignal.com/2016 /06/30/a-dustup-at-unc-over-christmas-vacation-and-other-microaggressions/.

4. Jean M. Twenge, *Generation Me: Why Today's Young Americans Are More Confident, Assertive, Entitled—and More Miserable Than Ever Before* rev. ed. (New York: Atria Books, 2014), 1–2.

5. A search for "millennials' good qualities" yields many relevant articles and studies.

6. Patrick Nelson, "We Touch Our Phones 2,617 Times a Day, Says Study," *Network World*, July 7, 2016, http://www.networkworld.com/article/3092446 /smartphones/we-touch-our-phones-2617-times-a-day-says-study.html.

7. See also Kelly Wallace, "Half of Teens Think They're Addicted to Their Smartphones," CNN, July 29, 2016, http://www.cnn.com/2016/05/03/health /teens-cell-phone-addiction-parents/index.html.

8. Susan Weinschenk PhD, "Why We're All Addicted to Texts, Twitter and Google," *Psychology Today*, September 11, 2012, https://www.psychologytoday .com/blog/brain-wise/201209why-were-all-addicted-texts-twitter-and -google.

9. Neil Postman, *Amusing Ourselves to Death: Public Discourse in the Age of Show Business* (New York: Penguin Books, 2005).

10. Jean M. Twenge and W. Keith Campbell, *The Narcissism Epidemic: Living in the Age of Entitlement* (New York: Free Press, 2009). For the authors' assessment of the origins of the narcissism epidemic, see pages 56–69; that topic is then expanded through the balance of the book.

11. Ibid., 1.

12. Postman, *Amusing Ourselves to Death*, xii–xiii.

13. See, e.g., Luke 6:27–38; 14:11–14; 16:10–12.

14. See the verses cited in chapter 11, n. 262.

15. Matt. 5:43–45; Luke 6:32–36; see also Rom. 12:14, 17–21.

16. I heard this spoken directly by Rev. Bonnke in a sermon he preached in Pensacola, Florida, at the Brownsville Revival School of Ministry, October 23, 1998.

17. As quoted without source attribution in Stephen L. Hill, *On Earth as It Is in Heaven: A Classic Bible Reading Guide* (Shippensburg, PA: Destiny Image, 1993).

18. My friend is Scott Volk, and his ministry is Together for Israel (www .togetherforisrael.org).

19. "Socialism Makes People Selfish," YouTube video, 4:23, posted by PragerU, July 18, 2016, https://www.youtube.com/watch?v=l3GfCmbPDN0.

20. I first heard this phrase from Christian author Don Gossett.

Chapter 14: The Church's Great Opportunity

1. Louis Drummond, *The Awakening That Must Come* (Nashville: Broadman, 1981); Francis Schaeffer, *A Christian Manifesto* (Wheaton, IL: Crossway, 1981); John W. Whitehead, *The Second American Revolution* (Elgin, IL: David C. Cook; 1982); David R. Wilkerson, *Set the Trumpet to Thy Mouth* (Lindale, TX: World Challenge, 1983).

2. For a pre–New Testament reflection, see Wisdom of Solomon 8:19–20; see also Leviticus Rabbah 27:6.

3. This is widely attributed to Winston Churchill, but I am unable to confirm the original source of the quote.

4. In the New Testament sickness and disease are frequently associated with Satan and demons, as well as with sin. See Michael L. Brown, *Israel's Divine Healer*, Studies in Old Testament Biblical Theology (Grand Rapids, MI: Zondervan, 1995), 227–34.

5. I recognize and affirm that God can work through sickness and that sometimes the most godly, faith-filled people can be sick. I'm simply emphasizing what I understand to be the biblical emphasis, where God is revealed as Israel's Healer (when they obeyed his commands) and where Jesus healed all who came to him. See further Brown, *Israel's Divine Healer*.

6. Michael L. Brown, "God Is Moving Among Muslim Refugees in Germany!," The Line of Fire broadcast, August 1, 2016, http://thelineoffire .org/2016/08/01/god-is-moving-among-muslim-refugees-in-germany/.

7. See Matt. 5:13–16 (cf. John 8:12; 9:5); Eph. 5:8–14; Phil. 2:14–16.

8. Mark Tushnet, "Abandoning Defensive Crouch Liberal Constitutionalism," *Balkanization* (blog), May 6, 2016, http://balkin.blogspot.it/2016/05/abandoning -defensive-crouch-liberal.html?m=1, his emphasis.

9. Michael Brown, "Open Letter to Harvard Law Prof: The Culture Wars Aren't Over and Christians Aren't Nazis," *The Stream*, August 19, 2016, https:// stream.org/open-letter-harvard-law-professor-culture-wars-far-conservative -christians-anything-nazis/.

10. Wes Granberg-Michaelson, "Think Christianity Is Dying? No, Christianity Is Shifting Dramatically," *Washington Post*, May 20, 2015, https://www .washingtonpost.com/news/acts-of-faith/wp/2015/05/20/think-christianity-is -dying-no-christianity-is-shifting-dramatically/.

11. See Brown, *A Queer Thing Happened to America*, 129–33.

12. Cited in Robert J. Morgan, "The Sixth Great Awakening: America's Only Hope," *Huffington Post*, June 11, 2013, http://www.huffingtonpost.com

/robert-j-morgan/sixth-great-awakening-americas-only-hope_b_3391348. html. Morgan also cited this quote from Increase Mather, describing the spiritual state of his colony in 1702 [!]: "Look at how the glory is departing. You that are aged can remember 50 years ago when the churches were in their glory. What a change there has been! Time was when the churches were beautiful. Many people were converted and willingly declared what God had done for their souls, and there were added to the churches daily such as should be saved. But conversions have become rare in this day. Look into the pulpits and see if there is such a glory as there once was. The glory is gone. The special design of providence in this country seems to be now over. We weep to think about it." See also Donald S. Whitney, "Revival Was the Church's Only Hope," *Revival Commentary* 1, no. 2 (Fall 1996): 5–7.

13. See Joseph Tracy, *The Great Awakening: A History of the Revival of Religion in the Time of Edwards and Whitefield* (Boston: Charles Tappan, 1845), 26.

14. Brown, "Open Letter to Harvard Law Prof."

15. G. K. Chesterton, *The Everlasting Man* (Garden City, NY: Image Books, 1955), 260–61.

16. Michael L. Brown, "One Book on Homosexuality and the Church," Line of Fire broadcast, December 15, 2015, http://thelineoffire.org/2015/12/15 /two-new-books-on-homosexuality-and-the-church/.

17. See Larry Eskridge, *God's Forever Family: The Jesus People Movement in America* (New York: Oxford University Press, 2013), 11.

18. Leonard Ravenhill, *Revival God's Way* (Minneapolis: Bethany House, 1983), 127.

19. Frequently cited, but always without original source attribution.

20. John D. Woodbridge and Frank A. James III, Church History, Volume Two: From Pre-Reformation to the Present Day (Grand Rapids, MI: Zondervan, 2013), 597.

21. Oswald J. Smith, *I Have Walked Alone with Jesus: Day by Day Meditations of Oswald J. Smith* (Burlington, ON: G. R. Welch, 1982), October 1 entry.

22. See Luke 10:18; Matt. 28:18; Rom. 8:37; 1 John 5:4.

INDEX

SCRIPTURE INDEX

New Testament

ABOUT THE AUTHOR

———

DR. MICHAEL L. BROWN IS A REVOLUTIONARY AT HEART, AND HE burns with a holy passion to see God's people so radically changed by the Lord that we in turn will go and change the world. Having served as a leader in one of the most significant revivals in modern church history, he is an eyewitness to what God can do today and he lives in constant faith and expectation. Through his daily radio broadcast, the *Line of Fire*, through his TV shows on GOD TV and NRB TV, and through his books, articles, and videos, he seeks to stoke the fires of another great awakening and an even greater Jesus Revolution.

As an educator and mentor, he is committed to pouring himself into the younger generation, and as a father and grandfather (now blessedly married for more than forty years), one of his favorite emails of 2016 came from one of his granddaughters, asking him to recommend verses for her to read in her brand-new preteen study Bible. As a Jewish believer in Jesus, he is constantly engaged in debate and dialogue with his beloved people, longing for the day when all Israel will be saved (Romans 11:26), and as a preacher and teacher, he has the privilege of speaking around the world, having traveled to thirty nations on more than one hundred fifty overseas ministry trips. He and his team are very active on social media, and he would love to stay connected with you on Facebook, Twitter, or YouTube. And to be sure that you don't miss any of his new articles or videos (often more than five per week), sign up for his weekly emails at https://askdrbrown.org/. You can also check his itinerary there, since Dr. Brown likes nothing more than meeting you, his readers, face-to-face.